Strategic
Brand
Management

Strategic Brand Management

New Approaches to Creating
and Evaluating Brand Equity

JEAN-NOËL KAPFERER

THE FREE PRESS
A Division of Macmillan, Inc.
NEW YORK

Maxwell Macmillan Canada
TORONTO

The Free Press
A Division of Macmillan, Inc.
866 Third Avenue, New York, N. Y. 10022

Maxwell Macmillan Canada, Inc.
1200 Eglinton Avenue East
Suite 200
Don Mills, Ontario M3C 3N1

Macmillan, Inc. is part of the Maxwell Communication
Group of Companies.

Printed in the United States of America

printing number
1 2 3 4 5 6 7 8 9 10

Library of Congress Cataloging-in-Publication Data

Kapferer, Jean-Noël.
    Strategic brand management: new approaches to creating and evaluating brand equity/
Jean-Noël Kapferer ; [translated by Philip Gibbs].
        p. cm.
    Includes bibliographical references and index.
    ISBN 0–02–917045–1
    1. Brand name products—Management.   I. Title.
    HD69.B7K37   1994   93-42424
    658.8'343—dc20   CIP

Contents

PART II: BRAND MANAGEMENT

Introduction
Managing brand equity:
from brand value to brand values

Today, the primary capital of many businesses is their brands. For decades, the value of a company was measured in terms of its real estate, then tangible assets, plants, and equipment. However, it has recently been recognized that a company's real value lies outside the business itself, in the minds of potential buyers. In July 1990, when Bernard Tapie bought Adidas, the brand with the three stripes, he summarized his reasons quite simply: after Coca-Cola and Marlboro, Adidas was the best-known brand in the world. The truth contained in what many observers took simply to be a clever remark has become increasingly apparent since 1985. In a wave of mergers and acquisitions, triggered by attempts to take positions in the future single European market, market transactions pushed prices out of proportion with any established norms: Nestlé bought Rowntree for almost three times its stock market value, and 26 times its earnings. The Buitoni group was bought at a price worth 35 times its earnings. Until then, prices had been on a scale of eight to ten times the earnings of the bought-out company. Paradoxically, what justified these prices and these new standards was invisible, appearing nowhere in the companies' balance sheets. The only assets displayed on corporate balance sheets were fixed, tangible ones, such as machines and inventories. There was no mention of the brands, for which buyers shelled out sums much greater than the net asset value. The acquiring corporations generally deducted this extra value or goodwill from reserves in their consolidated accounts. The actual object of these gigantic financial exchanges and the disputed takeover battles that preceded them was something invisible, intangible, and unwritten.

1

What changed in the course of the 1980s was awareness. Before, in a takeover bid, merger, or acquisition, the buyer acquired a pasta manufacturer, a chocolate manufacturer, or a producer of personal computers or abrasives or whatever. Now, the prize in view is Buitoni, Rowntree (which means KitKat, pet food and After Eight mints), Atari, or Norton. The strength of a company like Heineken is not solely in knowing how to brew beer; it is the fact that people the world over want to drink Heineken. The same logic applies for Facom, Caterpillar, IBM, Sony, McDonald's, Barclays, and Dior. The distinction between brand and product is fundamental. Products are what the company makes; what the customer buys is a brand. The same is true of services. In paying very high prices for companies with brands, buyers are actually purchasing a position in the minds of potential customers, be it in the stalls or in the royal circle. Awareness, image, trust, and reputation, all painstakingly acquired over the years, are the best guarantees of future earnings. These justify the high prices paid. The value of a brand lies in its capacity to generate such cash flows.

For the potential customer, a brand is a landmark. Like money, it facilitates trade. Faced with a multitude of silent or "hard-to-read" products, whose performance cannot be assessed at first glance, customers are confused. Brands and prices make products easier to "read," removing uncertainty. A product's price measures its monetary value; its brand identifies the product and reveals the facets of its differences: functional value, pleasure value, and symbolic value as a reflection of the buyer's self-image. One word, one symbol summarizes an idea, a sentence, and a long list of attributes, values, and principles infused into the product or service. A brand encapsulates identity, origin, specificity, and difference. It evokes this information-concentrate in a word or a sign. This is why brands are vital for business exchange: when faced with, say, hundreds of personal computers, a buyer can use brands to structure this selection, to segment it, helping him to decide what he wants, looking toward the products whose brands indicate that they will satisfy his expectations, needs, or wishes. In markets in which technology and fashion mean that the choice is constantly evolving, brands provide a haven of stability, describing an identity and promising constant features and direction. Though the products may change, the spirit remains the same. IBM is synonymous with safety, Mercedes with German reliability and finishing, Facom with precision and fine workmanship, McDonald's with friendliness and service, and Coutts with financial skill and a personalized relationship reminiscent in some way of a select gentlemen's club.

Brands identify, guarantee, structure, and stabilize supply. They draw their value from their capacity to reduce risk and uncertainty. In a world in which everything is changing, brands posses a rare quality of stability. Who cares that the BSN group bought Nabisco Europe? What customers look for are Belin crackers or Pepito biscuits: they have an implicit contract with these brands. Dim hosiery has no less drawing power since it was acquired by Sara Lee Corporation; the same goes for Norton, acquired by Saint-Gobain, or Grundig, bought by the Thomson group. In acquiring these brands, these companies acquired the rights expected from these contracts; they also assumed the duties and requirements implied in them.

Like money once again, brands facilitate international trade. Brands are the only truly international language—a business Esperanto. Kodak is Kodak all over the world, just like Bull, Siemens, Michelin, Hilton, Lacoste, or Club Med. Not even money can claim as much: the pound sterling becomes a "livre" on the other side of the Channel. As for country names, Germans see their Deutschland become Allemagne in French. With brands, though, every buyer anywhere in the world knows what the seller is talking about.

Brands are the real capital of business, yet brand management is still in its infancy. At present, the tendency is to manage products that happen to have a name. Management is still living in the age of the product, but brand management involves other, specific approaches and principles. These are the focus of this presentation.

Management books and marketing bibles have not yet assimilated the full implication of the brand revolution and the new brand consciousness to which it has given rise. They speak only of products and services and of what is manufactured—not of what people buy. Young managers read about product life cycles, and how to divide them into phases from introduction to growth, maturity, decline, and retirement. Yet many dynamic and "modern" brands are actually more than a century old—take Coca-Cola, for example. Though products do die from natural obsolescence, brands can go on and on. The misguided belief that brands were simply the names of products was formerly so strong that brands have been thrown out with the products that carried them, once the product was judged to have reached the end of its life cycle.

Marketing manuals emphasize the process of launching new products. There, branding is merely a tactical decision at the end of the process, solely a matter of communication, just like advertising, packaging, and graphics. The reality, however, is very different. Henceforth, the strategic question facing businesses is whether they can grow using their existing brands, by expanding their range of action, or whether it is necessary to launch or acquire new brands. Traditional strategic management models speak of "product portfolios." The fact is that companies must manage *brand* portfolios. Yet in the very way that they are organized, many companies still have product managers, but no brand managers. Given that single brands are often expected to carry an increasingly large and varied number of products, this simply means that management of a shared asset is delegated *de facto* to several different decision-making centers. Without the benefit of integrating tools, decisions are made that over the medium term can erode brand equity.

A brand is not a product: it is the product's source, its meaning, and its direction, and it defines its identity in time and space. Businesses are discovering that brand equity must be managed, nurtured, and controlled. Brand consciousness is raising new questions for managers: how many brands are enough? How do you manage a brand portfolio? How should a brand be extended? What products and services should it encompass? Or, on the other hand, what should its limits be, even when a certain turnover is expected from it? Going too far can also weaken brand equity. How do you manage brands over time and keep them up to date, as technologies, products, and customers are changing? How do you change while staying the same? How do you provide consistent, synergic management of the range of products sold under a single brand? How do you optimize image in the relationship between products and their brand? How far can a brand be extended geographically? Does it have the potential to become a homogeneous geo-brand in all countries? Or is this impossible, or even undesirable? Many companies have the same name as their brand (e.g., Renault, Nestlé, IBM, BASF). What is the difference between managing a brand image and managing corporate and institutional image? Finally, given that brands do have a value, how can this be measured, so that it can be tracked and controlled? Should it be capitalized on the balance sheet, to indicate its true economic value to stockholders, investors, and financial partners?

These are all new questions, and each one deserves an answer. For the time being, such answers have been found intuitively, and decisions have been made by trial and error. Our goal is to provide a framework for comprehensive reflection and analysis, creating a rational means of finding answers. The models of analysis and decision-making presented here have grown out of research and have been tested in consulting situations and confirmed in practice. As demonstrated by the numerous case studies, the models offered concern brands in areas ranging from industry to service, from luxury goods and fashion to basic consumer goods and distributor's brands. These models are just as applicable in the United Kingdom as in Germany, or the United States and Japan.

Too often, brands are examined through their component parts: the brand name, its logo, design, or packaging, advertising or sponsorship, or image and name recognition, or very recently, in terms of financial brand valuation. Real brand management, however, begins much earlier, with a strategy and a consistent, integrated vision. Its central concept is brand identity, not brand image. This identity must be defined and managed. It is the heart of brand management. It calls for new means of thought and investigation; these are presented here.

I

Understanding Brands

1

What's In a Brand?

The logic of branding

Many corporations have forgotten why they have brands. A great deal of attention is devoted to the branding process *per se*, bringing in the participation of designers, graphic artists, and advertising agencies. This activity becomes an end in itself, receiving most of the focus of attention. In so doing, we forget that it is only a means to an end. Branding becomes the exclusive prerogative of the marketing and communications staff, thereby undervaluing the importance of other corporate functions to successful brand management.

While branding is an indispensable activity, it is only the last phase in a process that involves the corporation's resources and all of its functions, focusing them on one strategic purpose: creating a difference. Only by mobilizing all of its internal sources of added value can a company set itself apart from its competitors.

WHAT DOES BRANDING MEAN?

Branding is much more than the naming *per se* or the creation of an external indication that a product or service has received an organization's imprint or its mark.

9

A Brand Aims to Segment the Market

Brands are part of a strategy aimed at differentiating supply. Companies seek to better fulfill the expectations of specific groups of customers. They do so by consistently and repeatedly providing an ideal combination of attributes—both tangible and intangible, practical and symbolic, visible and invisible—under conditions that are economically viable for the company. The company wants to leave its mark on a given field, and set its imprint on a product. It is no coincidence that the word "brand" also means the actual act of burning a mark into the skin of an animal; of designating ownership in this way. When we talk of an Atari computer, it is like saying, "There's something Atari in this computer." Indeed, this is the first task in branding: defining just what the brand infuses into the product or service, and how the brand transforms it:

- What attributes are embodied in the product or service?
- What advantages does it incorporate?
- What benefits does it provide?
- What obsessions does it represent?

This underlying meaning of a brand is often forgotten or wilfully neglected. Some distributors are frequently heard to say, "For us, the brand is secondary. No need to stick something on our products." In so doing, they are reducing brands to their most superficial aspect, the label and the trademark on it.

Branding, however, is not based on what goes on, but on what goes in. The result is an augmented product or service which must be indicated in one way or another if it is to be noticed by potential buyers, and if the company is to reap the fruits of its efforts before they are copied by others.

On this point, it is highly significant that a product which has been "debranded" retains a greater value than a generic product. If it were true that a brand was something purely superficial, just like a label, then such a product would lose its value as soon as it lost its signs of brand identification. Instead, it continues to incarnate the brand: the brand's passing presence has transformed the product. This explains the value of Lacoste shirts without the Lacoste label, or Adidas shoes stripped of the Adidas name. They are worth more than counterfeit imitations, because the brand is present even when it cannot be seen. In contrast, though the brand may appear on an imitation, it is actually missing.

Brands are Built Up by Persistent Difference Over the Long Run

It is often pointed out that products bearing different brand names are identical. Some observers conclude that under these circumstances, a brand is nothing but a bluff, a device used to attempt to set a product apart in markets in which it is hard to differentiate among products.

This attitude neglects the time factor and the concept of competition. Brands become known through the products they create and bring on to the market. Whenever a brand innovates, it generates "me-too-ism." Any progress made quickly becomes a standard to which buyers become accustomed. Competing brands must then follow suit if they do not want to fall beneath market expectations. For a short time, the innovative brand will enjoy a monopoly, but it will be a fragile one unless the innovation is patented or patentable. Simply put, the role of the brand name is to protect the innovation—it creates a "mental" patent.

Take the example of Kellogg's, who created a new cereal that was natural and rich in fiber, two highly valued aspects of modern nutrition. In the light of its success, other manufacturers produced similar products. If Kellogg's had given its cereal a generic name such as "natural fiber cereal," consumers would soon have discovered that manufacturers such as Quaker and distributors such as Marks & Spencer and Aldi also had their own natural fiber cereal. The chosen name Country Store makes the innovative product specific. Like any proper name, it designates something unique. The product name makes the innovation exclusive and protects it against imitations. This is nothing other than the just reward for innovating, making an effort, and taking risks. And yet, while this corporation innovates by introducing products like Cocopops and Smacks one day and Country Store the next, no capitalization emerges from these efforts alone. These biscuits do not make their creative inventor famous. It takes something more than specific product names to obtain such capitalization: it takes the establishment of a brand name like Kellogg's. By producing such innovations, Kellogg's develops a capital of consumer trust and an image of a playful, high-quality creator. It can then reap the benefits of innovating repeatedly. The brand is what makes it possible to capitalize on innovation, for both the buyer and the seller.

A snapshot of a given market will often show similar products. A dynamic vision, however, reveals who has innovated and pulled the competition along in the wake of its success. A brand protects the innovator, granting momentary exclusiveness and rewarding its willingness to take risks. The meaning and direction of a brand and its economic purpose is revealed in the accumulation over time of such momentary differences.

Brands cannot be reduced to a symbol on a product or a mere graphic and cosmetic exercise. A brand is the signature on a constantly renewed, creative process which yields product A today, products B and C tomorrow, and so on. Products are introduced, they live and disappear, but brands endure. The consistency of this creative action is what gives a brand its meaning, its contents, and its character. Creating a brand requires time and an identity.

A Brand is a Living Memory

The spirit of a brand can only be inferred through its products and its advertising. The content of a brand grows out of the cumulative memory of these acts, provided they are governed by a unifying idea or guideline. Kellogg's, for instance, does not attach its name to any product: Frosties, All Bran, Special K, Rice Krispies all bear the marks of a single intention, marks that display certain values, attributes, and guiding principles. These are original, creative, healthy products for our times, universal products created with great refinement. This is a brand with flair, inventiveness, and a gift for quality.

The importance of memory in comprising a brand explains why its image can vary structurally from generation to generation. People who knew Gillette fifty years ago, when it appeared on the now famous blue blade, necessarily have a different conception of the brand from young fans of the disposable Gillette. The way we are introduced to a brand creates an anchor in our memories that shapes all future perceptions. This is the problem with two-track brands like Citroën cars: the brand image of those who discovered Citroën through the 2CV is diametrically opposed to that of individuals who first encountered it in the forms of the sleek DS or the XM. Then there are drivers who still remember its Traction Avant model, introduced before the Second World War. The memory factor also helps to explain why individual preferences endure. Within a given generation, people continue to prefer the brands they liked between the ages of seven and eighteen, as much as twenty years later (Guest, 1964; Fry *et al.*, 1973; Jacoby and Chestnut, 1978).

A Brand is a Genetic Program

A brand is both the memory and the future of its products. A genetic analogy provides a key to understanding how brands work. The brand memory that develops contains the program for all future developments, the attributes of later models, the characteristics they will have in common, and their family resemblance as well as their individual personalities. By understanding a brand's program, we can trace its legitimate territory and the area in which it can be extended, beyond the products that created it. The brand's implicit program reveals the meaning and direction of both former and future products.

A Brand Gives Products Their Meaning and Direction

The brand tells why products exist, where they come from, and where they are going. It also sets their guidelines. A brand is not a fact set in stone. It must be able to adapt to the times, to changes in buyers and in technology. Through subtle changes in what it produces, both in its products or services, and symbolically in its communication, this is how it stays up-to-date. A brand is built up from day to day; it is never set down once and for all. Of course its past must not determine its future too narrowly. But when a brand moves out in all directions, it can lose its meaning and become void of content.

The major brands have meanings that describe their content and their sense of direction. In the area of household appliances, for example, Siemens means durability, seriousness, and trust; it conjures up an image of careful, meticulous German workmanship. Hotpoint stands for practicality, carefree use, and the familiarity of a close friend who has watched the children grow up. Philips has acquired a reputation for innovating for the general public, putting technology at the service of the general population. It becomes apparent that on every market, each major brand has its own meaning. This meaning is very important, because it tells buyers what direction the brand's research, innovation, and other efforts are taking. One highlights durability, another practicality or innovation. Just as a word cannot have two meanings at once, since one is constantly dominant, no brand would attempt to embody all possible meanings. Each one follows its own path and leaves its own mark.

That similar products exist in the product lines of several brands does not invalidate those brands' existence, provided this similarity stays within limits. It is inevitable that certain models will be duplicated in the product lines of different brands. In the automobile industry, the cost constraints at the low end are such that it is difficult to manufacture a model very different from the competition. For economic reasons, however, a brand may be obliged to have an offering on this type of generally highly disputed market. By the same token, every bank must offer a basic savings account identical to that of all other banks.

These basic products represent only a limited fringe of each brand's offer (cf. Figure 1.1). Each brand maintains a sense of direction oriented toward its individual type of products, following a specific line of development. Suppose that brand A pursues durability, B practicality, and C innovation. Each product line contains products in which the brand demonstrates its guiding value, its obsession. These products embody the brand's meaning and direction. Citroën, for instance, is best embodied in its top-range cars, Nina Ricci in its fanciful evening gowns, and Sony in its Walkman or its Camcorders. This is why communication about such products is so important to a brand: they embody what the brand is about. Peugeot and Citroën cars, for instance, may have certain identical attributes, but the brands themselves have neither the same meaning nor the same identity.

Products cannot speak for themselves: the brand is what gives them meaning and speaks for them. It creates a resonance with them that builds and reinforces brand identity. The automobile industry is a case in point. Most technical innovations by one firm rapidly spread to the other brands. ABS braking systems are now to be found on both Volvos and BMWs, even though the two manufacturers hardly have

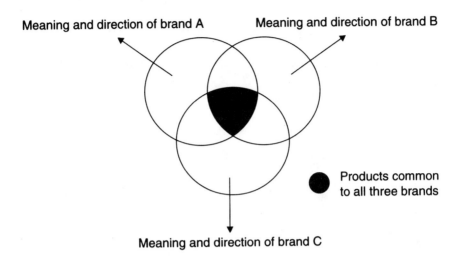

Meaning and direction of brand A   Meaning and direction of brand B

Products common to all three brands

Meaning and direction of brand C

Figure 1.1

Product line overlap among brands

the same identity. Is that a case of brand inconsistency? Not at all: ABS represents progress that everyone had to adopt. The brand gives its own identity to innovations

On the other hand, a brand can only be developed through long-term consistency that is both the source and the proof of its identity. Hence the same ABS (anti-blocking system) has a subtly different meaning for each manufacturer. For Volvo, a firm which preaches total safety, ABS is a necessity that serves the brand's values and obsessions. It embodies the brand's attributes. BMW, a high-performance brand, cannot discuss ABS in these terms—it would be a betrayal of its ideology and the system of values that galvanizes the whole organization and engenders the models that have made the Munich manufacturer famous. Instead, BMW presents ABS as a way to drive even faster. In the same way, safety-conscious Volvo accounts for its participation in European touring car racing championships by its desire to test its products better so that they last even longer.

A detail is never enough to establish a brand's identity, but the way it is interpreted lends weight to a broader strategy. A detail can only leave its mark on a brand if it resonates with the brand, deepening and amplifying the brand's meaning. This is why weak brands cannot

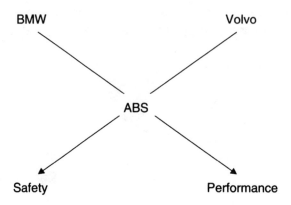

Figure 1.2

capitalize on their innovations: they cannot manage to put meaning into them and to create that resonance. Though the BX car was a commercial success, it scarcely rubbed off on Citroën's image. Only brands with a strong identity can claim to be innovators.

A Brand is a Contract

A brand becomes credible through endurance and repetition. With time, the brand's program becomes a commitment. By creating satisfaction and loyalty, the brand enters into a virtual contract binding it to the market. In exchange, the brand earns an automatically favorable opinion of any new products it introduces. This reciprocal commitment explains why brands whose products have momentarily declined do not necessarily disappear. A brand is judged over the long term: there is always a margin for failure. Brand loyalty leaves it a respite for recovery. Without this, Jaguar would have vanished long ago: no other brand could have withstood the way its cars diminished in quality during the 1970s. This is one of the benefits a brand brings to its company, in addition to the image capitalization it makes possible and the "mental patent" effect referred to earlier.

The contract a brand establishes is economic, not legal. Brands differ in this way from other signs of quality, such as quality labels and certification. Quality labels or seals attest officially and legally that a product meets a set of specific characteristics previously laid down by public authorities, producers, and consumers. These characteristics determine a superior level of quality that distinguishes the product from other similar goods. Seals are collective marks held by a certification agency which verifies production in accordance with a schedule of specifications. Certification is therefore never acquired definitively, and it can be withdrawn. In France, the "Label Rouge," a national agricultural quality seal, guarantees an objective level of superior quality. Woolmark is a special type of seal: it, too, is a collective sign, but it is managed and held by a private organization, the Australian wool producers, who are the only ones who may receive the seal. Neither a brand nor a certificate of controlled origin offers legal guarantees of an objective quality level. It is only through its existence over time that a brand progressively becomes a virtual contract.

The Internal Requirements Involved in Branding

A contract implies constraints. The brand approach assumes first of all that an organization and its various functions—R&D, production, methods, logistics, marketing, finance—all have a single, specific focus. The same is true of service brands. Of course, the R&D and production aspects are missing, but this simply shifts the duty to observe continuity and consistency onto the shoulders of personnel who have a key role to play in relations with customers.

The brand approach requires internal as well as external marketing. Unlike quality seal users, each brand sets its own standards. It must therefore meet them and must strive to outdo them continuously in order to satisfy the expectations of customers, who quickly become accustomed to the brand's latest progress. The brand must also make its standards generally known. This is a lonely task, aimed at differentiating the product and acquiring an aura of exclusivity. The brand alone must bear all the internal and external costs. What are these requirements and costs?

- Paying close attention to the needs and expectation of potential customers: this is the purpose of market studies.
- Incorporating technical and technological progress as soon as this can create a cost differential or performance advantage.
- Being able to provide product (or service) volume and homo-

geneity; this is the only way to ensure repeat purchases. It presupposes consistent quality in the offer.

- Controlling supply quality and quantity.
- Ensuring deliveries to intermediaries and distributors while respecting the deadlines, conditions, and formats they request, and doing so consistently.
- Being able to give sense and direction to a brand, and to communicate its meaning to the target public. This is what advertising budgets are for.

A strong brand becomes a symbol with the power to mobilize internally and to attract on the outside. It is the company's standard-bearer and its driving force. As such, it is greater than many attempts to establish guiding business or corporate principles. These last only while they are being developed, and are then forgotten, or may lead to fine phrases ("A Passion for Excellence!") on posters in the reception area. The brand, though, is the organization's external façade, maintaining a constant requirement and necessity to aim ever higher.

BRANDS AND OTHER SIGNS OF QUALITY

In many fields, brands coexist with other signs of quality. In the food sector, for instance, in addition to brands, there are also quality labels, certificates of conformity with standards, and controlled origin guarantees. This variety of other signs results from a twofold goal: to protect and promote products.

Certifications of origin (e.g., real Scotch whisky) are intended to protect a branch of agriculture and products whose quality is intimately linked with a specific place and know-how. The controlled origin is part of a subjective, culturally based concept of quality, rooted in the mystery and typicality bound up in a place. It segments the market by refusing the guarantee of origin to any product not made in a specific area according to traditional practices. In France, the July 2, 1990 law has established Roquefort as a controlled origin product. Even if Danish cheesemakers and Kraft could make a roquefort cheese in other regions or countries, which consumers could not distinguish from the roquefort made in the village of Roquefort according to ancestral methods, their products can no longer lay claim to the name "Roquefort."

Quality seals are promotional tools. These adhere to another, more industrial and scientific, concept of quality. According to this concept, a specific cheese involves objective know-how, using a given type of milk mixed with selected bacteria, and so forth. The quality label creates a vertical segmentation corresponding to objective levels of quality. The issue here is not typicality, but satisfying a stringent set of objective criteria.

The legal guarantee of typicality in a controlled origin marks a difference from a simple indication of source, which does not ensure any specificity based on natural or social factors—though it may be an attempt to suggest to buyers that one exists. Many modern cheese manufacturers attempt to cloud the issue further by adopting names that sound like the names of places or towns (e.g., German Camembert have French names) in order to evoke rustic, typical images. Quality seals, on the other hand, with their legal guarantee of objective quality, attempt to establish a hard factual aspect counterbalancing brand names chosen to suggest excellence. For instance, Rothschild, with its rich title, suggests the product offers high quality, yet it is recognized as a low-quality champagne.

Whether official indications of quality will continue to exist in Europe after 1993 will be a subject of debate between northern countries (e.g., the United Kingdom and Denmark), who believe only brands should prevail, and southern countries (e.g., France, Spain, Italy), who support official collective signs in addition to brands (Feral, 1989). According to the former countries, brands alone should be allowed to segment the market and build reputations for excellence around a name, as the fruit of production, distribution, and marketing efforts. These countries tend to favor an objective concept of quality: who cares if the Greeks' favorite feta is made in Holland or in the south of France, or if Smirnoff vodka is neither Russian nor Polish? The view of the southern states is that collective signs enable small businesses to make known their quality level or typicality, even though they use no specific brands. Their products cannot speak for themselves: a quality seal or certified origin gives them a position in consumers' minds. Clearly, behind the upcoming European debate on whether brands that have forged their own reputation are to coexist with official collective signs of quality, there is a second debate between the proponents of a free-market economy and the partisans of public authority intervention to regulate the economy. From the corporate point of view, the choice of a brand approach or the use of collective signs is a matter of strategy and of the resources that can be committed. A brand sets its own standards: legally, these do not form a commitment, but in practice, the brand comes to promise a group of specific attributes and values. It therefore seeks to become a reference in itself, if not the reference (as is the case for Société Roquefort, the very symbol of roquefort). By their fundamental nature, brands differentiate, but they do not like to share these differences. Strong brands are those that distribute values and manage to segment the market through their own efforts.

On an operational level, a brand, once again, is not simply an act of advertising. It embodies a proposal incorporating the long-term specificity of the products bearing its name, an attractive price, efficient marketing, and the projection of the brand identity through advertising. It is easier for a small business to earn a quality seal for one its products, through strict efforts on quality, than it is to undertake the demanding adventure of creating a brand, which consumes such quantities of financial, human, technical, and business resources. Even without an identity, the small business's product becomes less anonymous, thanks in part to the legal indicators of quality.

To create a brand, producers must often pool their efforts, preparing and marketing the products of independent companies under a single brand. This is the case with Yoplait. Organized collectively, this brand achieves uniform production, packaging, services, prices, delivery systems, and even communication, all around the world. A brand is a total responsibility and an external commitment to customers and distributors. This commitment leads those who participate in the brand to standardize their practices. Controlled origin guarantees and quality labels are much less demanding, since all they require of users is the observance of specific criteria, generally related to the product or service. Everyone remains free to design his own marketing mix.

Collective labels for segmenting markets are a windfall for small businesses: they motivate efforts to attain quality and distribute information on products that were previously anonymous and unable to speak for themselves. A collective label creates a message that partially compensates for the absence of brand message. It creates an objective or subjective hierarchy of quality that differentiates some productions from others. In so doing, by helping many businesses that do not have the means to pursue a brand policy, it weakens strong brands, because it enables small brands to make a statement about their level of performance and meaning. This explains why corporations with major brands are ambivalent about market-segmentation through collective labels.

Because a brand transforms a product, it rejects everything that associates it with other producers. For instance, Société Roquefort paradoxically has nothing to gain from the fact that roquefort is now a controlled origin. Until now, this brand—the first in French history, created in 1842—had become the best by dint of constancy, respect for tradition, and an obsession with quality. In the minds of the public and of connoisseurs, Société stands for the authenticity of a place and its know-how (i.e., typicality) as well as fine taste (i.e., quality). Suddenly, the segmentation it had created separating it from all other brands has been diminished by the creation of a collective sign of typicality: legislation has wiped away a part of the difference between the flagship brand and its competitors. Now Société will have to become for Roquefort what Chateau Margaux is for the town of Margaux.

A strong brand is one that projects its values and manages to segment the market according to its own standards. It seeks to impose these standards and to become the reference. It therefore keeps its distance from collective means of segmentation.

Some major brands find quality seals to be useful and necessary springboards. At the outset they participate in them by financing campaigns that make these seals known, in order to promote a sign of quality that will reflect favorably on some of their products. Then, as their importance in financing promotion of the collective seal grows, they choose to funnel these sums into building their own brand and differentiating it from the competition. Such a brand must go further than the seal, promising an even higher level of quality which it alone embodies.

The ambivalent relationship between brands and collective signs can be extended to the collective campaigns themselves, which seek to change the image of a sector or the product category as a whole. Sometimes an entire sector may be threatened. Accustomed to competing with one another, none of the brands may want to assume the task of defending the sector. This is the case when the market leader actually has a relatively small market share. In such cases, a collective campaign is called for, which sends a different message from those of individual brands.

In contrast, when one brand is dominant, it may want to incarnate the sector as a whole and to speak for the sector in its own name. While projecting a brand message, it does work that improves the image of the whole sector, though it reflects primarily on the brand itself.

OBSTACLES TO ADOPTING A BRAND LOGIC

Within companies, the brand approach often comes into conflict with other approaches. Unwritten and implicit, these are thought to be neutral, when in fact they create obstacles to a true brand policy.

Business accounting rules are currently unfavorable toward brands. This is because accounting is governed by a need for prudence: consequently, any outlay that is not certain to result in a future recovery is written off as an expense, rather than recorded as an asset. This applies to investments in communication, which spread the word about what makes the brand different. Because it is not possible to measure exactly what share of the annual communications budget generates returns immediately, or in one, two, or several years, the whole sum is taken as an operating expense which is subtracted from the profits for the year in which it is incurred. Yet advertising, like investments in equipment, talented employees, or R&D, contributes to the development of brand equity. Accounting methods therefore create a bias that handicaps companies with brands, because they lead to an underestimation. Take the case of company A, which invests heavily to develop its brand name. Because these investments must appear in its accounting sheets as expenses, this results in low annual profits, and its balance sheet will display only a small asset value. This comes during a crucial period for the company's growth, when it may need help from outside investors and banks. Now compare company B, which invests the same amounts in equipment and production, putting nothing into its name, image, or reputation. Because it is authorized to record these tangible investments as assets and to amortize them gradually over several years, company B can announce higher profits, and its balance sheet, displaying higher assets, will look healthier. B will have a better image in accounting terms, even though A may actually be better placed to differentiate its products.

The principle of annual accounting valuation also hinders the brand approach. Each product manager is judged on his annual results and the net contribution made by his product. This places too much focus on the short term in assessing decisions, and favors decisions that bring quickly measurable results over those that build brand equity more slowly, but more solidly for the future. In addition, product-based accounting discourages product managers from taking on an additional advertising effort that would serve essentially to bolster the brand, when the brand works as an umbrella, covering other products as well. Managers only see that this extra expenditure in the general interest will be charged to their own statement of earnings. For example, Palmolive is a brand that covers several products, including dishwashing liquid, shampoo, and shaving cream. A decision could be made to communicate only about one of these products, taken as an image standard-bearer. The investment made would then be higher than could be justified solely by the expected sales of that product, because the collective image would also be heightened by it. This extra expenditure will nonetheless be written as an expense and charged to the product in question, even though it serves collective goals and benefits all the products under the brand umbrella.

In a reaction against the short-term bias caused by accounting practices and the way that balance sheets underestimate their values, some British companies have begun to capitalize the value of their brands in their balance sheets. This has set off a fundamental debate over the legitimacy of accounting practices that emerged in the "age of commodities," when assets primarily took the form of real estate and equipment. Today, intangible assets (know-how, patents, and reputation) are what make the difference over the long run. But beyond the need for an open debate in Europe and the world on how to capitalize brands, companies must find a way to write the long-term advantages and disadvantages of short-term brand decisions. This is rendered even more necessary by the (excessively?) high turnover among brand managers themselves.

A high personnel turnover disrupts the continuity a brand needs. Yet companies today actually program the rotation of their employees through different brands! Brands are entrusted to young MBA graduates who are inexperienced, no matter how prestigious their degree may be. What they want is a promotion, which takes the form of being assigned to a different brand. Brand managers are thus forced to produce visible results in the short term. This helps to explain many changes in advertising strategy or programs and in decisions on brand extension, promotion, or discounts. They are actually caused by changes in personnel.

It is significant that brands which have maintained a continuous, consistent message are those belonging to businesses with stable brand decision-makers. This is the case for luxury brands: the presence of the same creator or founder establishes the conditions for sound, long-term management. The same is true of major distributors. Their executives tend to stay put, and often handle communication or at least make the final decisions about it. In addition to incorporating brand value into their accounts, companies are trying to alleviate the effects of excessive brand-manager rotation by creating a long-term image charter as a lens through which to view the task of maintaining brand identity. This introduces a vital touchstone and is a tool for continuity.

Business organization can also prove an obstacle to brand management. To be commercially efficient, EDP service companies, for instance, are organized into divisions, the better to handle the problems of their specific sectors or functions. GSI, a European leader in the field, has divisions for travel, transportation, economy and finance, human resources management, marketing, and so on. The problem is that it becomes difficult to make collective investments to foster the name they share, GSI. Company organization makes this difficult: each division manager is assessed on his own financial results, which he naturally seeks to optimize.

Another classic syndrome is creating a brand without a specific supporting organization that could give it form and content, and therefore consistency. This was the case with the brand France Télécom International, which was to be an umbrella brand for all of France Télécom's international activities. Unfortunately, its organization remained vertical and tightly compartmented. There was no real horizontal structure behind the brand. Potential customers found themselves passed on to other divisions or subsidiaries (e.g., Télésystèmes, France Cable Radio), each of which had its own identity.

The third syndrome involves the relationship between production and sales. The production units in the Electrolux group are specialized by product. Their focus is single-product and multi-market, as they sell this product to business units, whose focus is, in contrast, single-market and multiproduct (the products are covered by an umbrella brand). The problem is that these independent business divisions, each with its own brand, all want to take advantage of the latest innovation from the production division, to maximize their individual earnings. What is missing is a structure for managing and allocating these innovations as part of a consistent, global vision of the brand portfolio. As we saw earlier (page 14), there is no point in entrusting a strong innovation to a weak brand. In particular, this undermines the very foundation of the brand approach, i.e., differentiation.

Failing to manage innovations has a very negative impact on brand equity. By letting each business division claim the same innovation for itself simultaneously, Electrolux contributed to the collapse of its best brand, which was weakened by its sister brand in the group. The latter is an attractive brand for discount stores, positioned on its low prices. Yet it received the same technical innovations as the leader, positioned as a high-end, more expensive, brand. If a brand is to have meaning, this must be reflected in the way innovations are allocated.

In contrast, Peugeot and Citroën share many internal resources and automobile parts, to attain cost and scale economies. But this has not prevented the two manufacturers from developing two car concepts that are very different on the assembly line, as can be seen through different external components, as well as specific internal components, when these are essential to the brand's meaning. For instance, the Citroën XM "hydro-active" suspension is different from the conventional suspension on the Peugeot 605. Similarly, top-of-the-line Volvos have the same engine as the Renault 25. But Volvo has built its meaning on other aspects besides the engine, as has Renault. Having an engine in common does not handicap these brands. In contrast, as General Motors made more and more apparent all that its various brands (e.g., Pontiac, Chevrolet, Buick) had in common, it fell into decline on American markets.

Along the same lines, when a producer supplies a distributor's brand with the same product it sells under its own brand, it gradually erodes its brand equity and, more generally, the respectability of the very concept of branding. It is stating by its action that what customers pay more for in a brand is the name and nothing else. By dissociating the brand from the augmented product it identifies and represents, the brand is made into something superficial and artificial, with no legitimate reason to exist. Ultimately, companies pay the price for dissipating their brand equity, when discount distributors declare in their advertising that brands are used to exploit consumers, and that consumers can resist by buying generic products. (This was the official line of Carrefour's advertising from 1976 to 1978.) This also justifies the sluggishness of public authorities in the face of increasing trademark infringement by distributors' brands. Moreover, such practices generally foster a false understanding of what brands are, even among opinion leaders, contributing to the rumor that nowadays all products are the same.

Finally, the way that various communications services are organized does not lend itself to the requirements of a sound brand approach. Even an advertising agency that incorporates a network of services covering name creation research, packaging, graphic identity, and corporate communication, event creation or promotion, presenting itself as an integrated communications group, remains an advertising agency at heart. And advertising agencies think only in terms of campaigns, operating in a short, one-year timeframe. The brand approach is something else: it develops over a long period and requires a fully integrated approach, where all means used are contemplated together.

It is clear that a company rarely finds contacts inside such so-called communications groups who will take responsibility for developing an encompassing overview that is not based on advertising without feeling obliged to sell a campaign. Furthermore, advertising agencies are not in a position to answer strategic questions, such as what the optimal number of brands in a portfolio should be. Given that the answer influences the survival of the brands for which it does the advertising, the agency finds itself in the awkward position of being judge and jury. This is why a new profession, that of the strategic brand-management consultant, must emerge. The time has come for businesses to have access to a medium-range vision that is not confined to a single technique and that is capable of providing consistent, integrated guidelines for the development of their brand portfolios.

SERVICE BRANDING

There is no legal difference between manufacturers' brands and service brands. These are economic distinctions, but not legal ones. By restricting itself to branding *per se*, the law is of little help in understanding how brands and the branding process work, and their specificity in the area of products or services.

Service brands do exist, such as Europcar, Hertz, Ecco, Manpower, Cap Sogeti, Club Méditerranée, Hilton, Marriott, Sofitel, and Harvard. Each one identifies a specific set of attributes that take the shape of a definite, though intangible, service: rent-a-cars, temporary employees, data processing, leisure activities, hotel chains, or higher education. Some service sectors seem to be just entering the brand age. This evolution is fascinating to watch, as it highlights just what is involved in adopting a brand approach, and reveals the specificities of branding an intangible service.

The banking industry is a fine example. If bank customers were asked what bank brands they knew, they would probably seem dubious or confused. They know the names of banks, but not bank brands. This is significant: for the public, these names are not brands identifying a specific service. They are corporate names or insignia belonging to a given place. It is true that, until recently, bank names designated either the owner of the corporation entrusted with the customer's funds (e.g., Barclay's, Morgan, or Coutts Bank) or a specific area (e.g., Midland Bank, National Westminster), or its target clientele (e.g., City Bank or Home Owners Building Society). The emergence of a brand approach can generally be discerned from the outside by a contraction of the name. Banque Nationale de Paris becomes BNP, Banque de Paris et des Pays Bas becomes Paribas, and National Westminster becomes NatWest. Some observers take this to be a desire to make the name look simpler, according to advertising precepts favoring what is easy to remember. It is easier to recognize the name of someone who uses a short signature. But though its incidence cannot be denied, this idea limits branding to brand names per se, and to the realm of communication.

What these banks are doing fundamentally by contracting their names is to become or establish a contract. Up to that point, some of them were the local bank. Their name designated their location, with no other meaning, just as an insignia (from *in signum*, sign + in) refers exclusively to a specific area. Because banks were primarily perceived in terms of places or persons, these names became proper names which rigidly designated a reality limited in time and space. Brands, on the contrary, are atemporal and aterritorial (with the exception of distributor's brands). They identify a set of attributes and make a commitment to a long-term difference in the banking services themselves. In this sense we can speak of a brand contract. Though it is a noun, the brand works as an adjective and a verb, explaining how the service has been transformed, what attributes it has received, and by what values it is governed.

As they are contracted, these bank names come to represent a specific relationship instead of a person or a place. To make it visible, this relationship may take the form of specific financial instruments (or exclusive policies in the insurance field). But these visible and easy-to-imitate products are not what explain and justify the move to a brand. They are merely the external manifestation. These banks and insurance companies have understood the key to what makes them different: the relationships that develop between a customer and a banker under the auspices of the brand.

Finally, one specific aspect of service brands that contrasts with product brands is that the service is invisible. What does a bank have to show, except customers or consultants? Structurally, service brands are handicapped in creating images of themselves. This is why the brand uses slogans. It is not coincidence that slogans are voiced (*vocare*), representing *vocatio*, the brand's calling or vocation. The slogan is a commandment for internal and external relations. Through it, the brand defines its behavioral guidelines, and these guidelines give the customer the right to be dissatisfied when they are transgressed. It is not enough for a bank to vaunt its smile or its listening ear. These attributes must be assimilated by the people who offer and deliver the service. Human beings are intrinsically and unavoidably variable: this is the challenge for the brand approach in service industries.

In banking, the requirement of maximizing short-term business results is often contrary to brand logic, even though banks claim to follow this logic in every other aspect. Crédit Lyonnais sums up its specificity and its guiding principle in a now famous slogan stating why it is different: "We have the power to say yes." This demonstrates the corporation's intention to give broader powers to the personnel that have direct customer contact. More than just window dressing, the advisory function of these employees is to be supported by the capacity to take immediate action—it is impossible to dispense good advice without decentralizing power. Is this positioning compatible with the orders given to all Crédit Lyonnais employees to "sell" as many Popular Savings Plans (PSP) as possible, when this new savings plan is available in exactly the same form at all other banks? Many customers should be advised against opening PSPs, or should at least realize they might have little to gain from doing so. A real advisory vocation is incompatible with a policy of opening PSPs for everyone, whatever their circumstances. This example proves that, notably in the banking industry, brands are still perceived as a way of speaking differently about products or services, but nothing more. Brand logic has not yet been sufficiently assimilated by the production and distribution departments.

LUXURY BRANDS

In luxury markets, there is some confusion surrounding the relationship between the concept of luxury brands, which the French call "griffes," or literally "claws." The term griffe is sometimes used to describe a luxury brand if the brand is applied to several products (Botton and Cegarra, 1990). Others claim that brands can become griffes (Rastoin, 1981). In reality, brands and griffes must be distinguished, in the ground they cover and the way they work. This leads to the realization that Dior, for example, is a griffe for one part of its production and a brand for another. In fact, a griffe can become a brand, but not the other way around.

Here again, the law does not differentiate between griffes and brands. In legal terms, a griffe is the fixed image of a signature, set down to be used as a brand. Yet the very word griffe says much more. Its other meaning, "claw," suggests instinct and violence: it is something unpredictable, that leaps out and leaves its mark. In this sense, the griffe is the mark of an inspired and instinctive creator. Last but not least, griffe has the same root as "graphic," and it refers back to the hand. Its reference model is handmade work and craftsmanship.

The specific domain of the griffe is clearly the world of creation. It refers to the world of art, it employs handmade production, and it is obsessed with creating works of unsurpassable perfection which is visible to the eye. The word "works" is crucial: the ideal behind a griffe is a unique work of art which can never be reproduced. This explains what it fears most: copies. Brands, in contrast, are afraid of fakes. Now it becomes clear why Dunhill, Dupont, Ferrari, and Porsche are not griffes in this sense, but luxury brands. These products emerge not from the workshop but from the factory, and their focus is not a unique work, but the series (even when limited). Their production is based not on instinct but on streamlined production. Of course there is something ingenious behind both Ferrari and Dior. But Dior is a creative genius, while Enzo Ferrari is a fantastic engineer.

Workshops can become industrialized and move into series, then mass production. But the opposite has never happened: factories do not aspire to become workshops. This is why a griffe can become a brand, adopting a democratic approach through the quantity and consistency ensured by mechanization. Yves Saint Laurent is a griffe when he signs his haute couture dresses; his name becomes a brand when applied to lipstick, ready-to-wear clothing, or perfume. In contrast, luxury brands like Breitling, Dunhill, Dupont, or Ferrari are never, properly speaking, griffes. The fact that they cover a great many products has nothing to do with the issue: it is a process called brand extension. Behind each of these prestigious brands lie the structural parameters of any brand: research, method, and stability. A griffe is a matter of inspiration, intuition, and the unpredictable.

2
Brand Identity

Few firms know what their brands are basically, where lies their unique quality, their singularity, their identity. Recognition of this absence of knowledge is generally prompted when the firm decides to undertake an advertising campaign on the brand itself, in addition to those of its products. Findus had spent the fifteen years up to 1989 vaunting the merits first of their "ready cooked meals," then their "lean cuisine," their "fish in breadcrumbs," etc. The firm realized that the brand now needed to speak directly and not only through its product campaigns. The handling of the brand campaign soon appeared uneasy. Among its managers there was no real consensus of opinion as to what Findus stood for. Management opinions were voiced in terms of a desired image—how they would *like* Findus to be perceived. Unfortunately, while a newly-created brand has absolute freedom to take any path it desires, such liberty of choice is greatly restricted after fifteen years. The brand has already acquired its own level of existence, its autonomy and identity. All this is lodged in the public mind and memory.

Others suggested that the problem should be approached from the customers' point of view—their image of Findus. But image is only a measure of what has been received, decoded. The real question is not "How is the brand seen?" but "What is the brand; what is its basic uniqueness?" It is not for the public to say what the brand should be—the brand must have its own identity. Answers to such questions will not be gained through classical advertising methods. Every advertising campaign is based on a copy strategy, which may change from one campaign to another. However, few brands follow a real brand charter of their individuality over a certain period. Nor can the answers be found in design or graphic guidelines which focus on the outlook of brand communications, packaging, etc. True understanding of the brand cannot be reduced to a graphic exercise. It should be an investigation of its very substance—the facets of brand identity. This chapter aims to explore these facets and to suggest the foundations for a brand charter.

In defining a brand's make-up we can answer numerous frequently-posed questions, such as:

- Can the brand sponsor a certain event or sport?
- Does the advertising campaign suit the brand?
- Is the opportunity to endorse a certain new product within the brand's field of legitimacy?
- How does the brand change its style of communication while keeping the same core identity?
- How can one expand to regional or international level while retaining the brand's singular identity?

All such decisions pose the problem of brand identity and definition—vital prerequisites for brand management.

BRAND IDENTITY: A NECESSARY CONCEPT

Brand identity is a recent idea. Is it just a fashionable phrase dreamed up by marketing and communications theorists, or does it have a real importance in an understanding of the brand?

What is Identity?

To appreciate the meaning of this significant concept in brand management, we shall begin by considering the various current usages of the word.

For example, we talk of an "identity card," or "ID" (which may be in the form of a passport, charge card, driver's license, etc.)—a personal nontransferable means of establishing who we are and, to some degree, our particular features. We also hear of "identity of opinion" between persons, signifying that they have an identical point of view. In communication terms, this second use of the word suggests that identity is what seems to spring from a single source, transmitted in terms of symbols, messages, and products themselves. This is important, since the more the brand extends and diversifies, the more the customer is inclined to feel that he is confronted with different brands and not a single one. If each product and its associated communication exercise traces its own path, it is difficult to retain the idea that all these paths emanate from the same brand source.

To talk of identity raises the question of permanence and continuity. Identity cards are updated. Individuals may change in status and outward appearance, but they still have basically the same fingerprint. The graphic signs of the brand certainly do have to evolve, so does advertising itself, but this brings into question the brand's ability to remain unique and permanent through time.

A third meaning of identity lies in the "identity crisis" label which psychologists attach, for instance, to certain adolescents.

Having yet to "find" themselves, youngsters seek to model their identity on one person after another. In wishing to resemble James Dean, Marlon Brando, or Richard Gere, the teenager reveals a feeling of insufficiency. These continuous changes create a void and force the basic question, "What is the real me?"

Finally, in a study of social or minority groups we often speak of "cultural identity," when people are bound by history, values, or by a feeling of participation in a common plan. Thus it can be said that minority groups have a strong identity, but their offspring are still in search of identity. For example, children born of immigrant parents can feel that they belong neither totally to their host community, nor to their parents' country of origin. In seeking an identity, they seek a pivotal basis on which they might pronounce and confirm not only their inherent difference but also their affinity to a cultural whole.

Brand identity may be a recent notion, but many researchers have delved into the identity of organizations (Reitter and Ramanantsoa, 1985; Schwebig, 1988). If we draw lessons from these varying meanings, having an identity means being as you are, following your own stable but individual plan. The essence of brand identity lies in the answers to the following questions concerning a particular brand:

- What is its individuality?
- What are its long-term goals and ambitions?
- What is its consistency?
- What are its values?
- What are its basic truths?
- What are its recognition signs?

These six questions point to the brand's definition and could indeed constitute its charter. (Advertising agencies such as BBDO and DDB make use of such questions to define brands.) In other words, such charters could form the basis for in-depth management of brand communication and extension over a given period. Communication tools such as the copy strategy do have their place in campaigns, but only in the short term. Other guidelines are necessary in building, layer upon layer, a one-and-only brand.

Brand Identity and Visual Identity Norms

Many readers will make the point that their firms already make use of graphic identity manuals. We do indeed find graphic "bibles" and other standard aids to visual identity in the company armory. Initiated by the disciples of graphic identity, firms have rightly sought to follow the common path in brand communication. But these visual norms focus on "descriptive recognition" and ask such questions as:

- What colors shall we choose?
- What design will look best?
- What type of print should be used?

Though this may be a necessary first step, it isn't the be-all and end-all. In any case, it puts the cart before the horse. The real problem is not one of graphic appeal—it concerns the very substance of that which is to be portrayed. Outward formal appearance—the look of the thing—is the expression of the deep-rooted identity of a brand. Choice of symbol presupposes a clear definition of the meaning of the brand. Though graphic manuals are now plentiful, it is still difficult to find precise definitions of brand identity within companies having such manuals. Normally, brand codes and style can be defined only after the six questions posed earlier have been answered. External signs of recognition must reflect the singularity of the brand; they do not of themselves compose this singularity. Citroën's identity, founded on an engineer's ideals of perfection, explains the typical design of its cars (DS, SM, CX, XM, etc.). BMW's family resemblance is clearly identifiable, but it is not a true identity. Its identity lies in the brand's individuality, goals, consistency, values, and vision.

Many firms have unnecessarily constrained their communication because they have formulated a visual identity charter before defining their brand core identity. Since they are unaware of the fundamental meaning of their brand, they continue to follow purely formal codes of practice, giving the greatest importance, for instance, to photographic style. Thus Nina Ricci's systematic adherence during twenty years to English photographer David Hamilton's style in their advertising program did not necessarily relate to this brand's deep identity. How often have we heard the anxious question, "What should be kept permanent in the advertising message from one campaign to another?" Looking at a typical brand advertising project, we wonder which features should be retained for permanent use. Do we focus on color, a cloudless sky, a posture—or perhaps a certain movement? Everything quickly becomes a code, and communication is frozen. Such dogmatism stifles the brand.

Knowing the brand identity, on the other hand, allows a certain freedom of expression, since it recognizes the preeminence of deep identity over the strictly formal features. Brand core identity defines what must remain permanent, and also what may evolve.

Identity: A Modern Concept

The emergence of a new concept—identity—is not altogether surprising, even though the world of communication is already acquainted with brand image and positioning. Today's problems are more complex than those of ten or twenty years ago. There is now a need for a finer approach to allow a better appreciation of the reality.

In the first place, we cannot cease to stress the state of overcommunication in which we find ourselves today. Everyone wishes to have a voice. Every small firm, every private or public body, even those in high (government) office—all wish to climb on the advertising bandwagon. One only has to look at the huge increase in advertising budgets, not only in the major media but also in the mounting number of professional magazines. It becomes extremely difficult to even exist in the hurly-burly thus created, let alone convey one's identity. For communication is not just the act of speaking, it is the ability to make oneself heard. Today communicating is not a technique, it is a feat in itself.

The second factor which highlights the urgent need for understanding brand identity is linked with the constraints weighing upon the brand. We have entered the era of "similarity marketing." When a brand is innovative it creates a new standard. Other brands must fall into line if they don't wish to fall behind in the field—hence the increasing number of similar, me-too products. Regulations are also a cause of similarity. Those governing bank operations, for example, contribute greatly to their inability to fully portray their individuality and identity. Market studies can also produce consistent trends within a sector. When they subscribe to the same lifestyle studies, companies draw similar conclusions, giving rise to identical campaigns sometimes voiced in the same ways. During the 1980s, how many bank slogans included the word "life"? If such companies rely only on a graphic format to differentiate themselves, the chances of conveying their identity are very slim.

Finally, technology is a cause of similarity. Why do cars increasingly look the same, in spite of their different makes? Car makers' concerns about fuel economy and drag coefficients, with their consequent restrictions on design, capacity, mechanization, and cost, result in similar outlooks. Moreover, when two makes of car such as Peugeot and Citroën share many identical parts (e.g., chassis, engine, gearbox) for production and economic reasons, they can rely only on each individual brand identity in order to end up with two dissimilar cars with the rest of the parts. Diversification also poses a serious threat to identity. New brands appear, penetrating new markets and fresh outlets. This not only creates a scattered or fragmented communication, but often gives rise to a patchwork image. The brand objectives do eventually pierce the confusion, but not in any coherent or integrative shape. Seeking to adapt to each of its markets, Toshiba presents a youthfully exuberant image in the hi-fi field, while being serious-minded in their microcomputer advertising, and waxing truly lyrical in their promotion of televisions and video recorders. With its ever-changing image, the brand loses its singularity and identity. The same signature may well endorse each campaign, but do they all come from the same source?

With no theoretical or practical means of specifically analyzing the brand and its management, the firm either fails to consolidate the brand capital asset, or allows it to be gradually diluted.

IDENTITY AND IMAGE

What contribution can the notion of identity offer which brand image cannot? Firms, after all, lay out vast sums to measure their brands' image.

Why Do We Now Speak of Identity and Not Image?

Image is on the receiver's side. Image centers upon the way a certain public imagines a product, brand, political figure, firm or country, etc. The image refers to the manner in which this public decodes all the signals emitted by the brand through its products, services, and communication program. It is a reception concept.

Identity is on the sender's side. The sender's duty is to specify the meaning, intention and vocation of the brand. Image is a result thereof, a decoding. In brand management terms, identity necessarily precedes image. Before portraying an idea in the mind of the public, one should establish exactly what is to be portrayed. As Figure 2.1 shows, the customer forms an image through a synthesis of all the signals emitted by the brand (brand name, visual signs, products, advertising, sponsoring, patronage, press releases, etc.). The image results from a decoding, an extraction of the meaning, an interpretation of the signals. Where do these signals come from? There are two possible sources, brand identity being the most obvious. There can, however, be extraneous influences ("noise," or parasitic factors) whose purpose may be removed from that of brand identity, but which nevertheless act as a mouthpiece for the brand in achieving meaning.

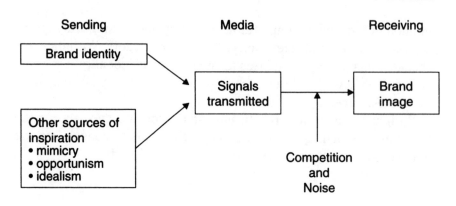

Figure 2.1

Identity and image

What are these extraneous influences? With no clear idea of their brand identity, certain firms resort to mimicry, imitating their own competitors' communication. Secondly, trying to please all segments and to come close to their "ideal brand" leads managers to forget the identity of the brand, and instead to swim with the changing tide. Yesterday the customer sought glamor, today he must be cocooned. And tomorrow? Who knows? Opportunist and popularity-seeking, the brand loses its substance. It is just a cosmetic camouflage having no meaning in itself.

The third source of noise is that of fantasized identity—the brand as one would ideally like to see it, but not as it actually is. Its effect is to create a message which later becomes detached from the customer's vision of the brand, to be considered as insincere and possibly forgotten.

A new sense of priorities in identity structure promises to avoid this drift away from communication precepts. Citroën does not set its store in engine power like its sister make, the rally expert Peugeot. The image of wild horses once presented in its advertising features was, therefore, out of character.

To summarize the concept of identity, though all things are possible when a brand is first created, after a time it acquires an autonomy and its own meaning. Starting as a nonsense word attached to a new product, year after year, it acquires a meaning, composed of the memories of past emergent communication and products. It defines an area of

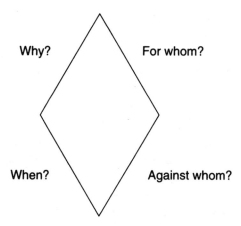

Figure 2.2
Positioning

legitimate possibilities, yet appreciates its own limitations. We cannot expect the brand to be anything other than itself.

The brand should obviously not go into a shell and cut itself off from the public. An obsession with image tends, however, to attach greater importance to appearance than to inner reality. So the horses of its advertising have trotted back to the Camargue, and Citroën has once more found its identity in the highly technological and elegant XM car. Instead of trying to please the public, brand advertising should better express what the brand believes in, its own ideals and vision of the world.

Brand Positioning

It has become common to analyze brands according to their positioning. The term applies to a process of emphasizing the brand's distinctive and motivating attributes in the light of competition. Positioning refers to belongingness and difference: to what product segment does the brand belong, and what is its specific difference? It is based on an analysis of response to the following four questions:

- Why, or for what? What is the specific consumer benefit or exclusive motivating attribute justifying the brand? Sony

brings innovation, Bang and Olufsen design and sophistication. Stouffer's "lean cuisine" provides fewer calories.
- For whom? This indicates the target. For a long time Schweppes was the drink of the refined set, Canada Dry a soft drink for adults, and Seven Up for teenagers.
- When? This indicates the occasion on which to use the product. Jacobs' "Night and Day" coffee makes a clear statement concerning this facet of its positioning.
- Opposed to whom? In today's context this question points to the main competition—those brands from whom one aspires to capture clientele. Hence such well-known campaigns as "Pepsi Challenge" and the "Un-Cola."

Positioning is a useful concept. It reminds us that a product is nothing unless it has been clearly positioned in people's minds versus the competition. The American Gaines Company, for example, brought out a new dog food. It was a semidehydrated product presented as a red minced meat—a hamburger. Unlike normal tinned pet foods, moreover, it did not need to be kept refrigerated, nor did it exude the smell normal with opened cans.

At this stage the company saw several possible positionings for the product. They could, for example:

- Home in on the canned food market by appealing to well-to-do dog owners. The thrust of their message would be: the can without the can. In other words, the meat without its unpleasant associations (smell, storage, etc.).
- Attack the dehydrated-products sector by offering a product which no longer causes the owner to be guilty of refusing the dog meat for reasons of practicality. The further attraction of minced meat could justify this line of reasoning.
- Target owners who feed their dogs on leftovers, pointing out that this is a complete energy-giving supplement—a sort of Wynn's for dogs (and no longer, as in the two preceding proposals, just a main meal).
- Take on the whole canine world by labeling their product as an energy-giving reward—a sort of doggy Mars bar.

The choice between these four strategies was made by assessing each one against eight criteria:

- Is the product suitable in its present form for such a positioning?
- What strength of motivation can be expected among consumers through such positioning?
- What size of market would correspond to this positioning?
- Is this a credible positioning?
- What financial budget does this positioning demand?
- Is it a specific and distinctive positioning?
- Does this positioning make the most of the product's main qualities?
- Does this positioning allow the possibility for change in the event of a setback?

The firm launched its product on the lines of the first positioning, i.e., homing in on the tinned food market, and gave it the name "Gaines burger."

What else can the notion of identity offer to that of positioning? Why do we need yet another concept? In the first place, because positioning is more a reflection of a product. It was necessary for Gaines burger to assume a precise position in the market. But the Gaines brand covers many more products than just this one. What then is the significance of the positioning concept when applied to this multiproduct brand? How can these four questions on positioning be answered if we are not referring just to a particular product? We can locate the various Scotch-Brite abrasive products and also Scotch video cassettes, but what does positioning mean for the Scotch brand itself and, *a fortiori*, for the corporate brand 3M? Here the concept of brand identity is more applicable.

Secondly, positioning stifles the rich meaning of the brand in not taking account of all its potentialities. The brand is choked within the positioning diamond. Positioning doesn't allow us to differentiate between Coca-Cola and Pepsi-Cola, Anais-Anais and l'Air du Temps, Dannon and Yoplait—that is to say, brands with closely-related strategies. The four positioning questions do not cater to such subtleties. They do not allow us to explore the identity and singularity of these brands.

A greater problem arises, since specific positionings can leave the advertising communication too open to creative whims and momentary changes in style or approach. Positioning has no voice where tone, style, form, and manner of communication are concerned and constitute the main message. In the audiovisual age, discourse does not rely only on speech, but incorporates pictures, sounds, colors, movement, and style. Positioning can only handle the text, the words, leaving the rest to creative chance and pretest uncertainty. Brand language should not be abandoned to mere creativity. Creative inspiration is only useful if it falls within the brand's legitimate territory.

The form of a message is a brand's substance coming to the surface. We can no longer dissociate brand substance from its form—the way in which it is written, seen, or heard. Brand identity provides the framework for total brand coherence. Through it, we can establish its positioning limits, regulate its means of expression, and ensure its individuality and durability. The concept of identity reminds us that one brand cannot accede to every positioning. A brand may be potentially all-embracing at birth, but time and the symbols which it adopts give it a meaning, a territory—and consequent territorial boundaries. In short, its etymological meaning imposes limitations. Brand identity forbids certain positionings and guarantees others. Positioning must be credible. It must be justifiable for the brand in question.

THE FACETS OF IDENTITY

Each market condition gives rise to concepts and methods to adapt to such conditions. When products weren't so abundant, one simply resorted to an old USP (unique selling proposition). After the era of image, positioning, and brand personality, we have entered into the brand identity era.

To become a power brand and to remain so, a brand has a duty to be faithful to its identity. Brand image is a volatile and changing notion—it is concerned too much with the appearance of the brand, and not enough with its very being. The notion of brand core identity expresses a willingness on the part of the communication strategist to go beyond the superficial and to investigate the brand at root level. The concept of identity is formulated on the basis of three qualities:

- Durability
- Coherence
- Realism

It is not prone to idealism, fickleness, or opportunism, as is the case with brand image.

The Prism of Identity

Brand identity may be represented diagrammatically by a six-sided prism:

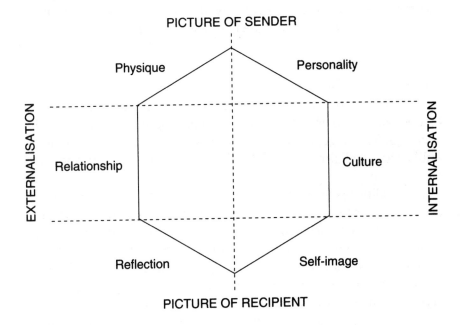

Figure 2.3

Brand identity prism

PHYSIQUE

A brand first has a physique—a combination of independent characteristics which may be either prominent (springing readily to mind when the brand is mentioned) or dormant (though nevertheless distinguishable).

La Vache qui Rit (the laughing cow) evokes the picture of foil-wrapped cheese portions in a red and blue round box. Citroën forms a vision of highly technological suspension, original outline, and boldness. Volkswagen means durability, BMW evokes performance and speed.

Physique is the brand basis. Taking the analogy of a flower stem, without the stem the flower dies—it is its independent tangible support. This is the traditional basis of communication, corresponding to brand know-how and standard positioning. It derives its features from certain key or prominent products of the brand. For instance, the physique of Rossignol is linked to skis, that of Salomon is "tied" to bindings. This is why Rossignol evokes fun and dynamism, and Salomon precision and security. Physique is a necessity, but not, of itself, sufficient, forming only the first stage in brand construction.

PERSONALITY

A brand has a personality. It acquires a character. If, as often happens, we identify the brand with a person, we gradually form a picture of that person by the way in which he speaks of products or services. La Vache qui Rit is a generous, benevolent soul. Peugeot is conservative, unlike the idealistic Citroën. Atari loves the competition and challenge.

Personality has been the brand focus since 1970. Numerous American agencies have made it a prerequisite in all communication campaigns. Ted Bates created a new USP (unique selling personality), while Grey gave their own definition of brand personality. The Euro–RSCG agency made physique and personality the two main pillars of all brand communication, and considered these the source of its style. This explains why brand characters like those of which we have just spoken have blossomed forth. The easy way to bestow personality on a brand is to provide it with a spokesperson, a star, or an animal. It is restrictive to summarize the brand as simply having a physique and a character. As we shall see, power brands have further depth.

CULTURE

The brand has its own culture from which every product derives. The product is the physical embodiment and vector of this culture. Culture implies a system of values, a source of inspiration and brand energy. The cultural facet relates to the basic principles governing the brand in its outward signs (i.e., products and communication). A deep-seated facet, it is the mainspring for the brand. Apple is the product of a California culture, in the sense that that state symbolizes eternally new frontiers. Even without the presence of the founding directors of the Apple organization, everything continues on the basis that Apple has something revolutionary to offer to firms and—on a wider plane—to mankind itself. This dream, this vital source of inspiration, becomes established not only in its highly original computer products and services but also in its advertising style.

Culture seems to both influence and infiltrate major brands (Benetton, Coca-Cola, Adidas, etc.). Advertising strategy has neglected this essential facet in its insistence on mere personality. We shall see this when considering retailers' identity, too: the leading retailers are those which have personality, but also a culture. Citroën's culture stems form its typical engineers' ideal—progress through the application of science. Mercedes personifies German values, with order and strength prevailing. The three-box bodywork and overall symmetry characterize the brand's physique, while the Mercedes symbol on the front is a further epitomization of order. Adidas is embedded in a collective culture: unlike Nike's or Reebok's highlighting of the virtues of individualism, Adidas is linked to the values of collective sports (soccer, etc.). The cultural facet is an essential one. It has only recently come to the fore, coinciding with a realization of the link between brand and product.

Brands do not simply identify products. The brand legitimates the product. Findus is not just the name given to a range of frozen foods. It was a voice of opposition to time-honored cultural determinants of eating habits—religion and social class. In speaking loudly through advertising, Findus announced that women were no longer to see themselves as housewives: Findus were going to take them away from all this. Would the product have taken off if there had not been this insistence on new cultural implications? Since the brand was speaking loudly it soon enjoyed a social standing and thus was able to influence new patterns of behavior. It was to be a further harbinger of female emancipation. In this sense we can agree with Fourcade and Cabat (1981) in saying that a brand speaks less about the products themselves than about their legitimacy as new behavioral habits. The brand provides meaning to products and consumers' behavior alike.

Cultural associations are evoked in brand countries of origin. In Coca-Cola we see America, in IBM we see Wall Street, in Ralph Lauren we see Boston. A product such as Mars, however, has somewhat lost its apparent roots in becoming a totally international brand. The names Canon and Technics do not conjure an image of the Rising Sun, whereas Mitsubishi, Toyota and Nissan speak for themselves. One of the bonuses for Evian and Perrier exports is that they signify a part of French culture. However, this is not the only factor adding to their value. When Americans buy a Perrier or an Evian they are not just paying for the cultural facet but for all six facets of these brands.

The cultural facet provides the link between brand and firm, particularly when they bear the same name (e.g., IBM, Sainsbury, Renault, and Nestlé). Its culture prevents Nestlé from becoming regarded solely as a provider of mouth-watering delicacies. As a puritan and austere corporation it could not be otherwise; this would not do. A brand's degree of freedom is largely dependent on the corporate culture, of which it becomes the most visible sign. It isn't just by chance that Renault as a brand built its identity on features such as capacity and comfort (whence the brand slogan "cars for living"). Nor was it the result of a market study implying that this was what a large proportion of car owners required. Being a semipublic firm (termed "France's social workshop"), Renault's corporate values naturally tend more toward human relations than toward mere performance and competition (cf. BMW). The presence of Renault in Formula 1 is designed to counterbalance this. However, Renault has other fundamental values.

RELATIONSHIP

A brand is a relationship. It often provides the opportunity for an intangible exchange between persons. This is particularly true of brands in the service sector and, as we shall later see, for retailers. The Yves Saint Laurent name has an air of seduction—an underlying sensual man–woman relationship permeates both his products and their customer appeal, even though no personal presence may be evident. Dior's relationship is more grandiose—somewhat showy, in the progressive sense, flaunting the desire to shine like gold. La Vache qui Rit is at the heart of a mother–child relationship. To Coutts Bank is attached throughout the world a selective connotation: it is not supposed to be an open bank but one which selects its clients, in the manner of most prestigious clubs.

REFLECTION

A brand reflects a customer's image. When asked for their views on such-and-such a make of car, the consumer's immediate reaction is to think of the type of driver that it would most suit—a rep, a family man, a poseur, or an older type. There is often a confusion between this reflection and a brand's target. Target describes the brand's potential purchasers or users. Reflection is not necessarily the target, but the image of that target which the brand offers to the public. It is a type of identification.

Though its reflection is restricted (young people), Coca-Cola has a much wider clientele. Such a paradox can be explained by adults' identification with youth values.

The confusion between reflection and target still causes problems. Many advertising managers fail to realize that the public cannot be targeted in a simple, transparent way. This approach ignores the fact that the brand buyer does not want to be portrayed as he/she is, but as he/she wishes to be seen as a result of being an adept of a particular brand. Brands are used by consumers to build up and convey their own identity. They have an emblematic value in the eyes of the beholder.

Thirty years ago, when David Ogilvy portrayed the man in the Hathaway shirt as a one-eyed man, a sort of British colonel who was injured at El Alamein, he did not mean that the Hathaway shirt target was this type of person. Similarly, not all persons wearing Lacoste shirts play tennis. Tennis is not the target market of Lacoste. It is its cultural root and a source of positive image for people buying the brand.

At l'Oreal, all brands have a written portrayal of the reflection of their customers. The Lancôme woman is exactly the same throughout the world. The same holds true for all l'Oreal shampoo and cosmetic brands.

If a brand does not manage the customers' reflection attached to its name, the competition will do it. Virgin's store reflection makes a formerly established competitor look rather old hat. To justify the physique of their products—microcomputers identical to those of IBM, but much cheaper and with a better performance—Victor projected a reflection of the IBM customer in a deliberately negative way in its advertising. He is a person who will seek the apparent security of an IBM screen rather than take the risk in availing himself of better efficiency and price.

SELF-IMAGE

The sixth facet of brand identity is customers' self-image. If reflection is the target's outward mirror, the self-image is the target's own internal mirror. Through our attitude toward certain brands, we develop a certain type of inner relationship with ourselves.

Many Porsche owners, for example, are simply proving to themselves that they have the ability to buy such a car. Such a purchase may be inconsistent with their career prospects, and to some extent a gamble on their materialization. The brand, therefore, acts as an obligatory motive for self-improvement—hence Porsche's advertising copy stressing the race against oneself, the only race which never ends. As we see, Porsche's reflection may differ from the self-image it evokes.

Even if he is not the sporting type, studies show that the man who buys a Lacoste sees himself inwardly as a member of a sporting club—a club where there are no distinctions of race, sex, or age (see Figure 2.4). This is because sport knows no such divisions. One of the characteristics of people who eat Gayelord Hauser dietetic brand is that they see themselves not just as consumers, but as followers of the brand. When two Gayelord Hauser fans meet, their conversation is such that one might think them members of the same religious sect.

These are the six facets which define brand identity and its potential territory. The brand identity prism demonstrates that these facets form a structured whole. The content of one facet echoes that of another. The prism structure is derived from one basic concept—that the brand has a voice. A brand does not exist unless it communicates. It would decline in strength if allowed to remain silent and unused for too long. Since the brand has its own means of referring—when speaking of the products which it encompasses, or endorsing the products which it promotes—it can therefore be analyzed like any communication.

Rhetoric teaches us that speeches always convey a picture of the sender. Likewise the case with products or shops: their type of communication allows us to imagine who is speaking behind them—the sender. It is a figurative process in the sense that, in the case of the brand (as opposed to the firm's direct voice) the sender does not physically exist. Nevertheless, customers, when asked, can immediately describe the brand's communicator—the one who personifies the brand name. The physical and personality facets surround this figurative sender. In focus groups they imagine and describe Mr. Pepsi or Mr. Lacoste, the founder. Naturally they do not describe the real R. Lacoste, but the one constructed by the communication.

Every form of communication also points to the presence of a recipient, as if a certain type of person or audience were being addressed. The reflection and self-image facets surround this figurative recipient, who in turn forms part of the brand identity. The final two facets—relationship and culture—are the bridging points between sender and recipient.

The identity prism also incorporates a vertical division (*lit caesura* see Figure 2.3). The facets to its left—physique, relationship, and reflection—are the social facets which give the brand its outward expression. All three are visible facets. The facets to the right—personality, culture, and self-image—are those incorporated within the brand itself, within its spirit.

Brand Diagnosis

The identity prism allows us to examine the brand in detail in order to detect its strengths and weaknesses. It puts the brand under the microscope of each of its facets and comes up with diagnoses which could never be obtained by stumbling blindly through a mass of image research data.

Why is Atari a rather shallow brand compared to IBM or to Apple? The answer does not reside in the comparison of sales or of the products. Atari has been a successful company since it was reoriented and managed by Jack Tramiel, the former president of Commodore. The Atari products fare well and sell well, too; but the brand itself lacks depth. As shown by a comparison of the three identity prisms, many facets of the Atari brand identity are empty. This is no surprise. Nowhere in its communications has the brand tried to convey why it exists; what are its sources of inspiration, its vision of computers, of organizations, of man in his relationship with machines. Atari is only the name of smart and surprisingly inexpensive microcomputers.

In this market, where fanaticism exists, brands are almost a religion. They have their adepts, apostles, priests, holy grails. Customers meet within clubs and communicate through professional journals. Some people think only of Apple, others will never betray IBM.

One does not build a successful religion by simply exposing the

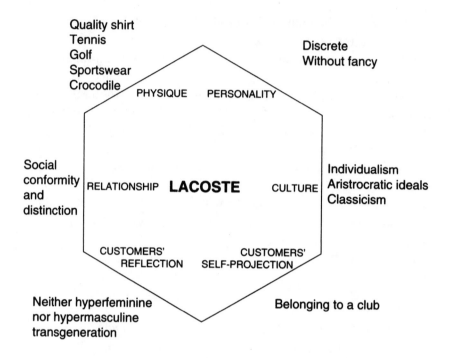

Figure 2.4

Lacoste identity prism

pros and cons of products. The managerial motto of Jack Tramiel and his associates worldwide is "Technology advances, prices retreat." This is a company or managerial slogan, not a brand philosophy. Atari as a brand has never made clear what it is the symbol of. Since the Atari name came from the video-games market, a halo of game identity still existed, but this ran counter to managerial plans to enter professional segments. What should Atari have done?

It should have explored the latent significations attached to the product category and to its own signs (the name Atari, the logo) and products. This exploration of the potential but still latent meanings would have revealed the facets of its identity (Figure 2.4).

The name Atari sounds rather like the kind of shriek uttered by karate or kendo fighters. There is an undertone of violence within the name, and it may be no surprise that Atari products attack the major brands, not by discounting but by implementation of better solutions to solve similar problems. The Atari brand likes competition and power. When Macintosh included only 8 bits, the Atari 520 ST had 16 bits. There is an emergent coherence behind all these separate facets of the brand behavior. Symbolically, if Apple means creation and IBM order, Atari is a weapon. The power included in its machines is not gratuitous. It is more power in the hands of users. The world of Atari is that of competition.

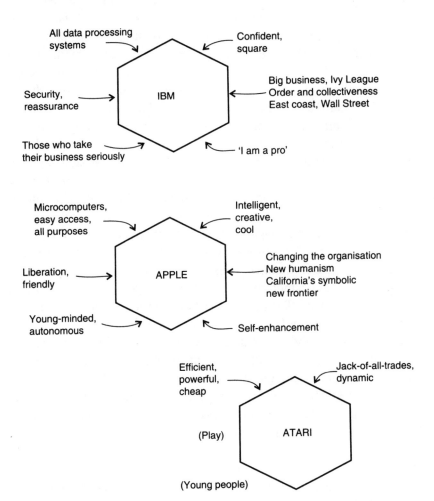

Figure 2.5

Identity prisms of IBM, Apple, and Atari

RETAILER IDENTITY

In 1988 the now multinational retailer Carrefour changed its advertising campaign. The new baseline was: "I act positively." As with each new campaign organized by this major multiple retailer, the questions were endless. What was Carrefour trying to say this time? Why was Carrefour changing?

Carrefour was in reality saying nothing more than it had been saying since 1975. Few multiretailers have retained such a consistent identity. Campaigns may change to take account of the ups and downs in competitive marketing. Carrefour, however, has remained loyal since its beginnings to one basic value and pivotal asset of the company—rationalism. The fact that this quality should be specifically included in their latest slogan was not an exploitation thereof. All Carrefour's communication since 1975—the era of "produits libres" (unbranded products)—bears the mark of the company's cultural facet and of its positivistic approach. What was Carrefour already saying in 1975? Produits libres, the company flag-bearers, epitomized an ideal—to sort the real from the imaginary needs created by marketeers. This latest campaign set the real world of the genuine product—the physical item—against the suspect environment of carefully designed packaging, symbols and advertising. Carrefour's prism of identity is defined in its basic sense by this rationalist ideal. An air of serene optimism permeates the company image—not one of aggressive devil-may-care. They see their duty to the customer in didactic terms, as can be seen from the company newsletter which they provide. "I act positively" sums up the self-concept of the Carrefour customer. It points to his good judgment in patronizing the store. The customer has seen the light. Carrefour did not advertise in the classical sense: it started a crusade to promote its view of the world, its ideals, its ambitions as to consumption habits. Inspired by Sainsbury, Carrefour now makes its own brands and products.

There are many examples of strong identity with a psychological depth among retailers. Many retailers however are graced only with a physique (Toys 'R' Us, C&A) or a character. They certainly create the picture of a sender, but their cultural facet is shallow and their relationship unimaginative. It was thought for a long time that physique and character were sufficient both for the brand and for the multiple retailer. Examination of leading retailers demonstrates a source of inspiration in their cultural values and the relationship facet which derives from these. These two facets deserve careful consideration, both in the service sector and in the retail trade.

Strong identities have a coherence which underlies strategic decisions ranging from store layout, product choice, and type and level of service and sales approach, to the very tone of the message. This coherence also explains the impression of permanence given by these multiple retailers, even though in reality they are continually changing. The sector leaders are self-willed retailers inspired by a doctrine and in search of a utopia. This gives greater legitimacy to their price/product/service positioning in consumers' eyes. Far more than being merely a graphic sign on the front of a store, their mark has become the symbol of a very specific relationship and of shared values and vision: this holds true throughout Europe for Marks & Spencer and for discounters such as Aldi.

3

Sources of Identity

How do we define a brand's identity? How do we determine the contours of its territory—and its limits? Everyone dealing with a well-established brand notes that, year after year, the brand has acquired a specific autonomous meaning. If, at the birth of a brand, all things seem possible, nevertheless over a period the brand loses degrees of freedom, while gradually gaining in conviction. Its facets take shape, indicating those products and themes whereof the brand is or is not legitimate, which it can or cannot endorse. Tests reveal this progression. Certain products or services nowadays do not seem to tie in with a brand, while others may show a close affinity—as though the brand were itself echoing their consumer benefits and giving them an added power of conviction.

Studies into brand image provide no satisfactory explanation to this. We would get even less joy by asking customers what they expect from this or that particular brand. They usually either have no idea or can only give their views on the brand as it is now. Citroën does not have a large market either in Denmark or in the U.K.; a Citroën owner in these countries would consider the car not as foreign in make, but as foreign to customary choice. If asked what he expected of the make, he would probably like to see it perpetuate the cult of the out-of-the-ordinary, and by the same token give that marginal minority of owners—himself included—further cause to remain different. Obviously, if Citroën geared their program to such selfish expectations, their share of the market would remain most restricted.

Consumers are often interviewed in an effort to measure the profile of their ideal brand and the characteristics necessary to win over complete public approval. This approach only gives rise to average profiles and does not take account of consumer segmentation. It is typical for consumers to expect from banks that they provide expert advice and attention, together with competent on-the-spot handling of personal banking transactions. Such expectations constitute an ideal, in the sense that they are difficult to put into practice altogether. In pursuing this idealized expectation, many banks lose some of their identity.

Wishing to resemble at all costs the ideal image expressed by averaging consumers' answers usually leads them to eradicate their individual strong points. For instance, Coutts overseas might be tempted to look more open, catering to all needs and customers, hence losing its identity composed of selectivity and distinction. The error lies in the pursuit of a market ideal. Each brand should pursue its own ideal and promote its own consistent set of values.

Commercial pressures naturally require a firm to keep in step with the market. No brand wishes to be another Van Gogh—unrecognized in his lifetime and magnified after his death. There must, however, be a reappraisal of present brand management policy which supposes that the consumer holds the keys to brand identity and strategy. The consumer is incapable of carrying out this function. Firms should, therefore, think more in terms of what they believe in and what they want to say, than of simple message-reception. A brand constitutes a plan—a genetic program. It is often not a written plan (with the exception of those few brands which now have a brand charter). We must, therefore, infer the deep identity of the brand by analyzing the history of all its outward embodiments—advertisements, products on which it appears, and symbols by which it is represented.

The best approach to a brand's inner meaning is through its signs of identity—those attributes which make it specially unique over time. This necessitates scrutiny of the products or services themselves, the brand name, its personification, logo, country of origin, advertising themes, and style and packaging approach. An in-depth study at ground level is needed to discover the unwritten plan behind these communications, products, and symbols; more often than not, there is no plan, either conscious or unspoken. Rarely does any such plan follow a set pattern; decisions are more often the result of spontaneous daily activity. Even brand creators such as Yves Saint Laurent, Ricci, and Lacoste have not been aware of following a specific plan. While they could rarely explain it, however, they would have no hesitation in saying what the brand should or should not do. They in fact see the brand as themselves, although it could be argued that the brand does not really begin to exist until its creator dies. Then it no longer has a body or an instinct, but becomes a program and a plan. Pierre Cardin as a man wants to explore all activities he has not been in yet. His curiosity as a man is natural. But in so doing he probably puts strain on the brand, for consistency and coherence is the path to long-lasting meaning. This example shows why sometimes creators forget that, though they share their own name, brands are now separate from themselves and deserve specific management rules. Do the advertisements that Mr. Benetton likes correspond to the Benetton brand?

In making a brand identity study we often identify the emergence of several plans. While a brand's history shows the decisions made by those who have developed its program, there is no necessary continuity, especially if the brand has been sold to different manufacturers through time. Rather than attempt the impossible task of correlating these extremes of approach, the easy solution is to favor the one which management consider will give the brand more impetus in its anticipated market. Also, unless it is a strong brand, often no coherent plan seems to emerge. The brand is more a name on a product than a sourcing and persuading force. We therefore find ourselves almost back to the stage of brand creation—the brand is full of possibilities and little is barred, even though in this case certain seeds of its potential identity may already have been sown in the customer's mind.

THE PRODUCTS

The product is the first source of brand identity. A brand reveals its plan and displays its uniqueness through the products or services which it encompasses. The true brand does not content itself with being simply a name marked on a product—just some graphic device at the end of a production or distribution process. The brand is the inspiration of this process. The qualities which it injects into products or services accompany them right through to the point of sale. These brand qualities must therefore be applied to its most representative products. Brand qualities convey a meaning only when they go to the very heart of the product.

With this in mind, Benetton pinned the strength of their brand on color. Color is not just an advertising theme. It forms the basis of its brand identity and operations. It has in fact allowed the company to stay ahead of its competitors through its capacity to present the latest fashion—in other words, the in-colors at any given time. It is one thing to say something: the hardest part is carrying it out. Unlike their competitors, Benetton decided to dye their jumpers, sweaters, and pullovers after they were made and not before, to gain time. By delaying their decision on the final colors, they were better prepared for the caprices of fashion and last-minute changes. If it turned out that fuschia was to be the in-color this summer, Benetton could immediately fall in line. However, though their brand identity is built on the color advantage, this does not concern the single physique facet of the brand. The color projects its meaning on the other facets of the prism, and in particular on the cultural facet.

Far from being simply an indication of positioning (the "colored brand"), color becomes its outward vision—embodiment of an ideal, of a system of values, of a brand culture. In its very name—"United Colors of Benetton"—as in its early advertising depicting two babies, one white, one black, the brand expresses its inspiration and idealistic vision of a united world in which all colors live together in harmony. Color ceases to be simply a feature which distinguishes the manufacturer. It is a banner, a sign of allegiance. Youngsters who wear the brand are singing a hymn to color. Color is the brand's innermost value—it transmits its inspiration to products, the manufacturing process, advertising, and merchandising. Others may copy Benetton. They can imitate its physique, but not the significance henceforth attached to the name.

Orangina is a case of a brand in search of identity and psychological depth. For years Orangina signified a physique, a speciality product— a fizzy orange soft drink. It differs from the normal run of similar drinks in that the orange pulp is left in the liquid. Such was the importance of this feature for the brand that it was supplied in a specially-designed orange-shaped bottle, with a label reminding the consumer to shake the bottle well in order to disperse the pulp. The brand then took on a personality when its TV advertising features were set to the rap music so popular with youngsters.

The last stage in this brand advertising was intended to convey at last the full meaning of the brand: to do that the relationship between brand and product needed to be reversed. Until then, Orangina had only been the name of a drink with the orange pulp. The adoption of a modern approach did not change the structure of this relationship. Today the opposite question is asked: What values could a pulpy orange soft drink symbolize? Coca-Cola's popularity with teenagers cannot be challenged with only physique and personality as weapons. Coca-Cola is a brand with an allegiance to an American cultural type. Orangina must find its own source of inspiration—the model on whose values the product is based. The point of departure lies in one of the axioms of brand management: a brand's truths lie within the brand itself. It is not by asking questions of consumers and by consulting oracles of sociocultural change that one discovers who the brand really is.

Looking at the life of Orangina since its birth, one finds that the mood conveyed by the Orangina brand has always been one of spontaneity, humor, and likability. It is a healthy, natural drink—a mixture of water and pulp. Orangina symbolizes sunshine, life, warmth, and energy. All combine to give a typical taste and feeling of the South. Power brands always seem to be the output and expression of a certain culture—a system of values which is embodied in the brand. In the case of Orangina, Southern values which it abides to are a potent alternative to the North American values of Coca-Cola. The South epitomizes looking at life from another perspective.

The Lacoste shirt represents only 30 percent of the company's overall world sales. It is nevertheless the product around which the brand revolves, since it incorporates all its original values. The shirt goes back to the period when tennis was played in long trousers and shirts with rolled-up sleeves. René Lacoste asked his friend André Gilliet to design a garment which to all intents and purposes was a normal shirt (in deference to dress requirements at Wimbledon), but which would be more practical—aerated, strong, and with straight sleeves. Thus from a chance beginning the René Lacoste shirt has embodied an individualistic and aristocratic ideal combining spirit and elegance. Lacoste remains acceptable—satisfying social requirements while not adhering strictly to their letter. Lacoste is an enduring symbol of presentability in its self-established niche between fashionable fancy and rigid standards (see page 50).

All the major brands have a pivotal product—a heart which transmits the meaning of the brand. Chanel has its gold chain, Chaumet its pearls, Van Cleef its intricate arrangement of precious stones. These do not simply typify product ranges—they are the embodiment and very linchpin of the brands' values. Dupont, on the other hand, do not seem to offer the same impact. They certainly make excellent lighters, but beyond that, what values are these lighters bearers of? In the ready-to-wear field, the 501 is the heart of the Levi organization and of the informal ideology which the brand conveys. On this point, it is significant that the product most frequently worn with a Lacoste shirt is a pair of jeans. Many brands, however, suffer from never having had a real pivotal product—an item exclusive to the brand which signals its identity. Citroën is an example of a brand where only certain products are representative. The brand's creative genius came to the fore in the DS, the mythical SM, and then the CX and the more recent XM. The Ami 6, Visa, and BX, fine as they were, seemed the result of another intention and source of inspiration. As for the 2CV, it points to the ability of the brand to deal with problems as only an engineer knows how—in an abstract, mathematically correct but unesthetic manner. Many of the difficulties in making Citroën a global brand stem from the fact that the same brand was introduced in different countries with different products: the Germans know Citroën through the 2CV. For them it is an ecology brand, not a high-tech brand.

POWER OF THE NAME

A brand's name often signifies its intentions. This is apparent in names specifically chosen to convey certain characteristics of the brand, from both an objective and a subjective viewpoint. This does not mean that names chosen on a purely personal basis, and without apparent recourse to rational processes, cannot define the brand's legitimate territory. Take the example of Steve Jobs and Steve Wozniak when they chose Apple as their brand name. It did not emanate from some creative study, nor from any computerized software on brand names. Apple seemed the obvious name to these two creative geniuses. It further epitomized the same sense of values as those which had motivated them to create a revolution in the world of computers.

The point which does need explaining is why these two did not choose a name along the lines of those of the front-runners at the time—such as International Computers or Micro Computers Corporation or even Iris. Most business managers would have chosen this type of name. In deciding to call it Apple, Jobs and Wozniak were giving notice of the nonconformist nature of their new brand. The name of a fruit—and its visual symbol of a part-eaten apple—had no deep significance. However, its very choice bore witness to its sense of values—the refusal to place the computer industry on a pedestal. Apple was to be the forerunner of a reversal in the man–machine relationship. No longer would the machine be an object of veneration or terror, but one of pleasure. Thus the brand name incorporated the germs of what would later appear obvious—a new standard had been created. What was true for Apple, however, did not apply in the case of Apricot. There is a difference between the spontaneous injection of values into a name, and a form of imitation which only retains the principle of the name itself—in this case a fruit—but which is unable to recreate the corresponding values and products.

The name is among the most powerful sources of identity. When studying brand identity it is well worth delving into the name to uncover the reasoning which might have influenced its selection. In so doing we can discover the brand's intention and its program. As the Latin saying goes, *"Nomen est omen"*—the name foretells.

In studying the brand name, we seek to identify the factors which add truth to this saying—i.e., the brand program and its area of legitimacy, know-how, and ability. The word "President" does not invoke an image of a region or a particular area, but of an ambition. Such a name can only be justly given to the best in its field. As we have said, the brand is a contract. It urges the firm to be able to provide the characteristics incorporated in the brand name.

The international menswear brand Boss derives its identity from its internationally understood meaning. It sells clothes for successful businessmen around 35. (Actually, Boss was the family name of the early founders.) An insurance company named Commercial Union will naturally evoke specific qualities of service. Many brands do their utmost to acquire virtues not incorporated in the brand name, or which the name cannot evoke.

If the product does not match the brand-evoked attributes, one had better change the brand name. Many brands advertise while disregarding their names. The temptation for the brand to give scant regard to its name is due to a hasty interpretation of the principle of brand autonomy. Experience shows that the brand acquires such an autonomy—it gives its own meaning to words. When we talk of Naf-Naf clothes for teenagers, no one thinks of the slang interpretation. Mercedes is a Spanish girl's Christian name: the brand has turned it into a name symbolizing Germany. This peculiarity is not solely attributable to brands—it can also apply to persons' names. No Frenchman, for instance, raises an eyebrow on hearing reference to Sean Connery, even though the surname would normally refer to "damned stupidity" in that language. Again, we do not think of roofing when talking of Mrs. Margaret Thatcher. Powerful brands impose their meaning on the vocabulary—they give words another meaning. The reality of this process is undeniable, though it can take a fairly long time according to its complexity. It is reasonable to accept that the many banks throughout the world whose name include the word Trustee or Cooperative will never depart from their original meaning. The field of activity of these banks is circumscribed by their name. They have no need to seek to resemble the Chase Manhattan Bank, or Swiss banks—their program is spelled otherwise in consumers' minds. Their names signify openness, partnership, a friendly ear, and genuine public concern. To achieve a better understanding of the original aims of such banks, we should investigate the purposes implied in their names themselves. These names conjure up the idea of a unique type of bank. The adjective "cooperative" (as in "mutual benefit society") leads one to expect a closer relationship with the public, an ideal of friendliness, and a lack of barriers between the banker and the customers.

A name—like an identity—has to be managed. Certain names may have a double meaning. The aim of a communication program is to bring the one to the fore and to repress the other. The Shell symbol is intended to evoke an image of the sea, thus eliminating the bellicose connotation of the word in the English-speaking countries. Again, Ecco, the international temporary employment agency, has never exploited the potential link with economy suggested in its name. Far from doing so, it has seen the name as a natural focal point on which to center the high-quality service. Ecco's advertising makes full use of the dual inference—the replacement echoes the replaced.

Without resorting to a complete change of name, the brand program can benefit from a slight modification thereof. This is why Club Méditerranée became Club Med. To Japanese or American or South African customers, the Mediterranean Sea means nothing specific, whereas it has attracted all Europeans southward for centuries, if not thousands of years. More than a sea, it is a myth. However, the necessities of worldwide expansion of the Club concept of holidays made this name change inescapable.

BRAND CHARACTERS AND SYMBOLS

Many brands have long been represented by a character. In some cases they symbolize the creator of the brand (the Johnnie Walker whisky, Mr. Lindt, Sara Lee). Others are a direct symbol of the brand and its qualities (Snuggles' Bear, the Lyle's golden syrup lion, Mr. Clean, Bibendum Michelin, the Famous Grouse whisky). Finally, certain characters serve as a prescribed emotional link between the brand and its public (the tiger on a package of Frosties).

Such individuals speak volumes for their brands' identity. They were chosen in fact as brand portraits—in other words, as a representation of the brand's traits and features in the etymological sense. They are not the brand, but the manner in which the brand presents its own characteristics. To offer an analogy, neither Brigitte Bardot nor Catherine Deneuve are la République. Having, however, offered their face and other parts as a model for Marianne, they demonstrate the way in which la République is imagined at a given period.

When a character has been associated with the brand for a long time, it becomes part and parcel of it. Children do not eat portions of cheese spread—they eat the Laughing Cow. They love burgers, provided it is Ronald McDonald. As we have said, the character says a lot about the brand personality and the relationship which it builds with the public. Ronald McDonald is funny and tolerant: he is the kindly uncle with whom one learns and plays. The identification of the precise nature of this relationship is necessary if one is to maintain consistency through time.

Retailers have made wide use of characters, with varied success. Certain characters are able to express the individuality of a retailer in a forceful way, while others are less effective, or are even counterproductive. Mammouth has always signified expansiveness and price-smashing, two attributes applicable to any hypermarket. While this was fine at the time when hypermarkets were first vying for popularity, the Mammouth image is scarcely applicable to present-day market requirements: it is too generic. It still figures as the store's emblem but is no longer the mouthpiece. The beaver, on the other hand, is the perfect international archetype for the resourceful, shrewd, and friendly builder.

TRADEMARKS AND LOGOS

Most people know the Cutty Sark ship, the Mercedes emblem, the Rolls-Royce "Spirit of Ecstasy" hood ornament, the nest on the Nestlé label, Yoplait's little flower, the flying red horse of Mobil, or the tree, the emblem of Bull. These symbols have been deliberately chosen to reflect their brands' personality and culture. Personality and certain other values are considered of primary importance among the guidelines governing a company's design and graphic identity program.

The importance of these symbols and logos is not so much that the brand is identified by their outward display but rather that it identifies itself with them and their inner associations. For example, a change in logo always signals a fresh outlook on the part of the firm and its brand. Their former symbols no longer signify their new intentions, and these too must incorporate the change. On the other hand, to revitalize a brand, certain firms find it more appropriate to reclaim its identity by drawing on the power and aggressiveness hitherto dormant in its emblem. This happened with Peugeot and the lion—their long-term symbol of new potential horizons. In their case the manufacturer finally showed his claws! After having left it aside for many years, Esso called back its tiger in its European advertising. Just as the signature can reveal the character of the signatory, these symbols allow us to delve into the brand's inner being, and the impression which it has of itself.

GEOGRAPHICAL AND HISTORICAL ROOTS

The identity of Swissair is intimately associated with that of Switzerland. The same association with a country of origin applies to Air France or Barclays Bank at the international level. Certain products convey the identity of their country of origin in their brands. Others, such as Ford, Opel, and Mars are completely international. Yet further brands have done everything possible to erase their national identity. Canon bears no reference to Japan, while Technics has adopted an American identity—even though the company was founded in Japan. Kraft's Hollywood chewing gum has an American ring, but the trademark is registered in France.

Certain brands draw their source of identity and their individuality from their geographical roots. This is of their own choosing. For example, what identity is revealed in the Finnish company Nokia's range of Salora televisions? When we think of Finland we instantly see a country breathing competence and individuality. As its name suggests, Finland is the country where the earth ends—a cold, austere, far-off land where the sun never sets. This spontaneous vision enhances and supports a technologically futuristic brand which encompasses telecommunications and satellite programs all in the most refined form. If Salora can live up to this vision, the brand has a strong potential, since it is imbued with an identity and an image which stem from its very roots. If, on the other hand, these particular products should lose their individuality, the brand's implicit contract will be broken, thus devaluing itself.

The brand can also gain strength from values linked with its associated region. Apple has benefited from the California values of progress and innovation, both in technology and in social patterns. This California brand has suggestions of an "alternative culture"—not true of Atari or several other firms in Silicon Valley. IBM incorporates the order, power, and conservatism of the East Coast. Evian's image is associated with the Alps—or rather with the vision which has been ascribed to it. The Salomon brand draws on the Alps, too, to convey its identity representing the virtues of mountain folk. Bacardi leads us to believe that the drink was made on some paradise beach.

ADVERTISING: CONTENT AND FORM

We should not forget that it is advertising which writes the history of a brand, a retailer, or any company. The Marlboro identity was created by the advertising saga which accompanied its development—the same with Benson & Hedges, Coke, or the famous Hamlet cigars. This is logical. The brand has a voice, and it only exists through communication. Since the brand is the expression of products or services, it is only right that it should have the final word.

When we communicate we are saying far more than we might believe. Every message bears an implicit picture of the sender (we imagine who is speaking), of the intangible recipient, and of the tentative relationship between the two. The brand prism of identity rests on this inescapable tenet of communication theory. What actually conveys these implicit pictures, this message hidden between the lines? Quite simply, the advertising style. In the present age of audiovisual media, a thirty-second televised spot says as much about the brand's style and the intended recipient as about the characteristics and benefits of the product publicised. Managed or not, planned or otherwise, successful or rejected, every brand acquires a history, a culture, a personality, and a reflection through its cumulative communications. To give the brand its full potential, this gradual accumulation of ideas must be managed in the most favorable direction.

This is precisely what DDB did for Volkswagen. Though Volkswagen have their own marketing set-up, all their advertising is still handled by the DDB agency. The result is that all Volkswagen models appear under the same name, no matter what the country. Even though the old Passat name did not work well in France—in spite of the efforts on the part of VAG France—the new model was still launched under the same name. However, the individualistic style of this make is a legacy of Bernbach's expertise. He managed to persuade DDB to incorporate the same lines in their worldwide network. Materialization of the brand's style goes back to the time of the Beetle, when Volkswagen's field of activity was also first established.

In its advertising, both on the screen and in other media forms, great play was always made of the look of the Beetle—not to mention its logo. The car was to be viewed in a lighthearted manner, and nothing more. Such a mood was achieved by self-derision, a certain false modesty, a touch of impertinence in referring to the competition, and the use of paradox. In so doing, Volkswagen built a powerfully intimate relationship. They appealed to the customer's intelligence and called on his practical reasoning in putting necessity before the irrelevant.

The paradox surrounding Volkswagen lies in their constant ability to talk of a popular product in almost elitist undertones, while relying on humor to make it credible. This allows them to introduce minor modifications as though they were major developments. The basic arguments in promoting the range have nevertheless remained centered on certain practical values which have been there since its beginnings—quality of manufacture, durability, reliability in all weather, favorable price and trade-in value, etc.

But this advertising style, though created outside the Volkswagen Company, was not artificially attached to the brand. It fitted with the core identity of that brand. There was truth in it. What sort of person in fact could create a monstrosity of a car—the Beetle—which so completely defied trends in the American automobile world? It could be none other than a basically genuine idea painstakingly created by a reasonable man with a vision. The company had to raise the status and ego of those who bought the car and flatter their intelligence by acclaiming their decision to break for the moment from current American patterns. In the blink of an eye, the brand succeeded in promoting its values and its culture. The Volkswagen style is Volkswagen, even though it was created by Bernbach.

The David Hamilton–Nina Ricci partnership produced an unchanged advertising style between 1970 and 1989. Does this mean that the famous English photographer imposed his style on Nina Ricci? If we examine the brand's advertising campaigns since it first appeared in 1932, we find more importantly that this latest style brought out the means of brand expression which the firm had unconsciously been seeking. From its very beginnings, the brand had been symbolized by the veil (on the head or over the face)—in other words, the basic symbol of marriage and purity. The Hamilton approach roughly signifies a veil. Through the predominance in his photographs

of young women on the brink of womanhood, Hamilton was reinforcing the spiritual communion between his own style and the Nina Ricci
brand. Curiously, this same gradual assimilation occurred with a
closely-related brand—between Cacharel and the English photographer Sarah Moon.

   Although both created world best-seller perfumes, l'Air du Temps
(Nina Ricci) and Anais-Anais (Cacharel), we shall see (Chapter 5)
that, despite similar outlooks, each of these perfumes had a very specific core identity.

II

Brand Management

4
Creating a Brand

All the major brands examined so far—Apple, Lacoste, Sony, etc.—started life as up-and-coming brands. Over the years—more often than not through intuition or chance—they became major brands, established brands, powerful brands. Since these were necessarily new brands, we might ask ourselves what the established brands have—or what they have done—which the other brands have not. In the previous chapters, we made an in-depth examination of major brands and large retailers. Each had a rich identity and a well-determined know-how. They had acquired a brand personality and a system of values—that is to say, an authentic brand culture—and they proposed a relationship, a reflection, and a consumer self-concept. All these qualities enhanced their position. Every one of these established brands seemed to move in a set direction—in other words, they were motivated by a precise source of inspiration and by a recognition of where they were going in terms of those products or services which they were willing to encompass and set their name on. Here we have all the key requirements for creating a new brand. The best way for a new brand to succeed is to act like an old brand!

Put another way—as S. King put it twenty years ago, instead of

71

preoccupying ourselves with ways of launching new brands, we would be better served by asking ourselves how we might invent an established reputable brand. Most firms are totally blinkered in this respect, since they continue to see no distinction between the launch of a new product and launching a brand.

CONFUSING BRAND LAUNCH WITH PRODUCT LAUNCH

Marketing books devote chapters to the definition of new products, but nothing to the process of launching a major brand. Their advice is even sometimes limited to a choice of names for a new product. This confusion between product and brand stems from situations where the brand is only arrived at by chance. Most reputable brands, rich in meaning and values, started life as a simple name on an emerging product. This name was usually chosen out of the hat, without any thought or study. For example:

- Coca-Cola reflected the ingredients in the new product.
- Mercedes was the Christian name of Daimler's daughter.
- Citroën was a patronymic name.
- Adidas is a contraction of Adolphe Dassler; likewise, Lip of Lippman, and Harpic of Harry Picman.

The new product had to be given a name so that it could be brought to the public's attention. Through their advertising, firms could display the advantages of the new product and the qualities which the purchaser could expect. (The experienced reader will recognize the classical copy strategy.)

After a period of time, the new product becomes obsolete and is replaced by another product having a better performance. This new product inherits the reputation already attached to the existing name. Products change; brands remain.

So, at the outset, the firm boasted the merits of the initial product—call it X. With the natural waning of the product over a given period, notice is given of its resurgence, improvement, and change in the form of a product with a better performance under the same name. This signals the birth of a brand. It is no longer advertising which sells the products—the brand does the work (see also page 116).

Again in the course of time, the brand, in its role linking product and consumer, will gradually acquire greater autonomy and will detach itself from its original meaning, such as its reference to the firm's creator or a product feature. Few English people now think of "clean" when they speak of Kleenex, for instance. The product name has become a personal name, denoting nothing specific but charged with associations acquired as a result of products or services, usage, word-of-mouth, and advertising. These factors allow us to draw a picture, through its voice and means of communication, of what this X really is. What is its background, its cultural qualification, its system of values, its personality? To whom is it speaking? Over the period, X has changed direction—it is no longer a name attached to a product, but the meaning of products, both now and in the future. X, the reputable brand, has assumed values which it will pass on to the products it embraces—right from the production stage. In terms of brand creation, the lesson to be drawn is simple and final: if the new brand does not incorporate a system of values from the outset, there is little possibility of its success in establishing itself as a major brand in the long term.

On an operational plane, this means that in choosing a new brand, as much attention must be paid to its potential image as to the product itself. Why has Atari not yet attained the status of a major brand while Apple has already succeeded? As we have already seen, the fault does not lie in their products or software. The 520 ST, 1040, Portfolio, Mega, and Transputer products are unbeatable. They form the concrete expression of a manufacturing philosophy which is forever on the lips of the new Atari creator, Jack Tramiel, and of his subsidiary company managers: "Technology advances, prices retreat." A proving example is the Atari 1040 with laser printer, which is much cheaper than an Apple Macintosh, though less powerful. What Atari lacks is a meaning—an individuality which speaks for more than just the name of the manufacturer of the 1040, Mega, or Transputer. The brand has never made clear its heart, what motivates it and its source of inspiration and cultural base—the features which allow us to pinpoint the brand's mission, together with the objective and subjective values which it is attempting to inject into the microcomputer industry by means of its products.

In launching a new brand we must look upon it from the outset as being truly a brand, and not the mere name of the product which we see in its advertisements. We must not wait for the name of the product to perhaps become in the long term a deep symbol, imbued with a meaning which goes far beyond the product itself. Time is money, and long-term plans are hazardous. The new brand must be thought of as a full-identity prism from the start—in other words, we should focus on the functional and nonfunctional values which it incorporates.

By placing the accent exclusively on the launch of new products, marketing theorists confuse a brand's history with brand management. Certainly it has taken years to build present megabrands. What was at first a nonsense word, Kodak, has slowly, product after product, ad after ad, become synonymous with family, entertainment, reliability, friendship. Now Kodak has reached the status of a full-sense noun. Managing means drawing the lessons from history to save time. To create a brand is to look upon it from the outset as an established brand, rich in significance. This entails a few determining principles.

PRINCIPLES OF BRAND CREATION

Defining the Brand's Identity

It is not advertising which speaks of products—it is the brand. When considering the launch of a new product, the pertinent questions are those making up the classical copy strategy:

- Who is being targeted?
- What is the product positioning—its distinctive advantage and competitive area?
- What promises and benefits can the consumer expect?

In seeking brand creation, one preliminary question must be answered: Who is this brand? Before we can assess what the associated product is capable of achieving, we must first know who is speaking, why does the brand exist, what are its values, goals, etc. (Table 4.1).

As we have seen, defining brand identity does not simply boil down to a definition of a brand's personality or character. An analysis of powerful brands shows that they have a physique—know-how, and a pivotal product to which they are not entirely restricted. They also have a culture—a system of values—and propose a specific type of relationship, consumer's reflection, and self-image.

Table 4.1

Brand identity platform

Specifying Brand Program

---

1. Why does this brand need to exist?
   What would the consumers be missing if the brand did not exist?

2. Standpoint
   From where does the brand speak?

3. Vision
   What vision has the brand concerning the product category or the world itself?

4. Values
   What are the brand's core values?

5. Mission
   What changes does the brand want to bring in people's life?

6. Territory
   Where is the brand legitimate in achieving this mission, in what product categories?

7. Anchoring acts or products
   What acts or products best convey the brand mission and values, are prototypical of the brand program?

8. Brand's style and language
   What elements of style and language are typical of the brand?

9. Brand's imaginary client?
   Not the target buyer but the reflected buyer.

A preliminary definition of brand identity cannot be sought in the same way for product brands and for corporate brands. Many companies today are effectively brands in their own right. ICI is both a firm and a brand, as are Siemens, Elf, Akzo, British Telecom, IBM, etc. In contrast, Crunch is Nestlé's brand, and Mir one of the Henkel brands, while Ariel belongs to Procter & Gamble. Firms awaken to the fact that their name is actually a brand when they realize that the buyer or consumer is as important as the financial analyst in the markets in which they operate—when Main Street is as important as Wall Street.

From an operational point of view, creating a brand with no direct reference to the firm offers a greater degree of freedom. All things are possible, though this does not mean that everything is relevant or easier, as such.

It is possible, however, to invent a new brand identity. In the case of company-named brands, the brand becomes the major spokesman for the company. There must therefore be a relationship between the brand identity and the firm's identity. The company brand identity has less freedom than the product brand identity. The company-named brand is in effect the firm's external showpiece. It conveys a message to the wider public, who are made more aware of the firm. It is vital that the company workforce should identify with this brand. In this way, company-named brands are seen to take on the same cultural features as the firms from which they emanate.

The Renault brand concept "Cars for living" is by no means a fortuitous one. Since World War II, Renault has established itself as the social laboratory of France. Humanistic and social values dominate company policy—men are of greater importance than machines. The whole Renault corporate ideology is centered on access to quality of life—Renault factories were the first to close for the whole of August for "holiday." This corporate culture has transmitted itself to the brand. Renault's present emphasis on Formula 1 racing in no way contradicts this—the intention here is to reinforce the image of dynamic vehicle performance. The brand identity, on the other hand, has its source in an ideal of making "Cars for living."

The Nestlé brand could never assume an exuberant, greedy, or permissive identity. This is because it bears the same name as the company, whose identity shows none of these features. Even though the firm may not figure in the public mind, the Nestlé brand is nevertheless influenced by the all-important Nestlé company, which in the last resort either accepts or does not accept the brand identity. If harmony does not exist between the two, it is the brand identity which has to be modified to fall in line with that of the company. This far from signifies that the two coincide, but a bridge can be said to exist between them.

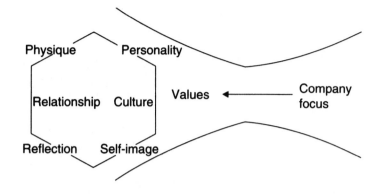

Figure 4.1

Transfer between company identity and brand identity when company and brand names coincide

Such a bridge normally operates via the cultural facet (Figure 4.1). There is a theoretical reason for this. A firm's identity is transmitted through its focus on one or two key values which mobilize its employees (Schwebig, 1985). These are the values which penetrate the brand, give it its perspective on the world, and stimulate its will to transform the product category. This "source value" passes its meaning to the brand. Renault turns the common automobile into a car for living. Citroën creates cars one step ahead of other cars, since the Citroën company focus is on progress through science.

After a time, the relationship between brand and company is reversed. The public image resonates, stirring the firm into far more action than all the here-today-gone-tomorrow "company projects." It is in order to take advantage of this that some change their name to that of their leading brand. For instance, the Tokyo Tsuhin Kogyo company has become Sony, Inc., while Tokyo Denki Kagaku has taken as its new name that of its well-known brand TDK. Tired of seeing its brand nowhere when its products are everywhere, the electronic giant CGE announced in April 1990 that it was going to change its name to that of its two well-known industrial brands, becoming known as Alcatel–Alsthom. CGE thus made visible its dual strategy (communications and energy) and its scope, personality, and culture.

Determining Its Imaginary Sources

We have already seen that major brands do not derive their identity solely from functional sources. This is why the choice of the brand's imaginary "source" is as important as the choice of the appropriate products of the range to advertise. In Europe, Chrysler, for example, had to make a choice. Was their brand identity to be based on the reference to an "American way of life and driving," or were they to follow Ford's path, making no reference whatsoever to myths linked to its heritage? Apple is steeped in a California allusion to high tech and counterculture. Atari give their products a high profile, yet without any particular underlying significance. The brand still conveys no feeling of depth—nothing to differentiate it personally from other products in the microcomputer field. Mitsubishi has its name on cars, but is not yet a brand in the full sense—we cannot perceive its values, its source of inspiration, its intention, direction, and guiding force. It is a name on countless products, a means of reassurance through its implied connection with the industrial power of the Mitsubishi group. It is the manufacturer's sign on packaging—an indicator of origin, not yet of a project; a sign without a design.

Choosing Products with a Meaning

The more ambitious the brand—and its system of values—the greater the degree of care required in choosing the product or service to launch the brand campaign. This should center on the product which best represents the brand's intention—the one which best supports the brand's potential to bring about change.

Not all the products encompassed by one brand are able to do this. A campaign should only be backed by a product which can reflect the brand's own image. Ideally, this path should be visible. The major car manufacturers are well aware of this. They see the vehicle's design as an outward manifestation of the brand's intention. The tapered outline of the larger Citroën cars (DS, CX, XM)—half car, half missile—is quite intentional. Product design can constitute a powerful expression of identity. Many cars on the market are outwardly similar, however, signaling a loss of their brand identity.

Product features also serve as a potential support for the brand.

The whole meaning and direction of Toshiba is illustrated by their portable computers. Atari has discovered the best support for its ideology in the tiny Portfolio. But what about the service sector? The performance of service brands is obviously intangible—there is no visual presence, apart from the customer and the service provider. From the invisible to the nonexistent is but a short step. Nevertheless, the same reasoning applies: choose the territory which best illustrates the brand.

One approach consists of making the invisible visible, by creating real "communication products." In other words, intangible services are presented in a packaged form—the service is given a name and dressed to create a physical existence in the service environment. For instance, British Airways advertises its Club Class services, as others speak of their "Guaranteed Satisfaction Plan." Well-considered sponsoring and selective patronage can be further clear manifestations of brand values.

Brand Campaign or Product Campaign?

Volkswagen has never centered its publicity on anything other than its products. From the outset, press ads have tended to depict their cars in all their visual purity. Though the caption might distance itself in a humorous, impertinent, or irrational way, the car remains the hero of the hour. Renault occasionally launches so-called "brand campaigns," which lay particular emphasis on the brand philosophy, epitomized by its slogan. Whenever a brand is created, there are two alternative strategies—to communicate the brand meaning, its imaginary significance, and its intention direct to the consumer; or to build it indirectly, by promoting a representative product.

The decision rests on the firm's ability to pick out a product which can convey the full meaning of the brand. It is not surprising that Volkswagen took the second option. The Beetle plainly demonstrated the touch of an original creator—a novel automotive concept embodying a different form of social expression.

When the American photocopier brand Nashua first appeared in Europe in 1979, several of the more conservative dailies allowed an otherwise rare full-page advertisement depicting the head of a Red Indian chief. The caption read tersely: "The most popular photocopiers in this country have an Indian name—Nashua, USA." This newspaper ad signaled the start of a brand campaign. Other full-page adverts followed featuring an Indian tribe, with each of the firm's products being depicted by one of the braves. This campaign described the very basis of the brand. It brought out the brand's central quality of reliability—both in men and in machines—and also its imaginary source-point, the mythical virtues attached to the image of the North American Indian. In this aggressive approach, Nashua was identifying itself not with Japan but with America—but an America different from that of Rank Xerox (the world of Manhattan) and of IBM. Nashua's America is that of the storied prairie, man's preeminence, the given word, lasting fraternal bonds. Reliability was to be the essential watchword as much in customer dealings as in the lasting qualities of their photocopiers.

The Nashua identity, founded on its central quality of reliability, satisfied the five demands against which any brand identity is judged:

- It was specific: no other brand than Nashua could lay claim to it. It was inscribed in its name.
- It was grounded: all present and future products represented its physical materialization.
- It was rewarding: its sense of security and reliability lived up to the expectations of those segments of the market for which it was intended.
- It capitalized on the insufficiencies of the competition: Rank Xerox, the leader in technological terms, was often reproached for its overbearing attitude toward customers, when it had come to monopolize.
- It inspired strong approval within the company itself: both production and sales teams involved in this new product saw themselves in harmony with the brand's own image. Its image reflected that of the company.

Nashua took the decision not to start life with a campaign which boasted of the reliability of one of its models, or the exclusive technical process behind its liquid toner system. Though durability is a product characteristic, brand identity does not boil down to durability alone—rather, it embraces this quality within a far wider ambit. The fact is that none of Nashua's products was capable of fully illustrating this far-reaching concept. In appearance, a Nashua photocopier is scarcely different from a Canon, Minolta, Toshiba, or Rank Xerox. Again, it only represents part of the brand's aim—functional durability. They therefore had to mount a brand campaign which would communicate more directly the purposes of this newly introduced brand. It was followed by a number of direct-marketing and trade-marketing segment-by-segment operations. Three years later, in 1982, Nashua held second place in the market, thanks to effective marketing and a communication program which quickly saw the brand take off, eager to announce new products each year.

A similar reasoning explains why banks show a preference for brand campaigns. As service companies, they have nothing to show. They can only point to their values and identity in symbolic terms.

Brand Language and Territories of Communication

Brand identity is rich in meaning. It cannot be reduced to a mere word or a concept. Even if, for the purposes of a campaign, a concept of communication is seized upon—for example, Renault's "Cars for living" or Nike's "Just do it"—the brand still shines forth through the other facets of its identity prism.

How then does it reflect its clientele, its relationship, its culture and personality? In the first instance, through its products or services. Macintosh products are a concrete representation of Apple's customer relationship. It must be remembered, however, that Macintosh is itself the name of a product—an original name not in the traditional run of computer identification. In language terms, the name is therefore a manifestation of the values on which the Apple brand identity is founded.

Today's vocabulary does not take a uniquely verbal form—one might even say that it has an overriding visual propensity. In a quick glance at television or a flick through the ads in a magazine, the picture stands out more than the words. Bull chose to speak in a visual manner through a language linked metaphorically with the tree. It means that any advertisement in any language depicting a tree reminds us of Bull. The brand has thus created a territory of communication, by according itself a combination of spoken and visual language. This has become their means of expression—in their view, everyone knows who is talking: Bull.

A territory of communication does not appear from nowhere, nor does it attach itself to the brand. It should emanate from the brand itself. Bull chose to express themselves in symbolic association with the tree, and not in factual terms, since the tree best synthesized the brand's specific features. Everything we wish to know about Bull is seen in its logo. On a physical plane, the main branches are the mini-computers, the smaller branches microcomputers, and the leaves software. This language can be understood both by the expert, in its clever analogy, and by the nonexpert, who is well able to figure out what is being conveyed. In terms of client service, each flow chart is a different variety of tree. The tree represents the different levels of computer operation proposed by Bull. The tree grows and changes shape as it adapts itself to its environment. The symbol plainly expresses the specific relationship between Bull and their public—that of adaptability and natural respect. Bull offers harmony. The power of this language lies in its truth, expressing Bull's identity. The language is international, applicable to all the company's products and services, and stands out in the sense in which every brand should be noticed.

Brand language allows the brand to hold forth more freely. Through lack of a personal language, communications are too often locked into a strangulating corset. In not knowing which language to speak, the same words or pictures keep reappearing, so that the whole brand message becomes clogged. From one campaign to the next, there is so great a desire to achieve a common image that they all end up as near-clones. The specific message which each campaign wishes to convey is masked by an excessive yearning for a common code.

The code may be rather artificial, but the language is natural. It expresses the speaker's specific attributes—personality, culture, and values—and allows the brand's products or services to be presented in an appealing way. Each time that Dim, the tights brand, embarks on a new campaign, it is based on a new product. Nevertheless, each is a typically Dim campaign. The accompanying music makes us aware of this, but such a device alone does not convey this general identical appearance. Dim's reflection is "la Parisienne," just as Marlboro reflects an unsullied, solitary, mythical man. Dim advances hand-in-hand with the female—epitomized by the Parisian woman—both in its products (liberating tights) and in its values. Such a sense of current values led to a change of name from Dimanche (Sunday) stockings to Dim tights.

Brand language finally serves as a means of decentralizing decisions. Guided by a unified format in which to express themselves, different subsidiaries worldwide can adapt the theme of their message to local market and product requirements while respecting the singularity and indivisible nature of the brand—in short, the common language. Brand identity must reconcile freedom and coherence. This is the role to which expressional guides—also called brand charters or manuals—must contribute. These must not deal simply with descriptive or identifying features—e.g., where the brand should appear on the page, etc. They must also specify dominant aspects of style, literal and visual.

DOES THE NAME COUNT SO MUCH?

Manufacturers make products; consumers buy brands. Pharmaceutical laboratories turn out molecules, but doctors prescribe brands. In an economic system where brands are the focus of prescription and demand, the brand name naturally takes on a preeminent role. For although, in a notional sense, the brand encompasses all the distinctive signs—name, logo, symbol, colors, personality, and even its slogan—it is the brand name which becomes the subject of discussion, demands, and regulations. It is therefore natural that we should devote particular attention to this facet in the process of brand creation—the choice of name.

What name do we choose in order to build a major brand? Does an appropriate name-type exist for such a purpose? An examination of major brands suggests an answer to this frequently-posed question. Consider, for instance, Coca-Cola, IBM, Marlboro, Perrier, Dim, Kodak, Schweppes, and Adidas. Is there a common factor linking these brand names? Coca-Cola referred to the product ingredients when it was first created, while the original meaning of IBM (International Business Machines) has been lost. Schweppes is unpronounceable in some languages, Marlboro is a place on the map, Kodak an onomatopoeia, and Adidas a shortening of the founder's name. The conclusion to be drawn from this fleeting study is reassuring: To create a major brand, we can take any name at all (or almost any), and then by consistency in communication over a period of time give meaning to this name—the brand's own meaning.

Does this mean that there is no need to give much thought to the brand name, apart from the strict problem of ensuring that the name has not already been registered? Not so, since the choice of an appropriate name, and respect for certain principles in choosing, allow one to save time—perhaps several years—in the process of brand development and the creation of a major brand. Time is a crucial factor when the brand needs to conquer its territory. The brand name must be thought of in terms of the brand's future destiny, not in relation to the state of the market and the standing of similar products at its creational stage. Since the choice of brand name often ends having the reverse effect of that intended, it seems high time to draw attention to the usual pitfalls in choosing a name, and to give a reminder of certain principles.

Brand Name Or Product Name?

The choice of name depends upon a brand's intended destiny. We must therefore make the distinction between the search for a name for a real brand in the full sense—having in mind its likely international extension, future wide range of products, and its long life—and, on the other hand, the choice of a name of a product having territorial and temporal limitations. The two do not warrant the same approach in terms of emphasis, time factor, and financial investments.

The Dangers of Descriptive Names

In 90 percent of cases, manufacturers hope that the brand name will describe the product which the brand embraces. They love it when the name describes what the product does (an aspirin called Cephaline) or is (a brand of biscuit named Biscuito). This search for names which denote the product reflects a poor understanding of what a brand and its destiny really entail. As we have seen, the brand does not describe the product, it distinguishes it.

In choosing a descriptive name we also fail to exploit the possibilities of multimedia communication. The qualities and characteristics of the product will be known to its target public thanks to advertising, salesmen, direct marketing, trade magazines, and consumer associations. It would be a waste if the name were made redundant by the message of all these other communication media. Rather, the

name should be exploited in order to provide a further meaning—
the spirit of the brand itself. Products are mortal: their life cycle is
limited. There should be no confusion between the meaning of a
brand name and the characteristics of the product which it embraces
at its birth. The Apple management were very conscious of this
need. It would take only a few weeks for the market to realize that
Apple made microcomputers. There was therefore no particular
virtue in a name like Microcomputers International or Computer
Research Systems. By calling themselves Apple, they immediately
pointed to the long-lasting individuality of the brand, and not the
characteristics of its temporary embodiment, Apple-1. This individuality was more apparent in other facets of the brand's identity than
in its physique.

The brand is not the product. The brand name must not describe
what the product does, but must reveal or suggest what the brand
is—what its meaning is.

Making Provision for Copies

Every major product is open to being copied; this is unavoidable. In
the first place, manufacturing patents fall within the public domain.
Wherein remains a company's means of prolonging its differential
advantage and of gaining its just reward for research and development? In the brand name. There is no better example than in the
pharmaceutical industry. We now live in an age of generic products
which multiply as soon as a patent ends. Laboratories then produce
the formula in question without any research or development costs.
When one chooses a brand name which describes a product—in other
words a generic name tied to the function of the product—it no longer
distinguishes the brand when copies or generic products arrive on the
market. The choice of a descriptive name turns the brand into a
generic product after a while. The first antibiotics fell into this trap.
They were given names which indicated that they were penicillin-
based: Vibramycin, Terramycin, etc.

Today, the pharmaceutical industry is aware that the name is in
itself a kind of patent and a safeguard against copying. The name must
differ from the generic product. A unique name is inimitable.
Glaxo–Roche laboratories, for instance, discovered an antiulcer agent,

ranitidine. The brand name is "Zantac." Their competitor, Smith, Kline and French laboratories, isolated another antiulcer agent, cimetidine, which they sold under the "Tagamet" brand. This naming policy puts a stop to copies and counterfeits. The doctor may be of the opinion that Vibramycin is just as good as Terramycin. Tagamet, however, seems unique—as does Zantac. Those generic products which in due course will inevitably exploit the cimetidine or ranitidine patents will not have the pull of the Tagamet or Zantac name.

An original name protects the brand by extending its sphere of protection against fraudulent imitations of the name. It was considered that the Kerius perfume was, in its name, a counterfeit of Kouros. In a lawsuit, legislators are not concerned with similarity of properties but with similarities in name. Kerius was therefore changed to Xerius. A descriptive name, however, does not have this "patenting" function. A brand calling itself Biscuito would have a very limited sphere of protection. Only the "o" could be protected, thus giving scope for anyone to come up with a Biscuita! Coca-Cola itself could not prevent the name Pepsi-Cola. Quickburger, Starburger, Burger King all are similar in name, though McDonald's is difficult to imitate.

The protective inadequacy of descriptive brands has been widely exploited by retailer brands. Wishing to lure part of the clientele favoring major brands toward their own products, retailers have chosen names for their counterbrands which resemble those of corresponding prominent brands. This causes a possible confusion in the mind of the consumer. For example, Incore copies Nestlé's Ricore, while l'Oreal's Studio line shampoo is copied by Microline, etc. Even in packaging, imitation is a source of confusion, since the consumer tends to use appearance cues when searching along the shelves. Recent research has, in fact, shown a rate of confusion of more than 40 percent (Kapferer and Thoenig, 1991).

Confronted with the problem of copying, the attitude of the pharmaceutical industry is to protect itself by simultaneous creation of a product name and a brand name. For failing to do so, some brand names tend to take on a common designation and are used to refer to the product in general. The brand name Sellotape is now present in some dictionaries. It is a proof of fame, but also a sign of degeneration as a brand name. To avoid the generic risk, it is better to create a qualifying brand name (Walkman recorder) rather than a substantival brand name (Walkman). This can be achieved, if necessary, by the simultaneous creation of a name for the product itself.

Preventing Time Effects

Many names make a noose for themselves when it comes to natural evolution of the brand over the passage of time. For instance:

- The name Europ Assistance limits the territorial extension of this brand and has opened the way to Mondial Assistance.
- Calor is associated with heating technology (steam irons and hair dryers), leaving no scope for refrigerators. Radiola was never convincing as a domestic appliance brand—its brand name is too closely linked with a specific field of activity.
- As the years roll by, the French sport retailer's name Sport 2000 becomes less and less futuristic and progressive.

Thinking International from the Outset

Every brand should be given the capacity to go international if it so desires. So many brands discover at a late hour the restrictions which their name imposes when they decide to break into foreign markets. Nike, for example, is refused registration in certain Arab countries. Computer Research Services has problems with its brand name in France, as does Toyota with its M-R2 model. The worldwide company CGE cannot gain protection for its name in the United States because of the earlier registration of the well-known brand GE (General Electric). Before taking a brand abroad, careful thought should be given to its pronounceability, the image which the name might evoke in certain parts of the world, and, not least, its prior use elsewhere. These new demands explain why the 1,300 identical words in the seven principal European Community languages are the cause of such interest. Many of these, in fact, have appeared as brand registrations. It also explains a tendency toward abstract names which have no literal meaning, and can therefore acquire their own.

Finally, as a paradox, brand internationalization can have an impact on the names of brands of purely national standing. This was shown in the case of *Temps de la Finance*, a French newspaper intended for cir-

culation in France. It had to change its name since it was too sugges-
tive of being a translation of the London *Financial Times*.

No Strategy—No Creation

Creating a brand name requires several stages of reasoning. The
brand's foreseeable destiny must first be determined. The second
stage establishes which particular facets of the brand identity should
be conveyed in the name.

Once the name's mission has been mapped out, a name-research
company can be briefed. In this day and age, these companies not only
employ the normal tools of creativity but are also aided by dedicated
software (Botton and Cegarra, 1990). Nevertheless, as in the case of
an advertising program, clear and precise definitions of strategy and
brand identity are indispensable prerequisites in the search for a
name.

BRAND AWARENESS

The equity of a brand is partly measured by the awareness which it
evokes—how many people throughout the world know the brand, if
only by name? This is natural measurement, since the brand is a symbol. Brand awareness relates to the number of persons who recognize
the brand's significance, and who are conscious of the promise which
this symbol expresses. More importantly, how many can point to its
field of competence—the products and services which it envelopes?
A brand without awareness is but a blob on a product—voiceless and
devoid of meaning. The aim of investing in advertising is to reveal the
meaning of the brand and to spread it as far and wide as possible in
order to encourage people to try the products offered.

There are three customary types of awareness:

- "top-of-the-mind" awareness, which gauges whether the
  brand is the first to spring to mind when people are questioned on brands relating to a certain category of product
- unaided awareness, which measures the brand's prominence,
  the level of unassisted association with the product category
- assisted awareness, which consists of asking the target public

if they have already heard of certain brands—whether they
know them, if only by name

Each of these levels of awareness represents an increasing level of
attainment difficulty, ranging from the most accessible—assisted
awareness—to the most difficult, top-of-the-mind awareness. Such a
hierarchy may lead one to deduce that top-of-the-mind awareness
should be the objective of every brand. This would be a misconcep-
tion. Each of these levels of awareness has its own function and exer-
cises an individual influence. The necessity to invest in the
attainment of a high-level, top-of-the-mind degree of awareness
depends upon the market.

Assisted awareness represents a level of reassurance—consumers
have already heard of the brand. Since the brand is not totally unknown,
salespeople mention it to a potential customer. Unaided awareness
brings together the few brands which immediately spring to mind in a
particular field. It gives them an edge over other brands when the purchaser is not too concerned about choice and is lining up the few names
belonging to the evoked set of brands at the forefront of his memory. In
the industrial market, this is the approach which is most often applied.
It forms the point of departure for selection of the few brands which
will later undergo a deep analysis. Top-of-the-mind awareness benefits
the brand in all those cases where the customer has to make a quick
decision—choosing a soft drink or a beer, with a waiter breathing down
one's neck, for instance—or if, for fear of getting too involved, the purchaser wishes to keep matters simple, as is the case with many fast-
moving consumer products (Kapferer and Laurent, 1983).

The decision as to which of these different levels of awareness
should be pursued depends on the way in which customers are
expected to make their choice, and their degree of personal involvement. Major investment to acquire a high level of unaided awareness
is not always justified. A domestic appliance brand will not see its
sales double just because the level of unaided brand awareness has
doubled. Instead, if a satisfactory level of assisted awareness exists,
the brand might do better by extending its sales outlets and distribution. In the case of durables-a relatively infrequent requirement—the
customers are often unacquainted with certain brands and unaware of
the necessary criteria for choice. They make up their minds after a

lengthy comparison between the products on show. If a brand name is tied to positive attributes and favorable attitudes, it will greatly contribute to the choice. The unaided awareness of Hoover is poor, but its assisted awareness is most favorable, and its sales are remarkable in the vacuum-cleaner market.

Unaided awareness plays a greater part in the choice of less significant products, since the perceived risks are minimal—as is the desire to spend time in choosing. But experience proves that under certain market conditions access to unaided brand awareness becomes almost impossible. Assisted awareness of the brand increases, but not unaided awareness.

Unaided brand awareness has an emotional dimension. This is borne out by the fact that unaided awareness is correlated to measures of global preference, and vice versa. Awareness is therefore not simply the result of mere repetition, but is achieved by creating appeal and interest. An unattractive brand will find it more difficult to achieve prominence as a result of the well-known process of selective recall. The relationship between assisted and unaided awareness is shown in figure 4.2(a). Unaided brand awareness is always acquired to the detriment of another brand. If one brand increases in awareness, another automatically falters. This is a feature common to most market sectors, where those questioned quote on average three or four brands, without prompting. If the number of brands referred to is the sum total of their memory capacity, the inclusion of a new brand in the customer's mind suggests that another must give way. Consequently, when, in a given market, three brands achieve a high level of unaided awareness, in practical terms they prevent the access of other brands to unaided awareness (Laurent, Kapferer, and Roussel, 1987). These markets are "blocked."

This memory-block phenomenon does not exist in new markets, where no brand has a high level of unaided awareness. Investment in advertising will serve to attain such awareness. It is further desirable from a competitive point of view since, in addition to blocking, it exploits the advantages of being first in the field (Carpenter and Nakamoto, 1990; Nedungadi and Hutchinson, 1985), hence being its prototype.

In young markets, where the product category is still finding its feet, the first brand to spread its message far and wide benefits from

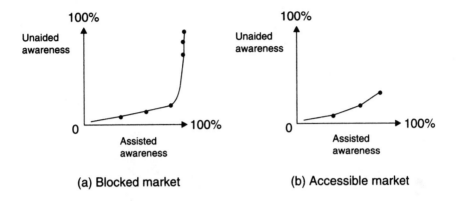

Figure 4.2

Dynamics of brand awareness

what we call the "pioneer advantage." Most brands which dominate a new market hold sway for decades afterwards, even in markets where the competitive edge is not achieved solely by technological know-how, experience, or productivity gains. One only has to look at Coca-Cola, McDonald's, or Xerox. The psychological explanation is that when a market is first created, its customers have no system of preferences or set criteria of choice. The first brand which comes to be known in this market becomes the prototype—the market reference. Put another way, it characterizes the ideal brand—it bears the combination of attributes on which the purchaser will henceforth base his ideal of satisfaction. It is this brand which will define values, and for this reason subsequent entrants to the market are handicapped. With their usual approach of "If they can do it, so can we," and their desire to emulate the pioneer, they lose something of their own character and merge into the background. This creates a structural handicap in terms of awareness.

It must be emphasized that the pioneer advantage exists only if the innovating brand gives satisfaction—if the product or service has a good performance. Otherwise, it is better to refrain from any form of communication, in order to avoid becoming the negative stereotype of the market.

5

Managing the Time Factor:
Identity and Change

Many apparently modern and up-to-date brands have actually been with us for a long time. Coca-Cola was born on 29 May 1887. The Michelin bibendum appeared in 1898, Gitanes and Gauloises in 1910, Camel in 1913, Dannon in 1919, La Vache qui Rit in 1921, Bull in 1933, Orangina in 1936, and Marlboro in 1937, to name but a few. These are brands which have survived—others have disappeared, to be forgotten for all time.

The perennial appeal of some brands reminds us that, though products are mortal, governed by a life cycle, brands can escape the effects of time. It is this resistance to time which has led companies such as BSN to refrain from writing off the value of the brands which they had included in their balance sheets. Nevertheless, brands themselves can also disappear. Why do certain brands show a resistance to time, displaying eternal youth, while others do not? Management of the time element lies at the heart of the problem.

The brand grows only over a long period of consistency. The concept of identity demands long-term and consistent measures and strategy on the part of the brand. In order to capitalize, the brand must maintain a precise orientation; continuity is essential to the brand's formation and longevity. However, a brand which does not develop becomes fossilized and loses its significance. Time merely reflects changes in consumers' lifestyles and expectations, in technology, and in competitive forces. Managing the time element therefore poses the questions:

- How do we develop while remaining unchanged?
- What do we change and what do we leave untouched?

Since the brand exists only by dint of its products (or services) and its communication, the management of time will necessarily involve these two vectors of evolution and continuity. On the communication side, we have the rare example of Marlboro, which initiated the image of the lone cowpoke in 1964. Few brands have in fact been so steeped in a myth whose image has been totally fixed in time and space. Coca-Cola, Volkswagen, Nestlé, Philips, and Adidas have had to update their customer communication and products to adapt to environmental changes. Brands must therefore learn to change their style and products in order to remain in fashion and up-to-date.

THE EFFECTS OF TIME

Time is only a proxy variable. It is a convenient indicator of the changes which affect society as well as markets, subjecting the brand to the risk of obsolescence on a double front—technological and cultural.

Technological progress and research and development maintain a permanent flow of innovations which the brand should incorporate, to safeguard against technological downgrading. In adhering too strictly to a temporal format, the brand becomes mortal. For a while, this was the case with Volkswagen. The brand covered a product, the Beetle, which, though unique and changed since its first appearance, was coming to the end of its life cycle, and both brand and product were going down together. It had not been understood that, though the product forms the brand's physical support, the brand should seek the support of other products in order to maintain its mission. Volkswagen was therefore no more than a single-product name. Without an ongoing renewal of its products or services, and without nonstop attention to its task, the brand falls by the wayside. Innovation and new products give the brand the opportunity to demonstrate its mission and direction, and to construct a coherent and specific image. This concerns IBM and Apple in the technological computer maelstrom as much as it does Coca-Cola. Certainly, the basic Coca-Cola formula has remained unchanged throughout the world, but its adaptability has developed in necessary response to changes in living conditions—e.g., family packs for the weekly shopping in hypermarkets, aluminum cans for more convenience when taking home and taking out, derivatives without caffeine or sugar, etc. Recognition of its purchasers' down-to-earth needs should be the brand's primary preoccupation, and warrants constant vigilance.

Cultural evolution is also tied to the time element, since values, customs, and behavior patterns are forever changing. What seemed revolutionary or even especially ill-chosen in 1978 is insignificant in 1992. This everyday feature of life threatens the brand which anchors its survival to one particular feature. Findus is the brand which gave credence to frozen foods. They were not content with being just an informing source on frozen foods—they turned out to be a legitimate force of a new social behavior. This, as we have seen, is one of the essential functions of brand discourse. Like a bolt of lightning, the advent of frozen foods helped shatter the traditional concept of the role of women. The Findus reputation and public voice gave authority to changes which women had long been seeking. Times have certainly changed—the housewife has been replaced by the working wife. The basis of Findus's original argument is now as outmoded as Women's Lib. If Findus had not developed, had not broken away from their earlier point of view, the brand would have become dated. The battle should not be fought just on the shelves, but in the whole media marketplace of ideas and symbols.

Time also brings about a natural drift away from former symbolizations. After the Second World War and its deprivations, the cow came to signify the abundance of nature. This suited La Vache qui Rit, the oldest of modern cheeses. Today, the cow is no longer such an omnipresent symbol of nature—we often do not even see it on milk cartons. The lovable old cow has gone back to being an animal. This causes a problem for the brand, since it now carries a rather infantile connotation and causes it to symbolize a cheese which a child stops eating just to show that he is no longer a child. Generally speaking, effigies can bog down the brand, closeting it in a symbolism which is prone to environmental change. Bibendum does not run this risk—it is an original symbol with no social significance. Only Michelin gives meaning to it, and vice versa. On the other hand, Robinson's golliwog has been affected by the social change in the meaning of its visual symbol—its crude representation of a Negro "doll" is now perceived as carrying with it certain racist undertones. It no longer has the same innocent and appealing symbolization that it once had. Uncle Ben's has escaped this obsolescence, for its jovial human figure is linked to a myth in time: the gentle black characters, playing the blues and suffering from slavery as in *Gone With the Wind*.

Brands created around a living personality also need to face up to changes in meaning. The personality has his or her own life and acquires a dimension and symbolization which may not always coincide with the brand's strategic interests. This is why celebrities signing contracts with Chanel, for instance, must agree to follow certain guidelines in their private lives (e.g.: to dress in a certain manner, or to eat in particular restaurants, etc.).

Over a period of time, the clientele advance and grow older. Those who took holidays in the first of Club Méditerranée villages will not see fifty again. The power of this brand lies in its ability to cater to the needs of its clientele without abjuring its faith or becoming a brand for oldies. The uncomfortable monoproduct of the time has since seen new products geared to the comfort requirements of everyone. Villages range from the desert-island hut to the five-star, marble-clad hotel, but the basic formula has remained intact, as demonstrated by the preeminence of sport and social enjoyment, whatever the country or type of village. The brand's success lies in its capacity to respond to the needs of a continuous sequence of clientele. In their failure to renew their clientele, many textile brands are now associated with an aging clientele, both as source of their sales and, worse, as the brands' customer reflection.

THE PYRAMIDAL MODEL OF A BRAND

Brand communication and slogans are bound to evolve. Positioning is the act of relating one facet of a brand to a set of consumer expectations, needs, and desires. As these change through time, the brand is obliged to follow suit. Thus Coke's advertising once spoke of thirst, later saying "Coke is it," and finally speaking of "the feeling." Coke commercials themselves have changed, although there is a definite Coke style, easy to recognize, and rather aped by many other brands. Over the longer term, it is remarkable how Coca-Cola, beyond the product's physical identity, has become an archetype, a value system which has remained largely intact since its birth, one century ago. The source of inspiration, or genetic code, of Coca-Cola seems never to have been betrayed throughout that period.

To manage a brand through time it is essential to analyze it as a three-tiered pyramid incorporating the time dimension (see Figure 5.1).

At the top of the pyramid is the brand's focal point, the source point from which the brand seems to speak and act. It is, to use an analogy, the brand's genetic code. This source point must be known but must remain unspoken of and invisible. It is the brand's deep identity, its core value. As such it is permanent over the long run. For instance, Porsche's core identity is not "fast cars" (this is actually a theme of its communication, and one of the attributes of its products): symbolically, Porsche's core identity is "the hero." Not the modern popular meaning of the word, but its archetypal meaning. Being associated with dangerous driving at times has never created a bad image for the brand, for risky situations are the natural fate of the hero. Naturally, one realizes how poor the effect would be of an overt statement that Porsche cars are for heroes. What is unconscious must remain so to be effective. It must remain hidden behind product arguments.

In the middle of the pyramid, we have the style and codes of the brand. Etymologically speaking, it is the stylus with which one writes and leaves one's mark and imprint. As one's signature, the style—a brand's specific means of conveying a message in words and images—is a reflection of the brand's core identity. As a consequence, style should not be random but should always be thought of in relation to the brand's deep identity.

At Guinness, all advertisements are tested, but top management is asked only one question: "Is it Guinness?" This "feel-right factor" measures the fit between the core and the way the brand portrays itself. Style may change a little to adapt to changing times. However, the truth is that identity becomes apparent only during a process of

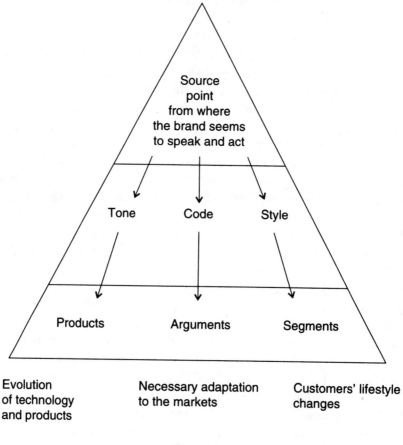

Figure 5.1
The pyramidal model of a brand

change. For example, depending on current fashion, women's clothes will be either in pastel or bright colors, short or long, loose or tight-fitting. To determine a woman's identity by means of a fixed code would be to ask her to dress in long-length pastel shades permanently, when everyone else was wearing short, brightly-colored clothes. Actually, a woman really portrays her identity by the particular and very personal way in which she "follows" the trends of the moment. Her process of choice from one year to the next, from one fashion to another, reveals the existence of a criterion and of a specific point of view, the mark of an identity. To remain modern, brands certainly must keep up with fashion, but twist it in their own way.

The lower stage of the pyramid relates to the communication themes, the brand's current advertising positioning. The customers look at the brand bottom-up. They discover it by its products, its themes and positioning, and the style of its communication. Brand management requires that if one is to build a long-lasting brand, there should be a clear understanding of the brand's core and source point. It works top-down: the style and style changes must not betray the brand's core identity. The communication themes and promises must fall within the brand's legitimate territory.

This three-tiered pyramidal model is also essential in managing international brands. Often the brand is not at the same stage of development in different countries, and, as a consequence, its advertising themes and products are not homogeneous throughout the world. This is not a problem as long as the same core value and style are present in all countries. Only in the long run will the product range and ads be unified.

There is a definite relationship between the six identity facets (the identity prism) and the pyramidal model (see Figure 5.2). An examination of advertising themes reveals that they refer to product attributes (physique), customer reflection, or the relationship (particularly in the case of service brands or children's products brands). They are the outward facets of identity, therefore they are communicated explicitly. They are those which are visible and material. The style, like one's handwriting, reveals the brand's interior facets—its personality and its customers' self-image. Finally, the genetic code, the brand's root source, inspires the whole structure and nurtures the brand's cultural facet. There is therefore a strong relationship between stylistic codes and identity. In Volkswagen's case, humor has been present in all its commercials and ads throughout the world, for decades. Humor is an effect of solidarity ("Volkswagen" meaning literally "people's car"), since it demonstrates a rejection of car idoliza-

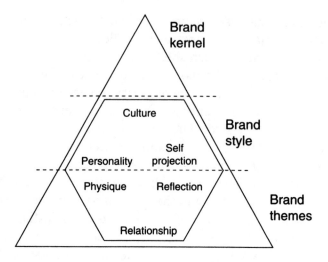

Figure 5.2

Identity and pyramidal models

tion, the cult which leads to a hierachical ranking of motorists according to the car they possess.

Brand-explicit communication can fluctuate between facets. In fact, there appears to be a sequence starting with physique, passing through reflection, and finally arriving at the cultural facet. Benetton started by promoting its colorful sweaters (the physical facet), quickly moved to relationship (a unifying force for the world's youth), and now promotes its culture, its vision of the world. Such stages are normal: the brand progresses from the explicit to the implicit.

The pyramidal model implies a varying approach in managing its three layers. The brand theme will change when it is neither motivating nor differentiating—there was nothing unusual in Coke's progression from "thirst" to "feeling." Every theme becomes worn, and the competition is quick to step in. As an expression of the brand's personality and culture, the stylistic code must be more stable, since it facilitates management of changes from one theme to another. The genetic code, on the other hand, must not be tampered with. To change it would be to create another brand, homonymous with the original but different. Even though Coke's advertising positioning has changed over the years, we are still aware that the basis of its identity has remained unaltered.

Finally, the idea of tiers within the brand allows particular flexibility to brands embracing several products. The message relating to these products must point to their specific advantages and must give rise to different promises according to each product—provided that they appear to represent the same point of view and to come from the same source of inspiration. In this respect the brand functions as a superstructure. This process particularly applies to umbrella brands and to global brands marketed in a number of countries.

Customers and even management are rarely aware of the brand's pivotal guiding force. In their minds they can reconstruct its visible facets and its codes, but without penetrating the brand's program. Nor is the brand's creator aware of it—its subconscious presence is naturally transmitted through his actions and choice. When, for example, Robert Ricci died in 1988, his successor commissioned an analysis of the identity of Nina Ricci, together with that of its best-selling perfume, l'Air du Temps. The death of a creator signals the birth of a brand—hitherto respected but not automatically understood. Identity analysis is a matter of brand archeology and delving in myths. The brand's symbolic products are identified and analyzed: from what unconscious program do they seem to emanate? Why does the Nina Ricci range sparkle with fabulous evening gowns? Why did Robert Ricci see a kind of revelation in the misty treatment by the English photographer David Hamilton, to the extent of signing a long-term and exclusive contract with him? What is the link between these dresses, l'Air du Temps, and David Hamilton? Once this link is known, the problem of replacing the David Hamilton style became less acute. In knowing what core symbol this style expressed, they were able to establish other means of expression which did not smack of direct imitation. Long-established brands seeking an overhaul should undergo an inner search before projecting themselves into the future.

In the past a classic error existed in relation to brand management—giving the brand a touch-up which actually modifies its inner self. Fiji offers a good example. Launched in 1966, it became one of the five most popular perfumes in the world, alongside Anais-Anais from Cacharel and Nina Ricci's l'Air du Temps. After years of advertising on the theme "The woman is an island; Fiji is its perfume," l'Oreal thought that they should modernize the message and bring it up-to-date in line with a more active, liberated image of women. The new creative brief was supposed to transform the brand's association "from the escapism to the instinctiveness of nature." Throughout the world there appeared posters of a woman with a snake, supported by a new slogan, "The perfume of paradise." Sales dropped from 7,280,000 units in 1980 to 6,730,000 in 1981; 6,052,000 in 1982; and 5,216,000 in 1984. Luckily the drop in volume was compensated for by a rise in price. In allowing the image of the snake to supersede that of nature, they had preserved the exotic envelope of the brand which had been paramount since the time of the perfume's conception. At the time of the perfume's conception, in 1965, Club Méditerranée was becoming fashionable, as was the theme of escape to tropical happiness. This was what led to the choice of the name Fiji. In so doing, they had selected exoticism as the brand's pivot of identity. Yet it was only a style, a mode of expression. The nucleus of the brand's identity, on which its success was founded, had probably escaped the notice of the creators themselves. By introducing a snake and an orchid, their successors were unwittingly creating another brand. Having failed to appreciate Fiji's motivating force, they had shattered its very substance. The mythical symbolization of the desert island is universal and well-appreciated—hence the perfume's original worldwide success. Unfortunately, they then focused on Fiji island itself and on the exotic factor—which proved to be of secondary importance. As for the serpent and the orchid—obvious symbols of seduction—they had no place on this desert island for untouched women.

BRAND THEMES, CODES, AND KERNEL

The three-layer model of the brand is essential for its management over time. Too often, brand managers do not know what their brand's kernel is, its genetic program. They do not know what to keep constant and what to change in order to adapt to changing times. They generally fall into either of two classic pitfalls:

THE EXCESS OF DEMOCRACY

Brand managers ask consumers how they would like their brand to evolve. Naturally, if this process is undertaken worldwide this leads to fragmented brands, each geographical area having remodeled the brand. Furthermore, consumers' expectancies vary like the ebb and flow. Brand management, unlike product management, needs a core project to start with. A brand must have a clear view of its ambition, why it exists, how it wants to transform the product category, and what its view of the world is, and then promote these views among consumers.

THE EXCESS OF CODE

Brand managers impose the same codes across campaigns and over time. But not knowing what should really be kept permanent (the significant codes of the brand), they freeze the whole picture. For instance, Nina Ricci has used the photography of David Hamilton (with its typically "fuzzy" style) far beyond the sixties and seventies, Hamilton's best-known period. Such overexposure of external codes actually hurts the brand, for it indicates a failure to evolve.

Not all brands have the three layers of meaning. Many brands are only a theme, a product benefit. As we have already observed, Atari lacks depth. Its theme is in its motto, "Technology advances, prices retreat." Atari has neither style, codes, genetic program, kernel values, nor symbolic meaning. Orangina was previously only a code. For decades it said "Shake me," because of the presence of orange pulp within the bottle. Its advertising imagery was also "shaking," as a visual metaphor of its oral theme. It lacked depth, a real value system. Only recently, as it aims at becoming a European brand, has Orangina unveiled its value system. One does not compete against Coke and Schweppes, which both have very precise value systems, without proposing alternative values. Orangina has found these in the mythology linked to the South (to be coherent with its fruit and origin). Its global advertising campaign is now a hymn to Southern life, sensitivity, and emotions.

Only by looking at brand kernels can one see the difference between lookalike brands. Beyond their envelope (the code), what do they say? For instance, two best-seller perfumes throughout the world are l'Air du Temps (Nina Ricci) and Anais-Anais (Cacharel). Looking at them, they seem like twins. Sarah Moon's photographic style for Anais-Anais is very close to David Hamilton's. Both perfumes aim at the young, adolescent girl. The codes, the envelopes of these two brands, are extremely close, but their genetic programs are very different. Anais-Anais portrays girls whispering to each other, almost looking alike, as if each girl were the mirror of the other. The advertising focuses on their faces, avoiding the body. The redundancy of its name (Anais-Anais) reinforces the mirror signification of the advertising: each person is the mirror of the other. Anais-Anais is fundamentally about narcissism.

L'Air du Temps does not uncover the same myth. It is noticeable that its ad depicts a young girl alone, lost in her thoughts, generally hidden by a veil (an image which is reinforced by David Hamilton's typically misty photographic style). In most cultures, veils are a sign of virginity; the time has yet to come when the young women is "unveiled" (literally and symbolically). L'Air du Temps' kernel is about initiation to femininity.

Knowing one's kernel provides much freedom to brand management through time. The external style may change, adapted to modern times, but the kernel must be respected. The basic myth, beneath the code, must not change.

Looking back at Fiji's example, one understands how a simple change for the sake of modernity and increased ad recognition was actually a deep change in brand identity. More recently, when Linda Evangelista, Fiji's top model, looks out at the ad reader or to the passerby close to the poster, she also departs from the brand's inner message. There should be nobody to look at. This change was probably undertaken after a focus-group meeting, or some advertising recall test. What is now needed is not brand managers but brand custodians.

The three-layered model calls for different research methods than paper-and-pencil consumer interviews. One now needs semioticians. Shell's basic kernel is in its symbol. This brand cannot be masculine, unlike Mobil or BP: it is a motherly brand, taking from the sea and earth to give to humanity. The universal meaning of its symbol acts as a genetic program within which the brand's actions find their coherence and significance. Shell cannot be hard, tough, mere technology, as can the other brands. Its kernel is different from theirs.

REVITALIZING BRANDS

We often see brands given a new lease of life (Berry, 1988; Saporito, 1986). This was the case with Sunsilk, and the car make Talbot. Sunsilk, a well-known shampoo of the sixties, was abandoned at the end of the seventies by Unilever. In 1988 the company decided to relaunch a complete range keeping the name Sunsilk. Starting again practically from scratch, this constituted a sort of brand creation and launch: most consumers had no recall whatsoever of the past identity of these names.

This does not apply to existing brands which have simply weakened, e.g., Audi, Citroën, and Atari. In their case, the process of revitalization first entails an understanding of their foundations, since it is these which will have to support new structures. Brand identity allows exploration of potential paths for recovery. Since there is still an awareness in the public mind, the new brand cannot carry on as though the old one did not exist. In 1984, Jack Tramiel bought Atari, the widely-known computer game brand. The latter had totally collapsed. Tramiel wanted to use the name to regain a foothold in the popular and business microcomputer fields. This basically amounted to an extension of the brand beyond its original territory. Since there was little need for advertising as a result of the already-existing level of brand awareness, it amounted to assuming the former basis of identity—i.e., the brand core. To be effective in a case such as this, the brand revitalization process must use this nucleus as a springboard and source of symbolization. In the microcomputer field more than anywhere else, products have no voice. They all claim a level of performance above the average, but their multiplicity and excessive claims render the offer indistinct. Brands are needed to structure the offer along coherent lines. Atari had to know its own core identity in order to determine which line to take. The video game is not the core—it is the territory of earlier products. Nevertheless, when related to the tiered pyramid illustrated earlier, the brand core could be partly inferred from this early territory. The video war games probably best personified the inspiration source of this brand. This basically signified that Atari should become a brand totally immersed in the spirit of competition. As we have already noticed, Atari's culture is not that of Apple or IBM. That the basis of identity should be the weapon does not imply a violent stylistic code! On the contrary, as exemplified in Japanese martial arts, the power is drawn deep within.

Revitalization therefore stems from the rediscovery of one's roots. The success of the Citroën XM is an instance of this. The car seemed to mark a revival of the Citroën brand after years in the wilderness.

The hydractive suspension clearly gave an unforeseen boost to its image. Echoing the brand's obsession with engineering, and its core identity, it also updated the brand image. It propelled the XM beyond the world of the fast car, toward that of the thinking car—in other words, beyond the "muscles but no brains" universe of its sister-make Peugeot, and the "cocooning" world of Renault. Their suspension is a tangible application of the brand's imaginary obsession: to get rid of terrestrial limitations. The XM revealed that Citroën had really come to life once more.

BRAND UPDATING THROUGH PRODUCTS

A brand is not updated only by means of communication, but also through its products. Years of spectacular advertising on the part of Citroën proved a delight to its agencies and to the communication microcosm, but affected its image not one iota. Such advertising was completely detached from the brand and bereft of identity. The revival of the real Citroën was announced in the sharp lines and characteristics of the XM. The updating of any brand is achieved through its products and through meaningful actions. It is striking to note how two struggling makes—Lancia and Audi—followed the same path. Audi now seems to be obsessed with technical progress and a positivistic approach. Its resurgence rested on two functional strengths: the exceptional Audi Quatro—the first four-wheel-drive car of its type—and competitions (in which they have usually been successful). The public were then made aware of Audi's progress through the esthetic Audi 100 and 80 models, founded on pure technical research. Lancia has staged a similar revival, drawing on the natural grace implicit in the make's Italian roots. Technology, and participation in many rallies and races, has signified the brand's revival and its intention.

Generally speaking, brands remain up-to-date by satisfying in their own particular way the fresh needs of their customers, and by renewing their clientele.

Monoproduct brands move to product differentiation, satisfying variations in taste and needs. In order to satisfy the needs of a clientele seeking light, sugar-free drinks, the Coca-Cola Corporation first launched Tab—leaving Coca-Cola as it was. This managerial philosophy has gone: the brand is not the product. Keeping the Coca-Cola brand up-to-date requires development in line with customer expectations, while keeping the taste and spirit of the brand intact. Diet Coke and caffeine-free Coca-Cola request attempts at making change while remaining essentially unchanged. On the other hand, the appearance of New Coke alongside Classic Coke, creating two tastes under the same brand, was a violation of its identity. The experiment was dropped.

In relentlessly improving its product, the brand reinforces its desire to keep up with latest user trends. Procter & Gamble's Ariel, for instance, was intended to become the top brand in the European detergent market. It therefore incorporates every progressive technological feature, provided they are reliable and significant. The brand also expresses a concern for the environment through the absence of phosphates and the introduction of easily-disposable refill packs.

The brand finally updates itself by extending its range to products outside its original territory. This general process—known as brand extension—certainly offers advantages, but also involves high risks. Brand extension is examined in the next chapter.

Promoting One's Values

If a brand is to survive, it must first be recognized as symbolizing lasting values—as a reference mark. The brand should not follow the market—it can swim with the tide but should always stick to its own values, permanently promoting them.

If one reduces a brand to the name of a product, the above paragraph seems to run counter to all the basic premises of good marketing. Shouldn't companies make the products people want? Naturally. But the brand is not a mere indicator of origin, it is the actual origin of the products to come. To become a reference mark it must have consistency in its meaning. Consumer tastes are like the ebb and flow of the tide. A brand which followed them would just be a weather vane.

The case of Gillette illustrates how, through time, a brand can lose its original goals and values, and how it can get them back again. In the 90 or so years that Gillette has existed, it has emphasized performance in shaving and has become a symbol of growing up, of manhood. Most often it was the father who determined the son's choice of razor. Hence Gillette was becoming an intergenerational favorite, a sign of continuity.

Around the early 1980s, the market changed drastically. The disposable razor offered cheap price, simplicity, and for a lot of people a pretty good shave. Women had started to influence purchasing decisions and bought these disposables for themselves as well as for their men. Convenience and price were important purchase criteria. According to classical product marketing, Gillette acted responsively and decided to sell its own disposable razor. In the process the weighting given to the Gillette brand name became subsidiary to the product name.

The brand had started to forget the fundamental principles on which it had been built. The values attached to the brand and the whole sector were being undermined by disposables. Gillette had to restore value—and values—to the shaving sector. It was decided to stop swimming with the tide and instead to divert it in the direction in which the brand wanted it to go. First Gillette stopped advertising disposables and focused instead on systems. "The best a man can get" summed up what Gillette as a brand has been all about since its birth. This claim was extended worldwide as the basic credo of the brand. In parallel, the "ultimate technology" of its Sensor razor was developed and launched simultaneously in 17 countries, providing men with—it was hoped—the best shave they had ever had. The brand had been faithful to its philosophy: the importance of understanding men.

How to Make a Brand Eternal?

All marketing textbooks remind us of the product life cycle. Products are born; they grow, mature, and die. Brands, however, seem to survive longer. Some of them are now more than 100 years old: Coca-Cola, for instance. What guidelines may pave the way to a long life, if not immortality?

First, the product should always be upgraded and adapted to the new demands of customers, as long as these do not run counter to the brand's core values (in which case the product needs to be sold under another brand name).

Second, the brand should avoid remaining a monoproduct. Even if the product life cycle can be slowed down, it cannot be arrested: the brand cannot run the risk of being carried away by the death of the product. This almost happened to the Damart brand in Europe. This brand is invariably attached to its historical best-seller, thermal underwear. However, what had been a great benefit in the 1950s became less so in well-heated modern offices, cars, and houses. The target customer became slightly restricted to those who most feel the cold: the old. Damart as a brand became a synonym of clothes for the elderly. When one knows that the senior market hates all brands or signs indicative of old age, one understands how Damart became a frontier brand, but a frontier few consumers wanted to cross. The brand had waited too long: it should have both modernized its thermal wear (making it thinner, mixing it with silk or other natural fibres) and communicated on new products to free the brand from its old-age image. This double-pronged strategy has been followed by Damart in the United Kingdom.

The emblems of the brand must be modernized and must be contemporary. This explains why packages, logos, and other graphic codes undergo periodic changes. The evolution of Benetton's advertising campaigns raises doubts as to its management. Beyond these images of death, illness, and despair, is it the same brand as the one which spoke of love, and friendship between races? Although it is still called Benetton, is it the same brand kernel?

These now famous cases indicate that a world-wide brand should behave rather like an open religion. If people want Coke, let's make it easy for them and suppress all the barriers preventing them from drinking it: caffeine, sugar for instance. The root product, the symbol of the identity, however, should remain preserved. Levis 501 jeans, for example, should not be retailored to follow modern styles. It is the symbol of the brand's values. The famous Lacoste shirt is the same as it was forty years ago. Such products act as flags: the last thing one wants to change.

6

Brand Extension

Brand extension is on the increase. When they enter markets where they had not previously been present, firms do so more and more under the name of one of their existing brands, rather than creating a new brand. Figures testify to this. According to the Nielsen Company, between 1977 and 1984, 40 percent of new-product launches in the U.S. grocery trade were achieved by brand extension. The tendency has since increased, both there and in Europe.

Brand extension is not, however, a recent phenomenon (Gamble, 1967). It has long been prominent in the luxury goods sector. Brands or "griffes" which began life in haute couture have come to embrace accessories, fancy goods, jewelry, timepieces, tableware, and cosmetics. The original own-label brands (Sainsbury, Safeway, St. Michael) covered several categories of varying products. Industrial brands have also extended their territory beyond that of their initial product, incorporating a diversification of activities under their name. Siemens, Philips, and Mitsubishi have long been exponents of brand extension.

WHY EXTEND THE BRAND?

Recent attention does not focus on the process of extension as such, but on the benefits which it promises. Firms have come to appreciate that branding does not just amount to an act of customer communication or a graphic exercise in packaging, but implies a total behavior pattern. The brand survives and fulfils its intention only if it permanently surpasses itself by improving its product and adapting it to ever-heightened consumer expectations. Innovation allows the brand to remain up-to-date and demonstrates an unceasing attentiveness to the changes in customer taste. Most brands which have pinned their fortunes on a single state-of-the-art product, relying on advertising to update their image, have fallen by the wayside. To be modern in today's world means being in tune with developments in user habits (e.g., in the food market, offering simplified meals and individual portions). This in turn requires integration of new technologies (freezing, vacuum packing, chilling, irradiation, etc.). If firms do not develop their own initial level of ability in line with such changes, they run the risk of being left behind.

A second major factor in brand extension is the cost of advertising. Brand reasoning proceeds on competitive lines. Gains in productivity must be sought, right down the line. This is only fully possible when it spreads the scope of its ambition from local to national markets, and then the worldwide market. Seeking the widest market possible is the only means of supporting the increasing costs of research and development and industrial investment. The only way to achieve this wider market is through advertising. If you add to this the need to outgun the competition, at least matching their share of voice, it is easy to understand the trend toward increases in advertising expenditure. Advertising is one outcome of permanent reinvestment in research, a quest for qualitative progress, and better performance in the market. The high cost of advertising makes it impossible to support an excess of brands—there is no alternative but to concentrate one's means on just a few major brands. Most firms therefore evaluate their brand portfolio at a given time and select those few which are to be the subject of advertising expenditure. These will be the brands with diversified, innovative products. Brand extension therefore results from the concentration of efforts on a few brands. New products which would previously have been launched as new brands, under their own name,

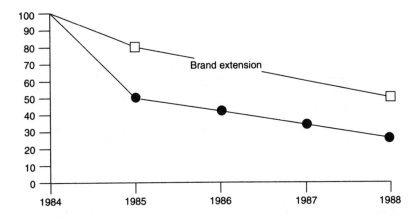

Figure 6.1

Rate of success of new brands vs. brand extensions

Source: OC & C

are now introduced under the aegis of an existing brand, but possess-ing the full authority of a strategic company brand.

The third factor explaining the vogue of brand extension is that it reduces the costs and risks of new-product launches. A recent OC & C study showed that only 30 percent of new brands survive more than four years. When new products are sold under an existing brand name, however, the survival rate is 50 percent (Figure 6.1). These are descriptive figures: what factors cause this positive effect of brand extension? According to OC & C, in the grocery market, naming a new product by an already-known brand increases the trial rate and the repeat purchase rate (Figure 6.2).

Back in 1969, Claycamp and Liddy measured the impact of family brand names on consumer responses. Building a model to predict new-product performance before market introduction, they found that "family brand umbrella" was the most important factor for predicting initial purchase.

Case studies testify the impact of an umbrella brand. In 1985, Kodak began marketing alkaline batteries under the Ultralife brand name. Instead of using the familiar yellow and red colors as with other Kodak consumer products, the packaging and the new battery had their own identity. The Kodak name appeared only in small type on the packaging. In the face of disappointing sales results, in 1988

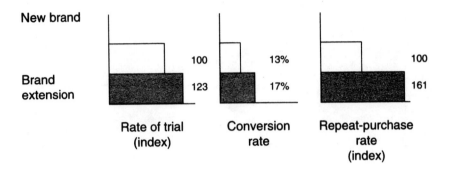

Figure 6.2

The impact of brand extension on the consumer adoption process
Source: OC & C

Kodak completely changed both the name and the outlook. They became a real Kodak product, named "Kodak batteries," with yellow and red packaging. Sales went up immediately.

The recent rapid increase in brand extension arises from technical progress, which places a greater onus on R&D costs, production economies of scale and, by way of consequence, advertising productivity. Firms tend to capitalize by allocating their innovations to one single brand, and not, as previously, to various new brands. In the same way, they seek productivity gains by exploiting the image value of one particular name which has accumulated over a period of time. This is how the way was laid open for such brands as Sony, l'Oreal, Dannon, Nestlé, and ICI, since they had acquired a very strong image where quality was concerned. They stand for promise, and carry a guarantee in their own right. It is normal for firms to turn this brand capital asset to their advantage by bestowing certain new products on the one brand.

The surge in brand extension is not, however, totally ascribable to technological factors. For a long time, brand extension was hampered by the classic brand concept.

The Classic Brand Concept

The classic brand concept rests on the equation:

1 brand = 1 product = 1 promise or customer benefit

So it is that Procter & Gamble give every new product a specific name, totally independent of all their other products. Ariel corresponds to a certain promise, Dash to another. Mister Proper is a household cleaner, and that is all. Compare this policy with that of Colgate–Palmolive. Palmolive is a toothpaste, a soap, a shaving cream, and a dishwashing liquid. Ajax is a scouring powder, a household cleaner, and a window cleaner.

The classic brand concept leads to an increase in the number of brands. If a brand relates only to one physical product and one promise, one cannot in principle use this to cover other products. Within this concept it is a strict form of designation, the name of a product—a proper name as surely as Aristotle is the name of a well-known Greek philosopher (Cabat, 1989). Such a concept gives little opportunity for brand extension. The brand in fact becomes the name of a formula or recipe. The only extension possible is line extension, either by permanently increasing the level of performance (in this instance the brand takes on a series number, e.g., Bold 1, Bold 2, or Bold 3), or by adding to the formats to cater to the latest user practices (e.g., packet, drum, mini-drum), or by multiplying the varieties (e.g., Woolite wool and Woolite synthetic textiles).

The classic brand concept is in fact restrictive. It fails to distinguish a brand's history and a brand's reality. A brand emerges as a mono-product—it is merely the name of that product. Only when the name loses this strict designatory status does it become a brand in the full sense of the word. The Laughing Cow is no longer the name of the triangle of cream cheese sold in a round box—it embraces a whole range of cheese products. Certainly in this case they are still processed cheese products, but their presentation, format, and taste all are different (in cubes as appetizers, in slices for hamburgers). Here the brand seems to have progressed to a second stage—that of a sign of know-how.

Through its means of communication (packaging, advertising, etc.), the brand is gradually endowed with features, images, and perceptions—all combining to form an identity, style, and way of being. The brand thus takes on a personality in addition to its know-how. Having progressed from its former function of designating its origins (the factory name) or the place where it is sold (the retailer's name), after a time the brand achieves a more refined significance engendered by its

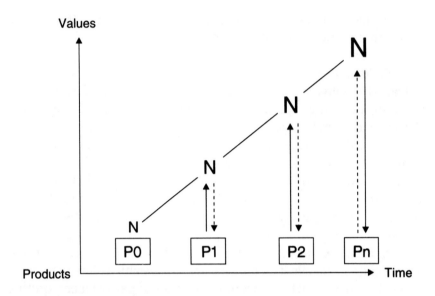

Figure 6.3

Time effects on brand–product relationships

physical output (products) and its communication output (advertising pictures, logos, other visual symbols of identity). The brand's relationship with the product is thereby reversed: the brand is no longer merely the name of a product—it is now the product which demonstrates the brand, in the sense that it exhibits the exterior signs of an interior imprint. The brand has marked the product with its imprint, transforming it by means of objective and subjective features. As a result of this reversal of roles, there are no further limits to brand extension than that of its capacity to segment new product categories—in other words, to bring about physical and psychological transformation of these product categories. The classic brand concept is nominal, in that the brand is the name of an object. Swatch is the name of a watch, not of sunglasses. If one transcends this object and asks what its plan is, what is its calling, one gains access to the full meaning of the brand. In other words, one sees in the object the sign of a transformation, according to the brand's core values and program.

In this sense, Swatch can sign sunglasses as long as they look "swatchy." A brand can go wherever it wishes. It is autonomous and sets its own ambitions. However, since it must take account of profitability, it must consider its own ability to effectively change any products which it appropriates, and must also ponder on the attraction of such change for consumers in that product area. What would be the effect on taste, texture, color, character, and attractiveness of a Camembert once it bore the Kraft brand? Would this new product be able to attract enough sales to economically justify this latest brand extension?

Consumers are less conservative than organizations and managers. The success of many brand extensions over the years has made an authoritative contribution to the realization of what a brand really is. One is now aware that the brand progresses from a name rigidly indicating an object to a symbol, an image, and symptoms of internal and external change. The first extensions are hesitant, tentatively relying on formulas closely resembling those on which the long-time root product was based. President is no longer exclusively a Camembert brand, but has also taken on a Brie and a Coulommiers. At a final level of extension, similarity of value is the only source of identity for products of a widely differing nature. Physical products certainly are different, but the brand concept endows them with togetherness, with "fit."

What connection is there between Palmolive shaving cream and its soap or dishwashing liquid? A common quality—gentleness. In line with this reasoning, the brand extends along an axis—a base value on which it can express such reasoning, loud and clear. Bic is no longer a ballpoint pen brand. It sees itself as a simplifier of utilitarian objects— as seen in the attribute "disposable." Thus it embraces ballpoint pens, cigarette lighters, and razors (its experience with windsurfers and perfumes will be analyzed later). Gillette defines its territory not in terms of a product (the razor) or an attribute, but in terms of everything which the modern man requires in the bathroom. Its mastery of the sharp edge clears the way for it to extend into feminine products (once suspect in the eyes of males): eau de toilette, body-care products, etc. The final level of brand extension is that in which the brand associates its name with a common spirit and an allegiance to shared values. How could we otherwise see a link between the Nina Ricci haute couture and Monsieur Ricci's men's ties?

Meaning of the Brand

The classic brand concept therefore takes the initial phase of the brand for its reality. Though we can accept that the brand starts with a product, it is not the product: the brand is the sense, the meaning of the product.

Products have no voice. A customer faced with a washing machine with no brand is confused. How can he gauge whether he will be satisfied with it? The brand signifies the intention of the creator—the values which he seeks to include in this machine. What has the creator sought to inject into this product—a love of tradition, the taste of a job well done, a respect for modern fancies, or finally a wish to find a happy compromise between innovation and durability?

Extension cannot go in all directions. It is the brand which defines this source of direction and the ultimate course. The brand carries within itself the code for future products which it will embrace.

What does this concept change in terms of brand extension? In the classic concept, extension scarcely ventures beyond the stage of technological know-how. The key concept is that of "skill." The only question which the businessman is asked is: do you or do you not have the industrial technique or know-how? Such a question is in itself a form of reasoning which still relates to the physical product—it shows a misunderstanding of the nature of brands. Following this line of reasoning, a Swatch car would make no sense. Swatch does not know how to make a car.

The wider brand concept implies extension beyond the sphere of the initial technique. The brand is not seen in terms of technological know-how, but as a way of dealing with products, transforming them, and giving them a common meaning. In that case, the idea of a Swatch car may be reasonable, for one can foresee how the Swatch values can segment the car market and give birth to a specific car. It suffices for Swatch to find a good partner: Fiat or Volkswagen, perhaps.

The case of Lacoste allows us to determine the effects of each of these brand reasonings. Having acquired its reputation with the knitted sports shirt (known as the 12 x 12), the logical extension for Lacoste would be to enter the field of other knitted products, and also that of polo-necks, T-shirts—in fact, sportswear and textiles generally. In this sense, shoes and leather goods are out (apart from tennis shoes). These do not require the same know-how as textiles and knitwear. In a wider concept, however, the Lacoste brand sets the wearer somewhat apart—he feels relaxed when wearing it. Lacoste stays outside the realms of fashion, since in following fashion there is no scope for distancing oneself. In this respect, Lacoste might well turn to shoes or leather goods, on condition that it preserved the brand's originality—never signing me-too products. The Lacoste brand could sign only those products which bear the brand qualities: suppleness, relaxation, high-quality finish, wear, fashion-consciousness, unisex appeal, etc. The factor which determines whether Lacoste can or cannot sign a product is not the physical know-how (which can always be delegated under license) but the degree to which the product conforms with the Lacoste core values.

At this time, formal strategic-planning models, such as those of the Boston Consulting Group, McKinsey, or A.D. Little, do not appear to have realized that brand reasoning is not parallel to product reasoning. The central point of their analysis is engineer-oriented: business units and business segmentation key concepts are that of know-how. The brand perspective is transversal and analyzes where the brand values can fruitfully segment the markets and be a source of profit. Furthermore, the need to nurture the brand capital should lead the corporation to enter new markets, even if it does not have the technical know-how, for these markets will provide modernity and dynamism to the brand image. Salomon, the world leader in bindings and in skiing and hiking shoes, has recently entered the ski market. It does not aim at competing directly with Rossignol, a world leader in skis. However, by means of a very narrow top-quality range, Salomon's presence in the ski market itself will boost its image, hitherto tied to the static connotation of its core product, bindings.

Having failed to catch on to the sunflower oil boom at the very beginning, Lesieur suffered for a long time from an image of being traditional, fuddy-duddy, and with no concern for the healthiness that the modern housewife most seeks. In fact, when Lever launched Fruidor in 1972, the sunflower market was in the balance. As far as their management at the time were concerned, Lesieur was the groundnut and the groundnut was Lesieur. Faithful to the classic brand concept, they had held on to a vision in which the brand referred to a know-how, to a seed (and vice versa). So instead of launching Lesieur Sunflower Oil, they entered this new market sector under a different name, "Aurea." In so doing, they admittedly succeeded on a commercial plane, since Aurea and Fruidor achieved similar levels of sales. However, it had the perverse effect of keeping Lesieur shut out from this new sunflower oil market—a sector favored by the younger housewife. Seeing that the sunflower sector was showing a considerable increase, Lesieur took a slight change of stance. Aurea became Lesieur Aurea, later becoming Lesieur Sunflower Oil. Having allowed Lesieur to become synonymous with the groundnut for so many years, and more so with the launch of Aurea, the Lesieur brand had acquired a negative connotation which adversely affected its sales of sunflower oil after Aurea was abandoned. Aurea therefore harmed the Lesieur brand, and Lesieur harmed the income from Aurea. They should have either stuck to a policy of maximizing their earnings by keeping Aurea, or should have foreseen the risks to Lesieur's brand capital asset in keeping the brand apart from the emergent trend.

TYPES OF BRAND EXTENSION

What are the various types of brand extension? Before dealing with this, let us remind ourselves that brand extension means more than just the expansion of a range. The latter refers to variations on a single product:

- in different forms of presentation (for example, a shoe polish with a sponge applicator was a more modern version of its normal tin)
- in different sizes (family or individual packs, etc.)
- in different tastes or flavors

Brand extension is a leap away from the initial technology. Here again we must make the distinction between associated extension or continuity extension and discontinuous extension. A brand of spark plugs can extend through its application to other car accessories (batteries, windshield wipers, etc.). This is the case with Bosch and Valeo. A major optics brand may extend to photocopying: this happened with Canon, Minolta, Kodak, and Agfa. A sports brand can embrace every sporting requirement (Adidas). Discontinuous extensions do away with technological affinities—the physical bridge between products. These are true diversifications. For example, Yamaha manufactures both motorcycles and classical pianos of repute. Retailer brands cover the whole field of consumer products, and even durables.

Some extensions are therefore far removed from the brand's initial territory, while others are in close proximity. This leads to brands with a narrow outlook—specialist brands—or brands with a wide spectrum (Philips, General Electric). Is it better to have a specialist or a broad approach? This question cannot be answered in general terms. We have to remember that the brand is arbitrary and can choose whichever path it desires. If Bic decides to put its name on windsurfers, nothing can stop it. If the company strategy is to give greater consideration to capitalizing on one name's saving on advertising, it will opt for a brand with a wide spectrum. Automobile parts manufacturer *leader* Valeo threw out all the specialized brands it had bought (Ferodo, Marshal) and substituted them with a single brand. Philips and Siemens opted for an identical strategy.

Each extension affects the brand and its equity in one of four different ways.

- *Certain extensions exploit the brand capital.* The product sells, thanks to the brand's contribution. This is the case when the product concerned scarcely differs from existing market competition: a typical case is Kodak batteries, or Rossignol's entry in the tennis market, adding rackets to its skis. The brand has not fully exercised its transforming role, but succors the product with its aura and its perceived risk-reducing consumer awareness. If this practice is applied too often, however— through a licensing policy, for example—the brand's capital asset dries up because of association with so many commonplace products.
- *Other extensions destroy the brand's equity.* Levi's slacks and blazers had no relationship whatsoever to the core values inherited from its mythical 501 jeans. Danger arises also when the extension is a top-down one. For example, the now disappeared Flaminaire brand decided to cover the lighter market by being present in all its segments: top of the range (to com-

pete with Dupont and Dunhill), midrange, and the disposable lighter (in opposition to Bic). This was fatal. The lower-range extension killed the firm's credibility at the top of the range, from which it drew its profits.

Similarly, it was a fortunate day when Porsche dropped their 924 model. The only thing which justified the considerable difference in price of these cars from those of their competitors was their prestigious name. None of the objective and subjective values associated with Porsche was found in the 924 model—neither the masculinity, nor the technology, nor their storied ability to surpass themselves. This model seemed to proclaim the end of the Porsche myth. Since at that same time there was no further talk of Porsche entering Formula One, or of having won in the Le Mans 24 hours, the only means of brand communication was through its advertising, a large part of which concerned the 924. To get back on their feet, they ceased production of the 924, and even of the basic 944.

- *Certain extensions have a neutral effect where brand capital asset is concerned.* The product simply falls in the line with what is expected of the brand. It is surprising how, in the electrical appliance field, brands are often credited with far more products than they actually produce. If these brands decided to make inroads in these directions, it would not change their image. This illustration reminds us that purchasers have a different vision of the brand from that of the manufacturer. They may attribute to the brand a wider field of ability, one not simply limited to its existing products.
- *Certain extensions help develop and nurture the meaning of the brand.* These extensions are extragenerative. They revitalize the brand and its nucleus, causing a resurgence of its basic values in a new and powerful way. The green blazer, for instance, is an extragenerative product for the Lacoste brand. It represents a rare symbiosis of the features which go to make up the Lacoste brand—conformity, discretion, social acceptability, and also a certain distancing effect. The green blazer gives a more relaxed look than blue (which is too much like a uniform for the Lacoste image), and recalls the turf of the lawn-tennis court.

Revitalization of Meccano's brand capital asset has been brought about through extension outside its field of origin, which was construction toys. The brand needed meaningful products which expressed its system of values. It therefore launched a line of children's clothes and stationery, and has its sights set on trail bikes, watches, and children's furniture. It is less a question of commercial opportunism than of research into areas where the brand can bring its distinct nature and personal values in line with current trends. The range of children's clothes would be very "Meccano"—very colorful, like the uniform worn by the US Navy and Air Force fitters.

To conclude this typology of extensions: certain brand extensions, while not desirable, are nevertheless necessary. They amount to preventive and defensive technical diversifications brought about in the interests of the imaginary capital. Above all, they are intended to block the use of the brand name by a third party in another product category. Take the instance of Cartier, who covers textiles and tableware. In reality, Cartier may not wish to develop these offshoots, but needs to prevent an Italian firm from registering the Cartier brand at the international level in the "textiles" category. The same applies to tableware. As a result of this tactical diversification, Cartier will prevent the stealing of the brand.

STRESS ON THE BRAND THROUGH EXTENSION

Not all brands lend themselves to extension. Certain brands are recognized by virtue of their precise know-how—they are positioned in areas where the consumer expects a sustained performance based on a mastered technique. The brand reduces the customers' perceived risk. This is the case with cosmetic brands (e.g., Clarins, Roc, Vichy, etc.), where the field of extension must remain within the bounds of an appropriate territory. Other brands, on the other hand, primarily impart a reflection. Dim is the symbol of the French woman, the young Parisienne. There is some scope for its extension into the male world, on condition that it concerns a clearly suitable type of man for this type of woman. Other brands have an almost quasi-religious dimension. St. Michael, the Marks & Spencer brand, covers everything from food to clothes and from toys to household wear and body care. In putting its name on these products, St. Michael is announcing that they conform with the Marks & Spencer ideology. With such a revered patron (etymologically, patron has the same Latin derivation as pattern, i.e., "to be followed"), the brand transfigures and elevates the products which it sanctifies.

Strategically, the firm could give the brand a restricted purpose—that of a highly-competent specialist. This is what the l'Oreal group has done with its many cosmetic brands. Should the firm decide, on the other hand, to opt for discontinuous extensions, it should take note of the conditions on which their success is based. Such extensions exercise a real pressure on brands, while also straining the credulity of the consumer. Is the Bosch of the electrical appliance world the same Bosch who makes car accessories? Do Peugeot electrical parts relate to the same brand as Peugeot cars? Many people do not believe this can be so. In their minds these are mere homonyms, just as there are Ariel cigarettes and an Ariel detergent, Mazda batteries and Mazda cars. They find it inconceivable that the same principle should lie behind the manufacture of both detergents and cigarettes.

If one wishes to prevent a brand from disintegrating and breaking up into disjointed units in the eyes of the purchaser, it is helpful to take notice of the prerequisites for wide-ranging extension. The more the brand extension covers categories of dissimilar products, the more it must draw on the deeper meaning of the brand. This supposes that there is one, or that the brand has the potential to acquire one. Otherwise, the extension would drain the meaning of the brand. It would be reduced to the simple rank of a factory brand—a reference to an origin but no longer a combination of features and with no more significance than a number.

Figure 6.4 illustrates the demands arising from brand extension. Each degree of product dissimilarity changes the meaning and status of the brand needed to cover these products. Close extensions (B) are compatible with formula brands—Lesieur can put its name on rapeseed, olive, and peanut oil. In both real and imaginary terms, there is nothing to suggest that the types of seed relate to different formulas or values. Extension one degree further (C) corresponds to a "know-how" brand. Palmolive, for instance, adds gentleness to everything it touches. Bic is the ultimate in simplicity, and therefore makes the disposable ballpoint as good a bargain as their lighters. The further extension (D), to be compatible with the first product (A), assumes a brand defined by its center of interest—its focal point. Habitat focuses its interest on the home, Gillette on men's facial care, Adidas on sport. When it first came on the scene, Sony was exclusively a high-fidelity brand. In a few years it acquired a name in television and video, and by the same token has seen its image and significance develop. Technology, sensitivity, and innovation, however, still remain its central values. The furthest degree (E) relates to a brand defined only by a deeper philosophy. Certain brands, or griffes, see a natural progression from haute couture to porcelain. They put their stamp of excellence on everything. This appears so natural that few realize that the famous Lanvin chocolates are not a product of the Lanvin signature. Yet people still see them as one and the same brand. The only way in which a brand can make dissimilar products fit together is by looking at them from a higher source-point. In order to give coherence to extensions which are further and further detached, the brand departs from its physique and relies on its source of inspiration and system of values, thus allowing it to provide meaning to each of the

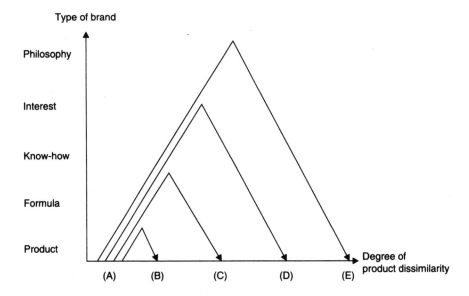

Figure 6.4

Type of brand and ability to extend

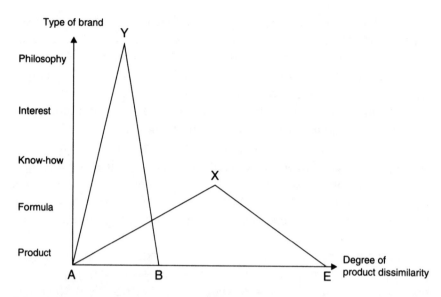

Figure 6.5

Under- and overexploitation of a brand equity

different products. A brand attempting to cover too many products would weaken, lose its unifying power, and fail. As a rubber band is weakened when it encompasses too many objects, so many overextended brands suffer in a similar way.

In concrete terms, brands having no depth, no identity apart from a physique (a product or formula), cannot support wide-ranging extensions. If they are extended, they decline and regress to the level of a protobrand—that of a factory brand with only a guarantee of origin. They become diluted, with no more meaning than a number (point X in Figure 6.5).

This is the case with Mitsubishi. Its name does not really relate to a unifying brand, capable of leaving its imprint. It is a corporate or factory name. It does not signify any meaning other than that of the generic image of Japan. Mitsubishi cars do not seem to manifest any particular ideal of design, nor do Mitsubishi televisions or machine tools, for example. It is also the case with Philips.

Originally this brand signified the know-how associated with their brown products (televisions, video, hi-fi). However, the brand did not convey any other meaning—it did not appear to be driven by an ideal, a value or other source of inspiration. Its extension into small electrical appliances, on the one hand, and white goods on the other, overstretched the brand. Consumer research testifies to this. Eighty percent of a sample interviewed declared that Philips specialized in brown products, and that these products were the mainspring of their ability. No more than 60 percent thought this was the case when it came to razors and small electrical appliances, and only 40 percent in the case of white products. Philips was therefore losing half its credibility where washing machines, refrigerators, and so on were concerned. In the case of these products the name was scarcely more than a simple guarantee, similar to that of a retailer's own-brand or an acceptable seal of quality. Subsequently, Philips decided to concentrate on its strong pivot, selling the white products to Whirlpool in 1989.

The Italian industrialist Carlo de Benedetti bought Buitoni because he perceived an unexploited latent potential in the brand. Until then Buitoni had been a brand signifying Italian know-how in the field of pasta and tomato sauce. De Benedetti turned it into a "solar" brand, giving it the authority to extend it into the realms of exotic spiced dishes (curried rice, couscous, etc.) and also cooked dishes, such as gratin dauphinois. By indicating that the brand's basis of identity lay not in Italy but, at a more abstract level, in the solar myth, Benedetti succeeded in diluting the brand equity.

In contrast to brands given too great a dimension, some are underexploited. These (point Y in Figure 6.5) cover only a narrow field of products, but have an inner mystique which could impart a significance to a wide spread of products.

A typical case of brand underexploitation is that of Dole. This brand had largely underestimated its worth and potential scope. The managers thought of Dole as a brand of pineapple juice. They misread the brand and the product. For consumers, Dole meant much more. Beyond its attributes (good-tasting, fresh, natural, Hawaiian) lay a deeper core: sunshine! Dole actually was a sunshine brand and could sign not only other fruits but go beyond the fruit segment altogether (introducing Dole ice creams, for instance).

A first result of this discovery was a change of the Dole logo, substituting a shining sun on the O for the former crown on the O.

La Roche aux Fées, a brand of chilled products dropped by Nestlé, would have had no trouble in putting its name on a line of children's clothes, a collection of books, or a publishing house. Its imaginary potential allows it to fall back on many categories of children's products.

PUBLIC REACTION TO BRAND EXTENSION

We now come upon a paradox. Being arbitrary, the brand can choose its own direction. There is nothing to prevent President from turning to an Emmenthal—or any other cheese for that matter—in an attempt to further extend its territory. Lacoste could make jeans, Uncle Ben's could enter the frozen-food or vacuum-packed food areas, Alcatel could provide a computer service.

Nothing, that is, provided President is still seen as a brand which is primarily centered on Camembert—in spite of the huge amounts spent in advertising its Brie and Coulommiers. Again, Uncle Ben's is considered to this day as a brand of rice and nothing else. The real-life public view seems to indicate a notion of legitimate areas—natural zones where a brand has the right to set foot, and others from which it is excluded. The brand should therefore be conscious of its limits. It cannot dictate its will to the consumer or industrial client. Brand changes are a perilous phase, and are never achieved automatically. If one speaks of a brand's territory, it means that there are frontiers which limit its extension.

In giving a product a certain brand name, we conjure up expectations in the minds of its potential customers, in the sense that they hope to find in that product those features which make up the brand program. Suppose a firm launched—under license—a line of washing machines and cookers with the name Mercedes. This would immediately provoke an image of the likely qualities and individual features of these machines.

By giving a new product the name of an existing brand, the firm has an eye not on easy savings, but on quick sales. The familiar brand name encourages people to try out the new product—in other words, it helps it to create a favorable impression. How does this attitude come about? What factors contribute to the opinion that such an extension is favorable or otherwise? Several empirical studies have recently addressed these specific questions (Aaker and Keller, 1990; MacInnis and Nakamoto, 1990).

What factors most explain the acceptability of a brand extension? The first factor is the global image of the brand which will support the extension. Does it have a generally strong, fair, or poor reputation? Consumers are only inclined to give a well-known brand a try. This does not mean that only powerful brands are open to extension. On the contrary, it could be vital for a brand with only a fair image to extend to products which will inject new blood and new life. In such a case it is not the brand which sells the product, but the product which gives the brand a boost.

The second factor, independent of the first, concerns the firm's ability to manufacture this new product. On this point the public will question its capacity to transfer skills and know-how, and ask whether it is able to mobilize the financial and human resources required in the production and commercialization of the product or service. It is a question of perceived—rather than actual—credibility. The public might therefore under- or overestimate the difficulty. For example, many consumers confuse a domestic and a domestic*ated* product. They undervalue the mass of research, technology, and other intangible necessities involved in the mass production of high-volume consumer products. How many people can imagine the years that were spent before 3M put the finishing touches to its Post-it notes? The public turns to heuristics to gauge the firm's credibility: Will the new product share one of the attributes which make up the present brand products? In addition to turning out simple, no-nonsense pens, Bic can do likewise with lighters or razor blades. The fact that the new product is a substitute for current ones further favors the perception of credibility. The firm no longer appears to show its strength through product ability, but through consumer advantage—through a centralized interest. In this respect, a Crest chewing-gum could represent another means of dental care, practically replacing the toothbrush.

The third contributory factor to brand extension lies in the look of the new product alongside existing ones; whether it appears comfortable as part of the range. This is more likely to be the case with complementary products—no one is surprised to see Rossignol skis next to ski suits, anoraks, and sunglasses.

Research has come up with a fourth influence on the acceptability extension—the perceived difficulty in manufacturing this new product. Certain product categories are considered easy to make. The consumer therefore perceives little variation between the top and bottom of the quality scale in this market. This applies to types of goods from handkerchiefs to refrigerators—these days the main criterion in buying the latter is volume. Other categories, however, are subject to major variations in quality—e.g., computing, insurance, holidays, and champagne. Aaker and Keller (1990) showed that a nonlinear relationship existed between this perceived difficulty and the acceptance of brand extension. When the public sees little difficulty in manufacture, there is no great advantage for a brand with a powerful image over those with a fair or poor image. For this reason the powerful image which a firm such as Thomson had acquired in the electronics, military, and video industries scarcely rubbed off on its televisions. It imparted its halo, but not its imprint. If the public finds that a brand is exploiting its name to sell products which are no better than the rest, they rebel in the face of this type of extension.

Being a powerful brand also counts for little when the public feels that it will be very difficult for it to manufacture the extended product. The Yamaha name means little when it comes to the art of making quality pianos. The public may even think that Yamaha motorcycles do not come from the same Yamaha company which makes the famous musical instruments.

The four abovementioned factors suppose that consumers' evaluations of brand extension result from a bottom-up process: implicitly, consumers are alleged to think mostly in terms of feasibility, technical expertise, know-how transferability, the perceived difficulty of making the extension. Basically, consumers would compare the products and the product categories. This is only a partial view of consumers' evaluation process, however: it actually explains only 26 percent of the extension evaluation variance (Aaker and Keller, 1990). The model ignores the fact that, in most cases, it is the brand itself which creates the link between the diverse products to which it is applied.

Looking at a list of products (perfume, shoes, portfolio, shirt, bag, pen, crystal, ring, watch, belt, tie), they may not seem to have much in common. However, as soon as one knows that it is Gucci perfume, Gucci shoes, a Gucci portfolio, etc., the same products fit together. The brand values endow them with commonality and togetherness.

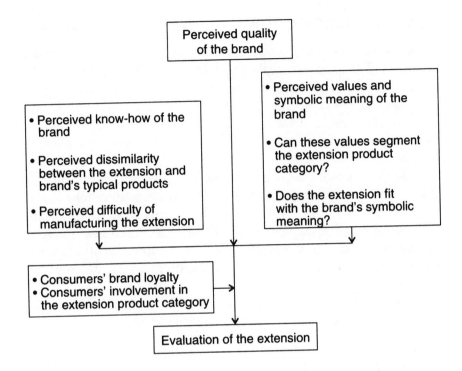

Figure 6.6

Variables influencing public acceptance of brand extension

Consumers' extension evaluation may take two routes:

- If the brand is merely a functional one (a formula, or know-how), they use a product-based evaluation; they rely on products' perceived similarity.
- If the brand has symbolic connotations, they use a concept-based evaluation and evaluate whether the extension remains within the brand's legitimate territory.

Research has therefore indicated the key variables which—on a psychological level—affect the level of acceptance of extension (Figure 6.6.). These variables form the object of a firm's research when exploring the possibilities of extending one of its brands.

BRAND EXTENSION: HOW?

Before setting about any practical extension, there are two preparatory stages. The first—an exploratory stage—probes all the associations with the brand which are present in the collective public mind. This stage allows conjecture as to which products would be compatible with the brand's meaning. Once this has been established, we have to turn our eyes back to the market. This brings into play the second study phase—testing the new product's ideas.

A decision cannot be made on the strength of this information alone. Brand extension is the result of strategic decision. It also involves factors linked with production, marketing, finance, and human resources. Extension always involves a certain risk—no form of study can accurately predict the effect of extension on the brand itself over a period. How will its status, its meaning, its equity be affected?

It cannot be over-emphasized that extension cannot be contemplated without complete knowledge of the brand's attributes:

- What are its attributes?
- What is its personality?
- What is its purpose?
- Where is its heart?
- What contract does it offer to customers and consumers?
- What is its latent potential?

These questions can only be answered through both quantitative inquiry (to establish the popularity of the brand and its image) and qualitative approaches. The brand's latent potential and source of inspiration are not revealed by mere image surveys. Access to its prism of identity and its motivating force requires qualitative investigation. Armed with this information, the second stage of the investigation process involves the extrapolation of the brand's distinctive features in order to assess their consequences. If Palmolive is a brand personifying gentleness, what other products need to be gentle? Scof is known for its place settings, so by metonymy could they extend to glasses, cups, or tableware in general? Since Rossignol is active in one area of sport (skiing), could it not also turn to tennis rackets and golf clubs? There may be a further metaphorical source of inspiration:

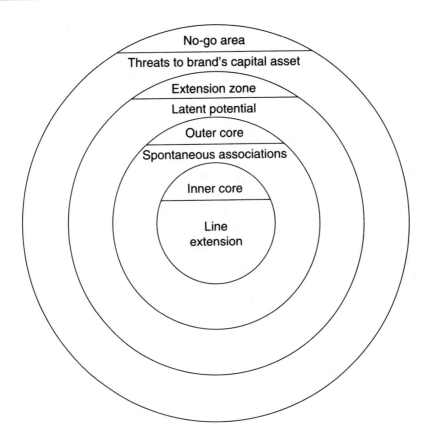

Figure 6.7

Perimeters of brand extension

for example, a razor blade skims over the beard, while a windsurfer skims over the waves.

The long list of ideas resulting from this process of extrapolation is placed under the microscope of feasibility. The short list which emerges can then be put to the target public, often by means of a market survey. For each proposed extension, the interviewee is basically asked a three-way question: whether the product interests them "a lot, so-so, or not much." One can thus arrive at a popularity chart of possible extensions.

This method has the advantage of simplicity and grading by numbers. Its one drawback is that it is conservative. When jumped upon with a list of products, those questioned tend only to comment on those salient brand features which spring immediately to mind. Back in the time when Bic was making only ballpoint pens, this approach would have ended up by exhausting the possibilities in the stationery field and would have established an absolute rejection of the idea that Bic should sell razors.

Within the concept of brand extension it is possible to distinguish several concentric zones (Davidson, 1987). Around the inner core lies the outer core, then extension zones, and finally no-go areas. Surveys based on limited questioning will reveal information on the brand's immediate vicinity (its outer core). In-depth qualitative analysis tells us about the extension zones. The task is therefore to indulge in qualitative investigation—to establish the brand's latent potential and to see whether or not it can adapt to each of the product ideas. In this way we should be in a position to decide if the rejection resulting from extensive polls stems from a conservative attitude on the part of interviewees, or if it is indeed due to the fact that the brand is incompatible with the product idea.

The qualitative phase is a constructive one. Bearing in mind that a brand transforms a product category, we seek to determine under what circumstances the proposed product could be suitable for the brand. In other words, what the objective or subjective attributes are which go to support the brand.

Along these lines, it is not sufficient to say that Lacoste could make jackets. We have to be more precise about what is a jacket bearing the Lacoste hallmark, as distinct from one outside its territory. The Lacoste prism of identity encompasses the following features: knit, finish, hard wear, discretion, harmony, social aptness, suitability, and adaptability. The reputation of the original Lacoste product forms a second protection—it induces that distancing effect which constitutes the brand's central value. It nurtures an image of supple transition between the personal and the social—bodily ease and social ease. The aerated mesh is analogous to the skin and its pores. This prism of identity defines the following territory which Lacoste should avoid, in order to prevent deviation from its meaning:

- The sporting ideal makes Lacoste suitable for all ages and sexes. It should not put its name on exclusively feminine

products (as in its failed line of aerobic gear) nor pander to the hypermasculine (e.g., hunting).
- Lacoste sells neither garish colors nor ephemeral in-products.
- As a "second skin," Lacoste produces neither heavy knitwear nor shiny leather clothes.

Leather jackets are not Lacoste; only the suede jacket is capable of possessing the Lacoste features.

The qualitative phase finally allows an understanding of the brand's function from the user angle. Is the brand one's own personal symbol, or a symbol for the multitude? Would one be seen on the slopes on a pair of Tesco skis? Where would one like to see the symbol displayed? This is an essential point in branding itself. What should appear on the pocket of a Lacoste blazer—the crocodile, Lacoste, or Lacoste Club?

This test phase sets out not only to determine whether the extension is consistent with the brand, but also whether the product will be considered superior to its competitors—whether the extension creates a desire. McDonald's, the fast-food brand, would have nothing specifically highbrow to impart if they entered the photographic sphere. However, they could very easily launch into, say, theme parks, on the strength of the McDonald's vision of family relationships, which transcends the hamburger but which would find its expression in a large setting such as a theme park.

A FEW CLASSIC MISTAKES

Brand extension is a strategy involving the brand's future and its equity. It is a delicate process calling for careful attention to sound methods and study of potential effects. There are certain potential pitfalls along the path of extension, which we shall now examine.

A Restrictive Vision of the Brand

Many firms have a limited perception of their brands. They consider them as descriptive names. The brand genetic program therefore encompasses just a few variations of the product bearing the name. It was this view which inhibited Lesieur from entering the sunflower oil market at the outset. Clinging to a notion by which groundnut oil = Lesieur, therefore Lesieur = groundnut oil, the brand became slave to the apparent virtues of a seed, misguidedly shielding its image from all the modern qualities of sunflower oil. It is still paying to this day. What a contrast with the Green Giant brand, which, in spite of its name, produces both yellow sweetcorn and white asparagus! And "Holiday Inn" has not confined itself to leisure hotels but is now a popular brand for businessmen, too. There are no olive extracts in Palmolive soap, nor in its shaving cream or dishwashing liquid.

All these brands would have had far more reason than Lesieur to restrict themselves in some way to a physical vision of their identity, since some such quality was included in their name: green, holiday, olive. To have done so would have been a mistake, since the brand obliterates the semantic association of words which serve to support it.

Does this mean that the presence of "olive" in Palmolive has been totally neutralized? The fact is that the meaning of the word has only been suppressed, remaining deep within. Palmolive benefits from this suppression. It is not centered on the restricted reality of the olive, but on the historical and mythical values and ideal which it inspires. The image of the olive conveyed in the name Palmolive is rooted in the objective and subjective qualities of the products which the brand embraces. There is no need for these products to contain olive extracts. It is the symbolization of the olive, rather than its actual presence, which forms the program basis in extending this brand.

Shutting Out the Brand

Having concluded that the Maggi image was rather old hat, Nestlé was quickly convinced that it should allow as little connection as possible between the brand and a new product line in instant mashed potato. The same thing happened again later, in the case of Bolino ready-to-eat pot snacks.

They had fallen into the trap of the "self-fulfilling prophecy." Their belief that the older Maggi brand could not be associated with new, modern products led them to shut the brand away in solitary isolation. This only served to reinforce its antiquated and outmoded image and to render it even less suitable for extension.

Many believe that the only way of saving a brand from this trap is through advertising and the adoption of current codes and fashion. A brand's modern image is judged by the new products it presents. The Maggi syndrome arises from a failure to remember that a firm builds up its brands through a long, gradual process. New products obviously must attain their marketing objectives, but the firm's continued existence depends on that small number of brands which will support a wide spread of products. Maggi is a vital prop to the Nestlé strategy. Had they looked more carefully at the brand's equity, they would have been happy to associate Maggi with the new line, thus reinforcing the brand and increasing its value.

When the Past Decides the Future

Another cause of excessive restraint on the brand lies in the emphasis on past decisions. You cannot drive a brand with your eyes glued to the rearview mirror. Admittedly, the brand is a memory bank where its products are concerned, but this does not mean that the future is an extrapolation of the past. Though the brand gains autonomy and inertia, it is still company strategy which determines its direction in the long term.

It sometimes happens that the decision on whether or not to extend a brand is influenced by managers' taboos about certain products. For decades it has been known that Gauloises was a packet of dark tobacco cigarettes. For years this created a taboo in the management: Gauloises being a dark tobacco, the brand could not be extended to a light tobacco. This classic confusion between the product and the brand is commonplace. Because the launching of a new brand, internationally, to compete against Marlboro was becoming too expensive, the Gauloises management was forced reluctantly to think of extending the Gauloises brand to the light tobacco cigarette market. Its success, coming as a real surprise, proved that there was an opportunity for a brand of light cigarettes endowed with the prototypical values of Gauloises: unconventional, nonconformist, individualistic, authentic.

As already mentioned, consumers do not share the same preconceptions about brands as do managers. For years, Mars was a bar; finally, the firm decided to exploit the brand equity and launched Mars ice creams, Mars liquid chocolate, and Mars chocolate tablets.

The first three attitudes that we have looked at so far have all served to restrict the brand. The next five have the opposite effect— not only is the range of extension too wide, but also the brand is prone to risk. Such attitudes most often result from commercial opportunism. Faced with the choice of exploiting the brand for a quick sale, or of entering into a license agreement, the firm considers only the effect on short-term profits, underestimating the risks involving the brand capital.

Extensions Can Dilute the Brand

Aware of the boom in the "light" foods sector, many brands have immediately rushed to enter this market. Some, however, were wrong to do so. In a market where it is difficult to be different, authenticity, excellence of taste, and respect for nature form the key bases of certain brands' individuality. With such a risk in mind, the President cheese brand was very careful to put plenty of distance between the brand name and its "light" line of products, calling it Pre-silege and basing its advertising program on codes other than those of the President brand. Similarly, not all beer brands should produce and advertise a light version.

Lipton's extension from tea to soups has also contributed to a weakening of the Lipton image. It is important that Tuborg should not sell its mineral-water tins outside of Greece. Tuborg's image of excellence could be hurt.

Opportunism and Inconsistency of Identity

Extension is rife in the luxury market, where licensing abounds. Go into a Nina Ricci boutique and you can buy china and cutlery. This constitutes a failure to understand the brand. What is all right for Hermès is not necessarily so in the case of Nina Ricci. Tableware is more appropriate to a brand such as Hermès or Dior, with their broader social aspects, or possibly to a brand relying on appeal, such as Yves Saint Laurent. It is outside the Nina Ricci scope of identity.

Persuaded to license their name to an American sportswear maker to launch a new line for aerobics, Lacoste soon realized, through the absence of sales take-off, that this was outside its legitimate territory.

Aerobics is a fad, and mostly a feminine sport—and these two characteristics are at odds with Lacoste's typical values.

In certain markets, a brand personifies the product category. It is
its prototype. Coca-Cola is the symbolization of all colas. Société indicates Roquefort. Levi's are the jeans. Having built a powerful brand
with an undisputed reputation known to everyone, the firm is naturally tempted to use the precious brand capital to support an unending
line of new products. In so doing, it runs the risk of destroying its
own credibility and authority within its original market.

Société launched modern products under its sacrosanct name (a
Roquefort cream to spread) and was considering salad sauces. Soon it
realized that it was no longer regarded by specialists and opinion leaders as the qualitative reference point for Roquefort.

Even though consumers might know full well that Société was no
longer produced on a local craft basis, they would still reject every
indication which pointed to a lack of authenticity. Nor should a prototype brand venture into categories where another prototype exists.
When this happens, the brand recognizes its opponent's authority and
tends to cower away. This is why Lacoste—the symbolization of
sportswear—would lose out if they strayed into the jeans market
dominated by Levi's, in both product and image terms. It would be
unable to stamp its mark—in other words, transform the product category and install its own attributes. There is nothing to prevent one
from sticking a crocodile on a pair of jeans. However, this would be
just a superficial deed which would weaken the brand, since it would
be seen as nothing more than an empty gesture. The brand ends up
squatting on another's territory—not acceptable in the case of a
major brand.

The Mundane-Product Trap

When there is scarcely any difference in quality between an extension
and its competitors, the extension could well bring about a short-term
increase in sales as a result of the family name but, over a longer period, it would adversely affect the brand and the confidence which it
inspires, by associating it with a product which the consumer does
not immediately find effectively superior to others of its kind. A true
brand is one whose image is embodied in the product characteristics.

Easily-made products cannot always relate differences in quality. An established brand which finds it impossible to transmit its know-how is left high and dry. Heineken could not in all reality transform popcorn. Thomson televisions do not fully benefit from the extreme level of competence gained by Thomson–Industrie in the fields of radar, weapons, and electronics.

Are Chanel T-shirts or Cardin cigarettes instances of this syndrome? The number of unimaginative products—handkerchiefs, socks, cigarettes, etc.—bearing luxury signatures under license is rapidly increasing. The only difference between a handkerchief and a Cardin handkerchief is the brand. There is, however, a structural difference between a Thomson television and a Chanel T-shirt. The television is the brand's own product—a concrete expression of some of its characteristics. The T-shirt merely supports the brand by way of its motif. Through this emblem the consumer associates himself with the brand.

The brand, as we have said, is additive—it is the sum total of its own attributes. The long-term danger for Chanel is that their T-shirt might come to be considered as an attribute of Chanel. It has to be said that it is a dull, even shabby garment worn by people who do not exactly have the Chanel look. Too wide a presence of the T-shirt is detrimental to the guarantee of refinement which is one of the pivotal features of this brand's identity.

When a brand not only proliferates in every direction, but makes use of uninspiring products such as cigarettes, handkerchiefs, ties, and accessories of every order, the brand capital asset becomes drained. Pierre Cardin is a prime example of this. When a name is splashed willy-nilly on anything that comes to hand, the signature loses its significance.

Finally, there are a number of difficulties associated with brand extension arising from forgetfulness on the part of the consumer and from the preeminence of a technological notion of the brand.

Complementarities Are No Guarantee

The brand extension graveyard is littered with *faux amis*. Campbell's, the soup brand, considered it quite natural to introduce a spaghetti sauce. Its appropriateness seemed to go without saying, since one of its product leaders is tomato soup. The sauce was a failure, and had to be relaunched under the name Prego. Similarly, Astra margarine has never been able to get Astra oil off the ground.

It is not the product itself which determines whether extension is possible, but an appreciation of the brand's main principles. Such a consideration explains the reticence on the part of Lacoste to put its name on jeans. It has been proven that the most popular accompaniment to the famous Lacoste knitted shirt is a pair of jeans. It would be tempting for any trader to try to capture the market with the complementary product. However—apart from the problem of there being a prototype brand on the market—it would have been a mistake. As an accompaniment to a pair of jeans, a Lacoste singles out the wearer. In putting its name on the jeans as well, Lacoste would turn the ensemble into a uniform—in itself a departure from the brand's identity. By the same token, Lacoste manufactures tennis rackets, but not the strings. The latter wear out more quickly than one would wish, and the player is disappointed. No brand proclaiming its durability could allow its name to be associated with such an ephemeral product.

From a technical point of view, a company specializing in canned, ready-cooked meals can, in practice, acquire a knowledge of frozen foods and vacuum-packed fresh commodities. So far, however, no wide-ranging brand has succeeded in making a simultaneous impression in all three markets. Customers do not consider the realistic problems involved in production techniques—they have only their own preconceptions of what is required. When consumers have no fixed image of production methods, they are not aware of the limitations which, in production terms, must exist. The French are conversant with the varying types of soil, producing individual wines differing from one region to the next. To an average Japanese or American, however, wines all are simply French wines, or German or Italian wines. Since a wine's regional individuality has little significance for them, they may well select a brand covering several vineyards or regions. The only things which matter are the country, the color of the wine, and the brand.

Clear Understanding of One's Brand Identity

Bic made its fortune with the ballpoint, and later with lighters and razors. It has failed with cheap, everyday perfumes for youngsters. This latter incursion came directly from M. Bich, without market studies. It was not the only idea to come from the top. When they expanded into windsurfers, it was also on the initiative of the boss, who was also a sailing buff.

The failure of Bic perfume was partly due to an error in assessing Bic's true identity. There is a principle behind this brand which controls its products. In spite of appearances, this principle is not the "disposable" factor. Its intention is to make objects totally instrumental, and functional to the extreme. The throwaway idea is a consequence of this principle—it is not the principle itself. The low price again is a consequence of it. One can instrumentalize tools, but perfume is not a tool, even though Bic hoped otherwise. Perfume appeals to the soul. Bic has functional quality. Actually Bic could have succeeded, had it been launching an air freshener instead.

If we do not ascertain the brand's main principle, the appearance of its products is the only indication of the brand's values that we can assess. Tahiti built its success on bath and shower products. The implications of exotic pleasure which these evoked made the brand indicate the direction of extension. However, it had no success with close products such as deodorants and eau de toilette. There was certainly close association of products, but not of the principles controlling them.

HANDLING THE CHANGE

What precautions and guidelines need to be considered in order to optimize the extension, once it has been decided to extend?

Anticipating the Risks

Certain extensions carry with them risks which cannot be ignored. If things go wrong, the ensuing publicity can rebound on the brand's other activities. In 1989, Wagon-Lits decided to enter the up-market travel scene with its elite clientele. When asked to put its name on this venture, Hermès eventually refused. The imponderables of the service sector—in particular the travel world—would have involved a certain risk which the brand did not wish to be exposed to. They can keep their eye on events in their Faubourg Saint-Honoré premises, but it would be a different matter when it came to hotels in Lhasa.

Fisher Price never entered the baby care market; accidents can happen with this type of product.

Anticipating the Risks to Extension

On a psychological level, brand extension assumes three hypotheses:

- that the brand's positive associations will be transferred to the new product
- that negative associations will remain in place
- that any positive feature of the brand will not become negative when applied to the new product

The aim of focus groups is to verify these hypotheses, and the role of communication to ensure that the second and third hypotheses remain true.

Returning to the notion of a Crest chewing-gum, such a product could well evoke a spontaneous pharmaceutical taste. This may be fine in the context of toothpastes, but would be a negative quality when applied to chewing-gum. It would be a mistake to center the communication around dental hygiene—which would only reinforce the negative associations which stem from the imagined taste. Communication should, on the contrary, emphasise the pleasure of the taste of this chewing-gum. In this way the communication will prevent the risk of transferring the brand's negative attributes to the new product. Crest has already acquired a strong image where health is concerned: it would be of no benefit to insist on it further.

Communication helped Lacoste's line in suntan products in much the same way. The brand, as it happened, lacked credibility in this sector. It had no real dermatological know-how, a factor which can make such products far less attractive in the eyes of purchasers. They therefore thought better than to call it the Lacoste Sun Range. It needed its own name—an upgraded meaning, to compensate for the Lacoste weakness in this area, and one which would provide the extension with all the technical credibility necessary for its success. The name they chose was Lacoste Sun Technics.

Generally speaking, the more the brand extends its field of activity, the more it is necessary to add specific stages of meaning in order to assist the extensions. Here we are entering the realms of brand architecture at different levels—the umbrella brand (parent brand), one made up of names of product lines (Findus Lean Cuisine, Atari Business Systems)—or of product names themselves (Sony's Walkman, Elf Optane, Milka Lila Pause). The problems posed by different brand architectures will be explored in the following chapter.

The Temptation to Underinvest

Many extensions are brought about for economic reasons. Due to the excessive cost of advertising too many brands, the brand portfolio may need to be pruned. Furthermore, when the brand name is already well-known, it would be normal to undertake an extension, reducing the expenditure normally expected for launching an actual brand. Analyses on the part of Nielsen Company under the guidance of J. Peckham (1981) point to the dangers of such an approach in fast-moving consumer goods. Nielsen studied 114 cases of new-product launches within three sectors: body care, food, and hygiene. Results showed that, after two years, new products launched under their own name gained twice the share of the market, compared to that of new products launched under the name of an already existing brand (6.7 percent against 3.3 percent in the case of body care, and 6.5 percent against 1.9 percent for food products). Could it have been a mistake to extend these brands?

Deeper analysis revealed the real reason for this performance gap. Products launched under their own name had budgets twice as high as those for brand extensions. To allow for this discrepancy, they recalculated the market shares on a proportional basis. The market-share calculations were then equal for both product categories. However, the research found that brand extension seemed more effective than a new name in the hygiene sector. This is probably due to a greater level of involvement in this product category—involvement founded on physical and social risk (as in the case of shampoos and cosmetics). People therefore are more disposed to seeking the security of a known brand (Kapferer and Laurent, 1984) to reduce their perceived risk.

Remembering the Brand Principle

The more a brand expands and concentrates its communication on extensions, the more it risks losing its unity. It must therefore firmly remind its customers of its founding principles, its deep-lying meaning and *raison d'être*. This is the purpose of brand campaigns where no product is shown in particular. It takes a long time to build up an image. Managers cannot rely solely on product campaigns to turn a brand into an integrated unit. They run the risk of having a patchwork brand made up of little segments, with no guiding principle, or an incomprehensible brand, the significance of which completely eludes consumers. The brand survives and remains current only by way of extensions, whatever their scope may be. Brand management calls for a two-pronged communication:

- offensive: working toward a widening of the brand territory
- defensive: reinforcing its present legitimate territory

This defensive form of communication brings into play the root products possessing the brand's basic attributes. In turning to further products (golf), Lacoste was very careful to update its roots by sponsoring the Davis Cup and the Roland Garros tournament. Concentrating their advertising on the symbolic crocodile and the 12 x 12 shirt, they were able to diversify on the strength of their original brand code. Levi's did the same in recommunicating on their legendary 501 jeans.

The Marketing Mix of the Extension

Brand extension is not limited to applying the brand name to new products, beyond the original brand market. It is sometimes accompanied by a different marketing mix from that involving earlier products.

Armani decided to target another, younger public with a line in half-price clothing. They called it Emporio Armani, and the goods are also marketed in parts of the world other than those occupied by Armani.

When Vuitton launched their watches, they sold them only in their famous long-established shops. Would they not have profited more from this extension by placing them in the best watchmaker–jeweler boutiques in New York, Tokyo, London, and Paris? Cartier took the opposite stance. They launched their Must de Cartier collection with the precise intention of using the brand's reputation to get away from the lofty world of jewelry and its certain clientele. Extension which is centered on price will be accompanied by a change in the distribution network.

To end this chapter: it appears that certain extensions may be a commercial success but can neutralize or sometimes even weaken the brand. Others, though showing more modest results, can revitalize the brand and render it capable of still further extension.

7
Brand–Product Relationships

In Europe, several firms have joined the American cookie bandwagon, in view of the craze for this type of biscuit. The French brand of biscuits, Lu, calls its cookies "Lu Hello," while Cadbury's has avoided any particular name, and is happy to sell them simply as Cadbury Cookies. What do these different names infer where identity is concerned? Why does l'Oreal include its own name in "Plenitude de l'Oreal"—its cosmetic line sold in multiretail outlets—while they are careful to avoid doing the same with Lancôme? Why does Alcatel name its brands Opus–Alcatel, Telic–Alcatel, etc? Is it a transition prior to the establishment of a single brand, in this case, a company-name brand such as Whirlpool, Siemens, AT&T, NEC, etc.? Why does Sainsbury endorse their products with their own corporate name, whereas other retailers steer away from this and offer an increasing number of exclusive brands which bear no reference to their endorsing corporate brand? Which of these is the right approach—or are they equally pertinent policies for a retailer to adopt?

All the above issues raise the general question of the brand–product relationship, of associations between brands and their products, lines or ranges, and the system of nominal and visual identity. Every firm has to face up to this question when it ceases to rely on a mono-product. This is particularly the case with large company groups. Mitsubishi has to keep its finger on the pulse of more than 25,000 products; 3M sells 60,000 products.

The difficulty these firms face is tied up with their brands' very essence. The brand has been defined as "a symbol serving to distinguish the products or services of one firm from those of another," and, in overall terms, the brand is seen to have two principal functions:

- Distinguish one product from another.
- Indicate a product's origin.

As the firm grows, and its range of products along with it, the problem of realizing these two objectives becomes a tricky one. Philips put their own company name on their televisions (what is usually called corporate branding). But what name could they give to their lower-quality range of cheaper televisions? To distinguish the two, they called the second range Radiola, in so doing concealing the product origin. In the opposite way, Holiday Inn preferred to emphasize the origin of their various range of hotels, calling them Holiday Inn Crowne Plaza, Holiday Inn Garden Court, and Holiday Inn Express. As one would suspect, continual increase in the number of products and ranges calls for advanced thought on a system of nominal and visual identity by which to organize the attribution of names and symbols to products. Such a system must clarify the overall offer, and structure it in such a way as to allow prospective purchasers to grasp its significance. It should be logical, based on a comprehensible format so that it can be applied by the various divisions within the company. The system should assist product sales and promotion in the short term and should help to establish brand capital asset in the medium term. Finally, it should anticipate future events and be adaptable to changes in product lines and ranges.

There are several type-models showing the relationship between brand and product. These we can now examine, together with their advantages and disadvantages. In the light of these examples, we shall look at the reasons why certain firms have opted for one formula or another, in order that we may deduce the criteria against which such decisions are made. We shall also identify the principal weaknesses and abnormalities occurring in brand–product relationships—in other words, in the brand architecture. In the following chapter we shall tackle the question of the number of brands which should be retained in one market or by one firm.

BRANDING STRATEGIES

Company practices reveal six types of relationship between brand and product (or service). Each confers a certain role on the part of the brand, indicating its personal status and its means of association (nominal and/or visual) with the products which it embraces:

- product brand
- line brand
- range brand
- umbrella brand
- source brand (or parent brand)
- endorsing brand

An alternative point arises with these six forms of brand–product relationship. Should the brand name be that of the firm, or should it be distinct from the corporate name? These six types allow us to piece together the brand's problems in every sector, whether it be services, industry, fast-moving consumer goods, or luxury goods.

Product-Brand Strategy

A brand is a symbol, a word, an object, and a concept—all at one and the same time. A symbol, since the brand has many facets—it incorporates all the figurative symbols such as logos, emblems, colors, shape, packaging, and design. A word, in that the brand is called by a name. An object, because the brand distinguishes the product from other products or services. Finally, a concept, in the sense that the brand's signature, like everything else, imparts its own significance—in other words, a meaning.

The purpose of product-brand strategy is to assign an exclusive name to a product, and one alone, and to accord it its own individual positioning. This strategy results in each new product receiving its own personal brand name. In this way firms have a brand portfolio

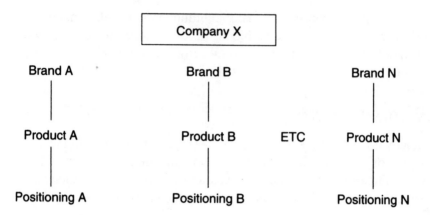

Figure 7.1

The product-brand strategy

which corresponds to their product portfolio, as illustrated in Figure 7.1.

Procter & Gamble have made this their brand management philosophy. It is seen in their detergents, with brands such as Ariel, Tide, and Dash, and also in their soaps—e.g., Camay, Safeguard, etc. Each of these products has a very precise positioning and occupies a particular segment of the market.

Firms in the food sector bring out new speciality products, each with an individual name. Their product-brand portfolio is therefore extensive. The mineral-water market is made up of nothing but product brands. You can ask for a bottle of Evian or Perrier, safe in the knowledge that you are getting what was requested. In this instance the brand is the name of a specific product, and thus a strict indication of identity. In an extreme case, this product can become so individualistic that it has no equivalent, and therefore becomes not only a product but a category of which it is the sole representative. Some have attempted to describe this phenomenon as a "branduct" (Swiners, 1979). The truth is that you cannot pin a name on a product of such a singular nature other than that of its brand. We see this in "Post-it" labels, Mars, Nuts, Bounty, etc. The product-brand concept takes account of this reality.

How does one manage through time the linking of name, product, and positioning? To begin with, the brand's only possible means of extension is to renew the product. The Ariel formula, for instance, has undergone constant improvement since the product was first launched, in order to maintain its original positioning. To this end, Ariel receives all that is best in technology and scientific improvement, as does its competing brand from Unilever (Kapferer and Thoenig, 1989). In order to signify a major improvement in the product, the manufacturer sometimes adds a number to the brand name (Bold, Bold 2, Bold 3). To cater to changes in consumer practice, the brand name can apply to variations in format, as, for example, in the packaging (packet, drum, micro-powder, or liquid).

After a time, attention to positioning will lead to a change in its supporting arguments. Ariel started life as a biological washing powder, with a promise to get rid of all stains. On the demise of the mangle and boiler, Ariel needed to maintain a high level of performance even at low temperatures—their promise to this day. This augurs well for brands whose names are not purely descriptive, since the brand must be able to cope with such changes in promise and technology, without any restriction. Ariel is not handicapped by its name. On the contrary, it humanizes the brand through its ethereal and feminine connotations—far removed from technical names such as Bold. The vowels (i and e) are symbolic in their inference of light, brightness, and energy (Collins, 1987)—which isn't a bad thing in the whiter-than-white market. Therefore, the name Ariel does not directly express its positioning, but lends itself to such symbolization, identity, and meaning.

What prizes are in store for the firm embarking on a product-brand strategy?

- For firms focusing their attention on a particular market, it is a strategic necessity. In carrying out a mass attack on one market—as did Procter & Gamble with four different detergents—the firm can occupy several segments having different types of expectations and needs, thus maximizing its share of the overall market.
- When these segments are not too different, choosing one name per product helps the consumer to see each as being different—a necessity when products look the same on the out-

side. Though all detergents have the same basic ingredients, the proportions will vary according to whether they are looking to optimize stain-removal properties, care of synthetics, colorfast control, or suitability for hand wash. Associating a specific name to a type of need underlines the physical reality of the difference between products.

- Product-brand strategy adapts to highly innovative firms who wish to preempt a positioning. If the first brand in a new segment turns out to be satisfactory, it inherits the pioneer advantage—it becomes the nominal reference for this innovation, or even the reference, full-stop. The name patents the innovation. This is particularly important in markets where success gives rise to copying. In the pharmaceutical world, where generic copies are always a certainty, every new product, as we have seen, is registered in two names: one for the product—the formula—and another for the brand. Even if they share the same formula, future generic products will seem different due to the originality of their brand name (Zantac, Tagamet, etc.) gives them a wide cloak of legal protection. On the other hand, wherever the law does not provide protection, forgeries and copies attempt to exploit the potential of the product brand by imitating its name as closely as possible. This is why, for their own brands, major retailers often make use of product brands or, to be more precise, counterproduct brands. Fortini copies Martini, Whip copies Skip, Quickcao follows Phoscao, etc.
- Product-brand policy allows firms to take risks in new markets. With the future of the liquid product uncertain, Procter & Gamble chose to launch it under a specific name. To have launched it as "Ariel liquid" at that time would have threatened Ariel's brand image asset. Had they brought out Dash liquid first, it would have incurred the risk of associating a potentially powerful concept with a weak brand and would have put that concept in the shade.
- Product-brand policy implies that the firm's name is kept apart from the public, and is therefore different from the brand name. In practice this allows the firm particular freedom to move wherever and whenever it wishes, particularly into new

markets. Procter & Gamble meandered from their first (1882) creation, Ivory soap, to the Crisco culinary aid in 1911; to Chipso, a soap for washing machines, in 1921; to Camay beauty soap in 1926; to Dreft machine detergent in 1933; to Tide in 1946; and to Joy for washing dishes in 1950; then on to Dash in 1955; Crest toothpaste in 1955; Jif peanut butter in 1956; Pampers diapers in 1961; Folgers coffee in 1963; Scope antiseptic mouthwash in 1965; Bounce kitchen rolls and Pringle potato chips in 1968; Rely sanitary tampons in 1974—and the list goes on.

- Since each brand is independent of all the others, the lack of success of one brand does not threaten to rebound on these others, nor on the company name. An incident involving Rely, which led Procter & Gamble to withdraw the product, had no impact on its other brands. The rumor of alleged ties between Procter & Gamble and some satanic cult or the Moonies had no impact on the sales of the firm's products.
- Finally, retailers' behavior weighs heavily in favor of this strategy. The shelf space which the retailer affords a company is in proportion to the number of its (major) brands. When one brand covers a number of products, the retailer stocks certain products but not others.

The drawbacks arising from product brands are essentially economic. Investment in multibrand strategy is not for the fainthearted.

- Each time a new product is launched it constitutes a brand launch. Considering the media costs in various sectors, one is talking of a considerable amount of investment in advertising and promotion. A further fact is that retailers, loath to take a risk with any untested product, will only try it out when tempted by heavy discounts.
- The increase in the number of product brands in one market, due to ever-finer distinctions in type, weighs heavily on the chances of a rapid return on one's investment. The volume of production required to justify such investment—in R&D, equipment, and commercial costs—makes the product-brand strategy better suited to rising markets. Here, just a small bite of the cherry would be equivalent to a high product capacity.

When markets are saturated, there is no such possibility. On the other hand, in a stabilized market it is sometimes more advantageous to perk up an existing brand by according it the innovation in question rather than attempting to give it product-brand status by introducing it under its own name.

Line-Brand Strategy

Renault sells many types of cars, from the small Clio to the largest models. Each model is available in a large number of versions: two or four doors, different engine sizes, automatic or manual. However, for each model, one of its versions is named Baccara. Baccara is a line brand, indicating leather seats, a luxurious interior, etc. The line brand extends its specific concept across different products, allowing for what is called a cross-branding.

In the beauty-care industry, firms make use of the same strategy: they launch at once a number of complementary products. For instance, balding men are not looking only for a treatment. They want a complete line of products to go with it: a mild shampoo, a daily lotion, etc.

The line is thus an answer to the call for like products with complementary features, all under the same name—as in the case of after-shave fragrances followed by a soap, a shampoo, a deodorant, a bath foam. L'Oreal's Studio Line follows the same idea, offering youngsters a structuring gel, lacquer, spray, etc. Again Calgon (a Benckiser brand) markets a dishwasher powder, together with a rinsing agent and lime-scale inhibitor.

A line can therefore be established by building on the success of the original product with practical variations of a closely associated nature—the typical approach followed by perfumes, for example. Alternatively, the line may be launched as a complete entity, offering several complementary products with the same inspiration—Studio Line allows youngsters to create their own hair style and take on a particular look. Possible extension of the line will cost no more than the marginal price of discounts and packaging, and will require no advertising. It must be compared with the marginal number of extra sales to be won.

Line-brand policy offers several advantages:

- It raises the selling power of the brand and creates a strong image of consistency.
- It leads to ease of line extension.
- It reduces launch costs.

The disadvantage of line strategy lies in the tendency to forget that a line has limits. One should only include new products or those closely associated with the existing one. Another problem is that the inclusion of a powerful innovation could slow down its development. Nestlé had to make certain that their new product, Bolino—a dehydrated ready meal—was not seen as part of their line in dehydrated packet soups. To be seen and appreciated in all its novelty, the product had to rid itself of this traditional descriptive tag.

Range-Brand Strategy

Weight Watchers groups more than ten products, all under one name and with one promise: Eat better and you will have longer-lasting results. In 1990, Findus embraced 135 frozen products under one unifying concept: "For Findus, only the best is good." Not all range brands are overabundant. Clan Campbell whisky has three quality levels: five-year-old, twelve-year-old, and the legendary twenty-one-year-old. Range brands bestow a single name and a promise on a group of products having the same level of ability. In range-brand architecture, products keep their current name (fish à la provençale, mushroom pizza, crêpes with ham and cheese, in the case of Findus). Clarins are even more specific in their product names: e.g., their purification mask with plant extracts, extracts of "fresh cells," multitensor toning solution, day or night soothing cream, etc.

Range-brand formation is found in the food sector (Green Giant, Dole), cosmetics, clothes (Benetton, Kookai, Rodier, etc.), kitchen equipment (Moulinex, Seb, Rowenta), accessories (Delsey, Samsonite, Vuitton) and industry (Dulux, Bosch). These brands bring all their products together under one promise or positioning, as shown in Figure 7.2. The advantages and otherwise of this formation are as follows:

- It avoids the random spread of communication by concentrating on one single name—the brand name—and by building up a brand awareness which can be shared by the products.

Moreover, through this formation the brand communicates by advertising its specific promise. On these lines, though the Pedigree range brand covers several products, it revolves its advertising around the image of exacting breeders. The film conveys the brand's focus of attention and the preeminence which it gives to the animal. Another approach consists of refining the brand concept by concentrating on specific products (called vector products) through which the brand can best express its meaning and contribution. This meaning can then be shared by the other products in the range not directly mentioned. Twenty-one-year-old Clan Campbell raises the quality of the whole range;

• The cost of launching such new products need not be great.

Among the problems posed, the most frequent is that of the brand's opacity as it expands. Gerble does not have too much of a problem with this since the majority of its products are based on wheat germ, and therefore reflect the brand. It has acquired a precise meaning, along with a depth and energy, which it imparts to its products in such a way as to make them quite different from those of Gayelord Hauser—the more glamorous brand favored by diet-conscious Hollywood stars.

Findus covers every savory frozen dish—135 in all. It is a good, quality, up-to-date brand, specializing in every type of frozen dish. For years, there were product names in their lower range which

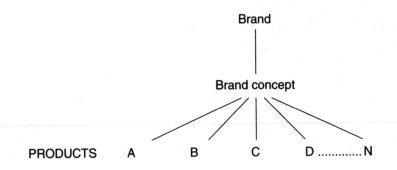

Figure 7.2
Range-brand formation

described the recipe. Such generic product names lack differentiation, and any brand can put its name on the same recipe. There were two clear necessities: on the one hand, the brand needed to be nurtured in such a way as to express its individuality; on the other hand, the consumer had to be assisted in sifting through the mass of 135 products in order to pick out those with appeal. The solution lay in an intermediate stage of meaning between the brand and the generic product name. To achieve this, they converted to product lines, as for example "Lean cuisine," grouping eighteen dishes recognizable by their white packaging; "Traditional," covering nine dishes, with maroon outers; and "Seafoods," comprising nine types of fish and assorted products (previously called quite simply hake cutlets, whiting fillets, etc.), in blue packets.

Such line names throw light on the products and structure the range, in the same way as shopkeepers organize their shelves. The criteria for making such divisions and groups depend on the brand. We can either make distinctions according to content (poultry, beef, pork—as in a butcher's shop) or by mixing the lines on the basis of consumer advantage (light, traditional, etc.).

The line structures the offer by bringing together products which are unquestionably heterogeneous, but which all have the same function. Thus Clarins, the cosmetics range brand, also structures its products by way of lines. To assist its consumers in making sense of the scientific wording on products, the brand puts forward lines as one would write a prescription. For example, the "soothing line" for sensitive skins comprises a daytime soothing cream and a nighttime soothing cream, as well as a conditioning fluid, and the "slimming and firming" line consists of an exfoliative rub, a slimming bath, a "biosuperactivated" reducing cream, and an "antiwater oil." Clarins products no longer form a long list of creams, solutions, lotions, balms, and gels, but are now a group of structured and coherent formulas, as we see in Figure 7.3. In order that the product structure may be seen where the purchaser most needs it—at the point of sale—many brands go to the extent of offering a minidisplay of the complete range.

The second problem occurring in the use of range brands stems from single communication on a whole range of products. For example, how do you adapt to a younger public when you want to sell fish

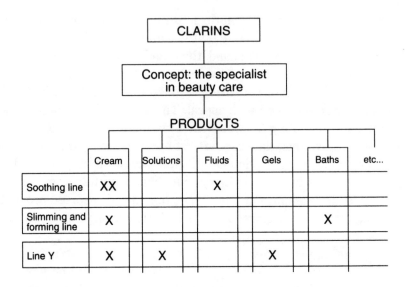

Figure 7.3
Range brand structured in lines

fingers? Since the main Findus message—in fact its only one—is "For Findus only the best is good," they have to manipulate it to suit the idea of fish fingers. Children would not be impressed by this theme, preferring the mateyness of Captain Igloo—created by the Igloo brand to tighten its relationship with the younger public.

Umbrella-Brand Strategy

Canon markets cameras, photocopiers, and office equipment, all under one name. Yamaha sells motorcycles, as well as pianos and guitars. Mitsubishi has a common interest in banks, cars, and domestic appliances. Palmolive manufactures household products (dishwashing liquid) and hygiene products (soaps, shampoos for all the family, and also shaving cream). These are all umbrella brands, in which the same brand supports several products in different markets—each with its own communication and individual promise (sometimes even with its own advertising agency). Yet each product retains its generic name. We talk of Canon cameras, Canon fax machines, and Canon printers. Figure 7.4 shows this formation.

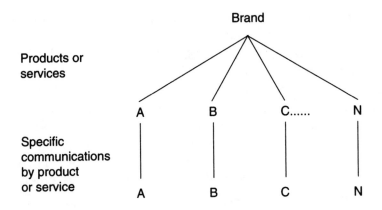

Figure 7.4

Umbrella-brand strategy

Chapter 6 was devoted to the question of brand extension beyond its original calling. Was Philips right in using the one name to cover hi-fi, television, light bulbs, computers, electric razors, and small electric appliances? The parameters of the decision have already been explained.

The main advantage of this strategy is the capitalization on one single name. Not one of their undertakings, products, or communications fails to contribute to the Philips reputation. Even the odd setback can add to public awareness of the brand. Umbrella brands are favored by multinational corporations marketing worldwide. Being already established, their name and reputation is a major asset in entering segments or areas which they had not previously penetrated. This awareness of the brand can bring about almost immediate approval on the part of retailers and public alike. Firms enjoying such awareness find the umbrella brand convenient in sectors where little marketing investment is required. In smaller sectors, they can even succeed with no specific communication. It also leads to considerable savings when they enter new strategic markets.

The importance of this last point should not be underestimated, particularly in the present era of overcommunication. In many markets today, the quest for awareness of a new brand is out of reach, when one considers the promotional advertising expenditure on the part of competitors. Advertising costs are a barrier to entry. This is what, in 1984, led Jack Tramiel, the former boss of Commodore microcomputers, to buy Atari—at that time a well-known name, albeit primarily for its video games. His intention was to make a fresh incursion into the family and commercial microcomputer scene. Tramiel chose to buy a brand with an established reputation—associated though it was with other products—rather than create another brand. The same reasoning is behind the practice of reviving former brands, to be used as linchpins for new products. Though most people will have forgotten this original product, the memory of the brand name will return once more. It is better to take advantage of a glimmer in the public mind than to start again from scratch.

The umbrella-brand strategy allows one to nurture the core brand by associating with it products with which it was not previously associated. Schweppes—until then a product brand—became an umbrella brand when it entered the fizzy drinks market occupied by Orangina, Pschitt, and Fanta. Their Schweppes Dry advertising brought modernity and youth—an effect which it had been difficult to achieve with their classic Indian Tonic Water.

Finally, the umbrella brand imposes few constraints. Each division within the organization handles its own communication, to get the best out of the particular market in which it operates. Toshiba hi-fi targets the younger generation with its own motto, and the microcomputer division pushes its outstandingly practical portables, while televisions are promoted on their picture quality. It is true that, in each of these markets, the overall brand will come up against one or more specialized brands. Awareness resulting from the umbrella effect is not sufficient: products have to prove their benefits in each market sector if the brand is to succeed. Peugeot Electric Tools is blessed with a major name. Even so, it must prove itself worthy when placing this well-known name in the car world on DIY products and materials. Assisted brand awareness does not automatically signify a legitimate product—even less so an excellent one—in the eyes of the purchaser.

The problems encountered in umbrella-brand administration stem from a failure to appreciate its demands. It sometimes happens that, in wishing to save money by diversifying under an umbrella brand, the firm forgets that the purpose of the brand is above all to earn money. Awareness is not sufficient in this respect. Each division must use its human and financial resources to best effect to show that its products or services are as good as those of specialist brands. No matter how strong the heart of the brand and its main products, it is vulnerable when extended.

The umbrella must not cast a shadow. When it was a subsidiary of Alcatel, GSI battled for years to keep away from Alcatel's system of giving its subsidiary companies names such as Telic–Alcatel, SMH–Alcatel, Roneo–Alcatel, etc. Realistically speaking, a data-processing service company should be duty-bound to show no apparent links with a worldwide manufacturer if it is to retain intact its own credibility. Extension of the name Alcatel to its own would have harmed GSI. Again, an accident occurring with one product can affect the other products under the same umbrella (Sullivan, 1988).

The more a brand covers different categories, the more it stretches and weakens, losing its force like an elastic band. It then becomes a simple name on products, indicating their origin—a manufacturer's seal, pointing to a guarantee of quality, or a retailer's own-brand, showing that the product is acceptable since it has been selected by him.

Only powerful brands with a precise meaning can cut across the system and embrace heterogeneous products, since they are able to impose their meaning on these products. Sony, for example, is an innovator. The brand can cover many categories, since the factors composing the Sony image are enticingly pertinent to these categories, no matter how unrelated their products may be. Palmolive seems to add softness to everything it touches. Its image is a basis of segmentation whenever a product comes into contact with the skin. The brand can therefore cast its net over hygiene as well as beauty—men as well as women.

The greatest handicap to the brand is not so much its horizontal extension, but its vertical extension, by which brands try to cover every level of quality and status. The Renault–Volvo relationship bears witness to this. The car market is a segmented one—the lower range, lower midrange, upper midrange, and top of the range, not to mention luxury and sports cars. It would be wrong to think that the brand program could exercise the same influence on every sector. Citroën's creative strength comes noticeably to the fore in the upmarket sector, but loses its edge when faced with the stringencies required in producing inexpensive cars. This factor signaled the death of Flaminaire lighters when they tried to compete with Bic and Dupont. They forgot that one name cannot be associated at one and the same time with both a refined product and an everyday product. This is why Carrefour ceased selling their "freedom products" line of quality products, which were priced less expensively than those of major brands. The problem was that at first glance they resembled the low-priced, low-quality group of products which other retailers had introduced, as a result of their plain white packaging. Carrefour's line was therefore classed as being of low quality—an impression which threatened to rub off on the corporate name itself. In the light of the future plans of Carrefour to use their name on products of a higher standard, Carrefour immediately ceased the freedom products line, to prevent any downward slide of their umbrella name.

The freedom allowed by the umbrella brand sometimes leaves the brand itself with a patchwork effect. It is one thing to allow each divisional manager to take care of his own product communication, but another to accept too many variations in brand style from one division or one product to the next. Managers are free to make detailed promises, in line with their particular market. However, though each product has its individual identity, the way in which the message is relayed should be identical in every case. Customers do not come across just one part of the brand—they are confronted with every product, each with its own particular message. The brand should be seen as an a coherent whole, even though it is organized in commercial and industrial divisions. The pyramidal model of the brand (see Chapter 5) helps to avoid this problem.

Source-Brand Strategy

This is identical to umbrella-brand strategy, apart from one key point—products are now directly named. They no longer come under a generic tag, such as eau de toilette or eau de parfum, but each has its own name, e.g., Jazz, Poison, Opium, Nina, Loulou, etc. This is a two-tier brand structure known as double-branding, illustrated in Figure 7.5.

Since this strategy is often confused with the following endorsing-brand strategy, it is important to specify the difference at the outset. When Nestlé puts its name on Dairy Crunch, Nescafé, Nesquick, etc.,

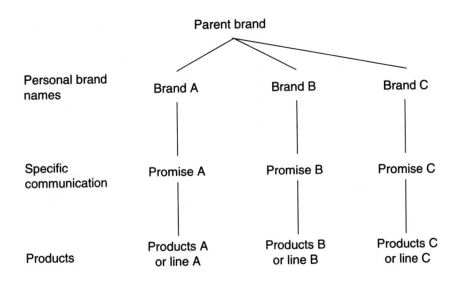

Figure 7.5

Source-brand (or parent-brand) strategy

the company is endorsing the quality of the merchandise. The Nestlé name dispels the uncertainty which some products can create. Nestlé takes a back-seat position only if the product itself is attractive, to the extent that few Crunch consumers attribute Crunch to Nestlé.

When we see Yves Saint Laurent on a perfumed deodorant such as Jazz, this name is much more than a simple endorsement. Here it is the brand name which holds sway and which accords Jazz the distinction and seal of approval which its own name would not normally enjoy. Jazz is another key to the door of the Yves Saint Laurent cultural universe. The problem with many brands is that they have converted from source brands to endorsing brands. Within the source brand concept, the offspring may have their own Christian names, but they are still tied to the family spirit which dominates. With an endorsing brand, however, products follow their singular paths under a simple common guarantee. It would be interesting to see how Cadbury's or Kellogg's see themselves here: are they still a source brand, or only an endorsement?

The benefit of source-brand strategy lies in its ability to impose a sense of difference and depth. The parent brand can promote its own significance and identity in a modified or enriched way through the name of its offspring, in order to attract a specific customer segment. Ranges having "Christian names" allow a brand—and its image capital—to profit from new consumer categories in hitherto unattainable areas. For instance, 50 percent of Coco buyers are under 29 years old, the majority of No. 5 de Chanel buyers are above 30. Coco brings youth to the Chanel clientele and image. No. 5 reinforces the classicism and elegance of the Chanel brand.

The one danger with a source brand is that of overstepping the limits of the parent brand's core identity. This means keeping within strict boundaries where brand extension is concerned. Only authentic names within the parent brand's field of activity should be used. Anais-Anais and Loulou benefit from their association with Cacharel. The names of both perfumes capture its romantic spirit present. If one is looking for greater freedom, endorsing-brand strategy is more suited.

Endorsing-Brand Strategy

Question: What is the common denominator of Pontiac, Buick, Oldsmobile, and Chevrolet in America, and of Opel and Vauxhall in Europe?

Answer: The two letters, GM.

No prizes, of course—it is the trademark of General Motors, the endorsing brand. Again, what name links Pledge, Wizard air freshener, and Toilet Duck? They are all Johnson products. Country Store, Rice Krispies, Frosties, and All Bran all have one thing in common: they are endorsed by Kellogg's, as Nestlé endorses Crunch, Golden Graham, Maggi, and Nescafé. The endorsing brand gives its approval to a wide diversity of products grouped under product brands, line brands, or range brands. Kellogg's normally tends towards product brands—Frosties, All Bran, Corn Flakes, and Rice Krispies refer to particular products. Putting aside their differences, Kellogg's stands as guarantor of their quality and taste. This apart, each product is still free to show its originality—hence the wide variety of names and symbols (each having its own animal).

Figure 7.6 symbolizes the endorsing-brand strategy. As we can see, "endorsing brand" is now placed lower down in its basic reassuring role. When it comes down to it, the customer is buying Pontiac or

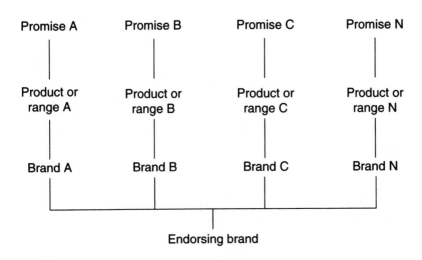

Figure 7.6
Endorsing-brand strategy

Opel, All Bran or Frosties, Pledge or Favor. General Motors, Kellogg's, or Johnson are supports and take a secondary position. The brand endorsement can be indicated either by an emblem next to the brand or as a simple name. Sainsbury uses its umbrella name on all products. In France the retailer Casino does the same with the exception of those products where they have no authority (champagne and perfume, for example). To cover the latter, they simply include their name in the small print with "selected by Casino." This comes down to the use of their name as an approval brand, a variation on endorsing. The manufacturer's identity remains, endorsed by the name of the retailer by whom it has been selected.

The main advantage for the endorsing brand is the greater freedom of maneuverability which it confers. It gives Nestlé, for example, unlimited scope. Once considered as a source brand with a specific image linked with baby food and with its roots in children's chocolate, Nestlé would not have been able to encompass the coffee market, the soup market, etc., under its single name.

Like the source brand, an endorsing brand profits from the advantages offered by specifically-named products. Each particular name evokes a forceful image of the product in one's mind, which in turn furthers that of the endorsing brand (at least in theory, as we shall see later in an analysis of dysfunctional brands).

Endorsing-brand strategy is one of the less costly ways of giving substance to a company name and allowing it to achieve brand status. Valentine, for example, added the ICI initials to their cans of paint, while the name of Rhône–Poulenc appeared on packets of KB garden products. The high quality of both brands was endorsed by these two major organizations. In an opposite sense, it also helped spread the name of ICI in France, as a result of the everyday presence on the endorsed products. Since the enhanced value and scientific and technical guarantee of their products had been taken care of by the endorsing brand, KB and Valentine could devote more time to expressing other facets of their identity.

As we can see, both participants in the endorsing brand setup have a shared role. The endorsing brand itself is responsible for the guarantee factor which all products need. Nowadays, this guarantee covers normal quality and scientific skill, plus elements of civic responsibility and respect for ecology. The other brand functions are carried out by the specifically-named products.

These six brand strategies all are case types. In reality, firms adopt hybrid configurations in the form of a range, umbrella, parent, or endorsing brand, according to the products. For example, L'Oreal is fully involved in its product "Floreal," endorses Studio Line, and has no visibility on Lancôme. L'Oreal's hybrid brand strategy indicates their willingness to adapt to specific consumer requirements in different market sectors (hair products, cosmetics, and perfumes) and to varied retail facilities (self-service or specialist stores). Nevertheless, many hybrid situations have arisen out of a series of small decisions taken over a period as new products are created. Failure to establish a preconceived plan of a brand's total embodiment and the relationship with its products often results in a total hodgepodge of branding policies.

A Case of Brand Proliferation

An interesting example of accumulation of separate branding policies structured at different levels, with as many as five denominational stages (i.e., quintuple branding) is provided by 3M. This is shown in Figure 7.7. The company focuses on high-tech research into the

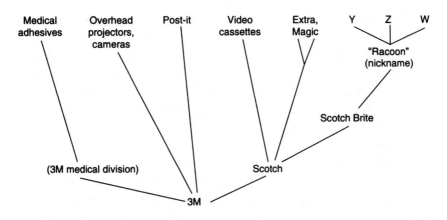

Figure 7.7

A case of brand proliferation and dilution of identity

industrial and domestic applications of adhesives. This covers a vast product area which includes instant glues, films, cassettes, medical plasters, clear plastic wrap, and overhead-projection products. The 3M name is synonymous with a serious-minded, powerful insistence on research and development which can leave the company image looking somewhat cold. The Scotch brand appears on most consumer products, sometimes with the 3M endorsement, sometimes alone (as with video cassettes). From Scotch came the international line, Scotch-Brite, covering their scouring pads. To counter the challenge of the equivalent Spontex product, particularly on the Continent, Scotch added to the generic denomination a specific name, calling it in French, for example, "The little raccoon." This parallels the impact of the Volkswagen Beetle name or, more pertinently, the Johnson Brillo pad. Applied in any language, such a personalized name gives the product a specific identity and imbues it with a closer, more friendly image. The "raccoon" itself has several variations—green, blue, red, etc.—depending on its shape and use.

The 3M situation is a typical case illustrating the problems created by brand proliferation. Although it ranks twenty-ninth in the Fortune 500 index and sells more than 60,000 products worldwide, 3M is rather poorly known. It has been found to have only 65 percent of aided awareness, and only 25 percent of people are familiar with what

3M does, and produces. This poor level of awareness creates a real shortcoming in one of the major roles of a corporate brand: to endorse. The fact is that 3M does not really act as it should: as a power brand. The roots of this situation lie in 3M's brand proliferation policy—it has 1,500 product brands, which are correspondingly specialized, and each one receives too little financial support to be properly supported. Furthermore, the effect is to create a screen, hiding the corporation 3M.

The worldwide response to this situation by 3M has been as follows: Since 3M relies heavily on product innovation, it needs very strong brands to "patent" these innovations in people's minds. This indicates a need for fewer but more powerful brands. A drastic change in brand policy had to be, and was, undertaken. Brands being too important to leave in the hands of brand managers, 3M created a Corporate Branding Policy Committee, whose tasks are:

- Establish corporate guidelines for brand use.
- Review the brand's world strategies.
- Approve any new brand requests.

Three new guidelines were soon introduced. From now on, the trademark 3M should endorse all products (with one exception, a cosmetic line). This was not the case in the past—for instance, the 3M trademark was totally absent on Scotch video tapes sold to the mass market. As a second rule, no products would carry more than two brands. In some countries 3M had become an expert in multiple branding, with three and even four levels of sub-branding, such as 3M Scotch-Brite XY! Finally, all brands will be global, which means no more creation of local brands.

The Corporate Branding Policy Committee developed screening procedures to evaluate new brand creation proposals. To be accepted, the new product it purported to name would have to meet a number of criteria. As a general rule, 3M would always prefer to use the name of one of its existing primary brands, to capitalize on them and nourish them. If such names could not fit, and would not be usable (for instance because of their image), then a 3M generic name such as 3M DS–HD computer diskettes should be used. There is only one condition allowing the creation of a new brand: will the product create a new primary demand? This applied in the case of Post-it.

As to sub-brands, they are allowed only when the primary brand alone does not accomplish sufficient differentiation (hence the creation of Scotch-Magic–type sub-brands). But the new philosophy emphasizes 3M's role as an endorsement brand.

This stance in branding policy created a deep change in management. In 1989, 244 new brand creation requests had been submitted. In 1991, only 70 requests were submitted. While 73 new brands (mostly local) had been created in 1989, only four were created in 1991. In ten years, 3M had cut its brand portfolio from 1,500 to 700 brands. It introduced a global policy to stop case-by-case decisions, a few power brands to cut trademark proliferation, and corporate management to replace subsidiary-based decisions. At 3M, what the Branding Committee says is gospel now. Dilution of identity has been stopped.

A similar policy was undertaken by Nestlé, whose corporate culture had hitherto led to decentralizing of major decisions. As a result, Nestlé also suffered from brand proliferation. Throughout the world, the most junior product manager could create a new brand to accompany any new product creation. These times have gone. In 1991, Nestlé created 120 new products, but only four new brands. Most of the new products were used to nourish existing primary brands, such as Maggi.

Taking a more general line, we shall now look at the main criteria governing the choice of one brand policy as opposed to another.

SELECTION CRITERIA

Which is the best brand policy? Does Procter & Gamble, firm supporters of product brands, have it right while their more flexible rival Colgate Palmolive is wrong? Is the retailer brand system adopted by Sainsbury better than that of Tesco, Aldi, or Kwik Save? Such questions keep recurring.

Each type of brand strategy has its advantages and disadvantages, as we have described. However, a simple list of pros and cons does not constitute as such a format by which a given firm can choose in accordance with a given market. Choosing a brand policy is not a stylistic exercise but a strategic decision to promote products with a long-term brand capital aim. It should be considered in the light of three limiting factors: the product or service, consumer habits, and the firm's competitive position. The above questions are again not easy to answer, since they call for final, binding answers in all-embracing terms. In reality, brand policy reflects the strategy chosen by a particular firm in a specific context.

The case of Calvet provides a good example. This Bordeaux wine merchant follows two contrasting policies—one in France and one abroad. In France, Calvet is a product brand which refers to a specific type of Bordeaux wine. Abroad, however, it becomes a multiproduct name—an umbrella brand covering not only Bordeaux wine but also Burgundy, together with other regional whites, reds, and rosés. This is to be expected. The French consumer is more accustomed to interpreting the various pointers to specification on a wine label: region, vintage, type of vine, year. In some cases, the retailer's name is also included if he has gained a reputation for choosing only the best wines on a price–quality basis. In this context, what can the name Calvet convey to the French consumer? The Calvet brand has meaning only when it can offer a plus which other Bordeaux cannot. This logically implies a brand strategy with a limited territory in mind. In France, Calvet is therefore a product name—a product brand. In other countries, however, particularly where there is no appreciable wine-producing industry, the consumer may not fully appreciate the meaning of "appellation," vintages, and other details. In Japan, they buy wine by its color and country. In Japan, therefore, French wines need a name which will identify them and reassure the customer. The umbrella brand is the best choice here. The Calvet brand can cover many generic French regional wines.

When choosing a holiday, the customer gets hold of a catalog six months beforehand. The catalog gives a complete description of each hotel, its distinctive characteristics, and even the cost. They also throw in a photograph. What, then, is the purpose of the brand in this context? There is nothing which the customer cannot see for himself. However in far-off destinations where promise and reality can be worlds apart, the customer needs to be reassured that there is little risk. This is where the Thomas Cook or Lunn Poly endorsing brand comes in. It presents itself as the final guarantor. The holidaymaker builds his dreams around the hotel name, with the risk-reducing presence of these endorsing names.

The high-flier sent to Ankara for three days to negotiate a deal has no time to dream. He knows the difficulties of the task ahead and can do without any unnecessary stress. This class of customer is looking for a flawless level of hotel service. He sees the brand as an indicator of a specific quality of service, facilities, comfort, and hospitality which does not deviate from one city to the next, nor from one country to another. The brand is a product brand. He rents a Hilton, a Sheraton, a Meridien, or a Sofitel room.

Club Med takes a third path—a range-brand policy. Although the range has come to be split into segments—from economy hutted villages to luxury golf hotels, summer and winter, throughout the world—the brand's name is unitary, and so is the advertising campaign. All the customer has to do is to specify his chosen geographical destination. This denominative policy is their strategy in a nutshell. Despite their differences, all these products share the same model and values. Their common features speak louder than their differences. The only notable development in their denominative policy has been the progression to the brand name Club Med—reference to the Mediterranean having become obsolete as a result of geographical extension, and being of little significance to an American, Japanese, or even South African.

As we can see, the decision to adopt a denominative policy is not prompted by any esthetic or formal desire. It results from a recognition of the brand's duties as expected by the customer, when compared with the function and meaning of other product-, range-, and line-brand names, including objective and subjective quality indicators such as packaging, catalog, advertising, and the retailer's own prescription and advice. Nevertheless, given the same customer reaction, two firms will not follow the same nominal identity program, since their precise strategies will differ. Their individual desires will infiltrate the branding process.

CORPORATE VERSUS PRODUCT BRANDING

Major corporations selling to both industrial and consumer markets must decide how much emphasis they will put on product brands and how much visibility they will give to the corporate name. It is noticeable that a trend now exists in favor of corporate branding. More and more corporations cease to remain hidden behind their product brands. Unilever, for instance, is starting an endorsement policy in Europe and adds its corporate name in small type under its Persil, Jif, Sun, or Sunlight brands. ICI is strongly present, close to the Dulux trademark.

For a long time, corporations remained hidden for security purposes: in the event of problems with one of the brands, the corporation would not be hurt. Reciprocally, the brands would not suffer from corporate problems. However, the advantages in the uncommon event of crisis are now outweighed by certain disadvantages. Huge corporations had become undervalued by public opinion, and even by professionals. For instance, although it was founded in 1969 and was one of the largest chemical companies in the world, AKZO remained largely unknown. No wonder: all the acquired companies had kept their own company names and brand names (Warner-Lambert, Stauffer, Montedison, Diamond Salt, etc.) AKZO gained a poor image in terms of its technology because of this lack of visibility. It had become the biggest unknown company in the world.

In many markets, too, customers have become more and more demanding and need to be reassured by knowing who stands behind a brand. Whenever there is some perceived element of risk to the consumer, the corporate reputation confers some security. Thus Johnson's products all are endorsed by Johnson's, despite their being strong product brands in their own right. ICI means technology and research, and adds this meaning to Dulux's own meaning.

In practice, the appropriate decision concerning the relative weight to give corporate and product names needs case-by-case analysis of what task each of them does best, or what targets are most relevant. Table 7.1 presents such an analysis. At ICI, three types of branding policy are now used:

- A top-down policy (umbrella-brand policy), whereby ICI signs a range of technical products which remain unbranded. The corporate name suffices: there is no need to further brand the products, for they are mostly tailor-made for their major customers. This is the case for ICI polyurethanes.
- A hand-in-hand policy (endorsement-brand policy), where ICI adds its corporate reputation and reassurance on technology and quality for the customers of famous mass-market brands.

For instance, Dulux, the biggest-selling brand of paint in the world, is backed up by the ICI logo. The same holds true for Perspex, the brand name of an acrylic sheet, competing against Plexiglas.

- A product brand–only policy. Thus Tactel, one of the best-selling fibers, makes no reference at all to ICI, since Tactel is serving the fashion industry, which is far removed from the imagery of the chemical industry. Karate, an agrochemical insecticide, also makes no reference to ICI, perhaps to protect the corporate name, since ecology has become such a sensitive issue.

Figure 7.8 presents the differential weight of the corporate and product brands *vis-à-vis* its different markets and activities. In a similar way, the greater the degree of industrialization, the greater the

Table 7.1

Shared roles of the corporate and product brand

Targets	Product Brand	Corporate Brand
Customers	+ + + + +	+
Trade associations	+ + + +	+
Employees	+ + +	+ +
Suppliers	+ + +	+ + +
Press	+ + +	+ + +
Issues groups	+ +	+ + + +
Local community	+ +	+ + + +
Academia	+ +	+ + + +
Regulatory authorities	+	+ + + +
Government commission	+	+ + + +
Financial markets	+	+ + + + +
Stockholders	+	+ + + + +

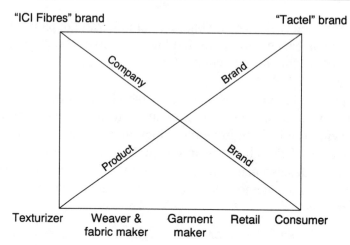

"ICI Fibres" brand   "Tactel" brand

Texturizer   Weaver &   Garment   Retail   Consumer
              fabric maker   maker

Figure 7.8

Corporate and product branding at ICI

emphasis on the AKZO name. Certainly, the well-known names are not suppressed, but must now acknowledge their origin (e.g.: X, part of the AKZO pharmaceutical division).

All companies must define strict guidelines with which to face these naming and branding decisions. Guidelines bring rationality and coherence to decisions so far made according to each manager's subjectivity. They become a tool of consensus and delegation. This is all the more necessary if the company is international and sells innumerable products. For instance, General Electric has created such a decision guide to help its managers choose one from among four branding policies:

- The monolithic one, whereby GE signs the product or company as single-brand (GE Silicones, GE Aircraft Engines, GE Motors). GE acts here as an umbrella brand.
- The endorsement type, whereby GE signs adjacent to a specific product or company name (GE–X).
- The holding type, whereby GE is discretely mentioned in such terms as (X, member of the GE group).
- The autonomous product or company, making no reference to GE.

The decision-making flow chart is made up of six criteria, creating a decision tree:

- Does GE control the company? (yes/no)
- Does GE have a commitment in this company? (yes/no)
- Has the product category an image value? (dynamic or not)
- Are there quality expectations of GE in this industry? (yes/no)
- What is the equity of the existing identity? (weak/strong)
- What is its impact on GE image? (high/low)

This example holds for corporate branding. Major consumer brands such as Dannon use similar decision trees to manage the balance between the parent brand and the product brand. All wide brands do the same.

PRODUCT NAMES: WHAT AUTONOMY?

Fiat distinguishes its cars by giving each its own name: e.g., Panda, Uno, Tipo, Regatta. For years, Renault chose to number its models: e.g., R4, R5, R19, R21, R25, but the advent of the Clio in 1990 to replace the R5 represented a policy change (the failure of the Fuego apart). BMW and Mercedes grade their brand on a numbered scale: the 3, 5, 7 series in the one case, and Mercedes 190, 200, etc, in the other. For some time, Citroën has codified its range in the manner AX, BX, and CX, although the appearance of the XM signals a development in this respect.

Dior launched perfumes under the names Diorella, Diorissimo, and Miss Dior, before changing to names such as Poison and Fahrenheit; its cosmetics had names such as Capture and Resultante, but then came Hydra-Dior. Taking the same products, Lancôme used the names Niosôme and Noctosôme; Clarins described its products as "Multi-Reducing" or "Multi-Restoring" creams.

In the computer service industry, the leading American company ADP takes the extreme stance in umbrella branding by giving no specific name to its personal software. We therefore have ADP Fast-pay, ADP Interactive Personal Package, and ADP Benefit System.

All these examples denote a certain relationship between the brand and its products—a choice between two extremes: complete autonomy or clear affiliation. Here we see the basic dilemma brought about by the brand's two concomitant but scarcely compatible aims of creating a distinction between products while retaining the notion of their origin.

It is possible to identify seven forms of strategy, with increasing degrees of autonomy:

1. We can buy Lacoste shirts, socks, jackets, sweaters, rackets, and eau de toilette. The products do not have their own names, and, as for that, do not need one. The brand changes everything it embraces, turning an uninspiring, everyday article into a product of distinction. This is the stamp of the powerful brand—its signature, or griffe. A sweater only has to bear the Lacoste name for it to stand out. Not only is it noticed, but the aura created by the brand sets it apart. The power of the brand releases it from the confines of the common lot. This is not solely characteristic of luxury goods-it can apply to any brand aiming to raise the overall status of its products. It happens in the case both of St. Michael and Sony. On the other hand, this policy is not suitable for weak brands, since they are unable to inject a common quality or spirit into the products bearing their name.

2. When Mercedes calls its models the 190, 200, and so on, the brand dominates the product. This policy emphasizes a brand whose image is reflected in every model. Whichever model he buys, the customer will discover all the objective and subjective attributes which go to make up the brand identity. The 190 is not an inferior Mercedes—it is the first Mercedes. Comparative figures deal only with product performance in such matters as engine power, and do not indicate that there is less of "Mercedes" in the 190 model than in the 300 model. Porsche made the mistake of forgetting this reasoning. The 924 bore no relation whatsoever to Porsche. Together with the basic 944, the 924 was only Porsche in name. The brand had failed to fully express its difference and superiority in this price bracket.

3. In naming its perfumes Diorissimo, Miss Dior, and Diorella, Dior provides a forceful reminder of the source brand. Each product is simply a variation on the brand's values deriving from a common core. Diorissimo is the height of Dior, while Miss Dior is a representation of the young woman in the world of Dior. This strict association between brand and product allows the rising brand to express its identity and system of values by means of those little extra touches. It has its limits in that the principle should not be

applied to too many products at one time, otherwise the source brand becomes nothing more than a technical prefix—a simple factory reminder linking together a random assortment of products. Too great a number of Dior–X products would exhaust the meaning of Dior. This is what is happening with Nestlé to a certain extent. Everyone knows that Nescafé, Nescore, Nesquick, and Nestea are part of the same brand, as are the chocolate and condensed milk, but they all go to give the brand a technical-process connotation.

4. When Lancôme calls their products Niosôme and Noctosôme, it is obvious that they wish to show, through the "ôme" suffix, an association between brand and products. The brand takes them under its exclusive wing, expressing their innovative qualities.

5. Clarins has such product names as "Multi-Tensing Gel" and "Multi-Restoring Fluid." Yet it would be wrong to see these as simple generic names. In fact, "multi" is part and parcel of the Clarins core identity, for two reasons. First, the prefix appears in all languages. Second, Clarins chose to capitalize on the term, even though it cannot be patented and is widely used in the pharmaceutical field, since "multi" infers a complete course of treatment, corresponding to the Clarins identity and intent—a product line rather than mono-products; several steps rather than a single one; a scientific approach, no magic.

6. The penultimate stage in autonomy advance (or, if one prefers, in filial retreat) is seen in the "Christian name." Dior's Capture and Poison perfumes, and Johnson's Pledge household spray all are examples. Clarins would certainly not have chosen the name Capture, as it has poetic and symbolic connotations, but it is acceptable to Dior since its nominal and semantic detachment allows Dior to extend without destabilizing the heart of the brand. In this instance, the relationship between product and brand is bottom-up. New meaning rises to the heart of the brand and the brand gladly accepts this new lifeblood. Exhausted or weak brands find this relationship therapeutic. In the car industry, for example, when a brand has insufficient energy itself, it cannot pass any on to its products, while the products are in no position to help themselves if they have non-names such as R5, R9, R19, R21, and R25. These products have to be boosted by their own energy, since the brand is unable to provide sufficient help. This is probably why Renault

turned to an "own-name" policy in 1990 with the appearance of the Clio, Chamade, etc.

7. The final stage refers to the totally autonomous product brand, with no offshoots or affiliations—brands such as Signal, Crest, Persil, Jif, and Sun.

Each of the above policies therefore has its own message and rationale. The choice between these policies depends greatly on the strength of the brand and its will, the strength of its new products, and the force of its commercial strategy.

A narrow relationship exists between the manner in which a firm sees its growth as opposed to seeing its choice of product names. Certain firms have an extensive growth policy in an effort to capture a larger share of the market, while others adopt a more intensive approach. In the first case, they set out to acquire new customers, to which end it is not desirable to present products as part of a range. It is far better to clearly distinguish them with specific names. Procter & Gamble do this with their multiple detergent brands. If, on the other hand, the firm opts for an intensive policy by developing their sales to existing customers, the products are better seen as part of a range. A customer introduced to this little enclave by one product should be tempted to purchase other products in what appears to be a complete range suiting his or her entire needs. Thus Apple calls its software MacWrite, MacPaint, etc.

RETAILER BRAND POLICIES

Nothing better illustrates the wide range of brand policies than a comparison of similar firms competing in the same area. This particularly applies to the retail sector. Faced with the same potential clientele, they opt for different brand policies reflecting their individual identities and strategic preferences.

The retailer brand is not a recent phenomenon. Sainsbury's began it as far back as 1869. The first retailer to officially register its brand in France was the Co-op, in 1929. Retailer brands have typically been umbrella brands, exclusive to the retailer, each covering a number of products within a similar sphere—e.g., groceries, houseware, and cosmetics. The retailers saw these products in an essentially defensive role, a reaction against reluctant manufacturers who were not supplying them.

In 1976, following the example of Carrefour, a new type of retailer brand known as "banner" brand began to make its appearance. The banner brand is itself an umbrella brand, in that it covers a large number of products. It appeared in no-nonsense packaging without artwork or embellishment, and in a single color (white, orange, etc.). It bore no retailer signature—only a guarantee in the visual form of its emblem and initials.

As its name perhaps indicates, the "banner brand" signifies an attacking strategy. Carrefour was thus able to present itself as the consumer's champion, hence the choice of the term "freedom" to name its new product line. Its stance was straightforward: as good as the national brands and cheaper (20 percent cheaper). These banner brands gave the retailers a new sense of emergence, and, for some, the beginnings of an identity. They were getting away from the price–choice–quality–service type of communication and were asserting their culture, motivating force, and basic intent. As the competition became more intense, a whole group of generic and unbranded products appeared on hypermarket shelves. Though admittedly of a lower quality than that of national brands, but 30 to 40 percent cheaper, these products came without frills, often in plain white packaging, bearing nothing but a bare description of the product (e.g., sugar, peanut oil, etc.). This caused a great deal of confusion in the consumer's mind as to the difference between low-priced generic products and banner brands. The problem was that the latter were originally intended to raise the image of the retailer and add a dimension of quality. The confusion threatened to have the reverse effect by dragging the retailer's image down. Carrefour therefore stopped selling its "freedom" line, and launched instead a policy of corporate branding: the store put its own name on many of, if not all, the products it sells.

The retailer-named brand is not new—Sainsbury's, Migros in Switzerland, and Jewel in the U.S. have used it since 'way back.

The fourth form of retailer brand is the "own-brand" or "private label," which has a different name from that of the retailer. St. Michael is the own-brand of Marks & Spencer. Own-labels can be used as a product brand, a line brand, a range brand, or an umbrella brand.

Recent own-labels share one essential difference from their earlier counterparts: in many cases they are product or line brands, designed to capture customers from the market leader, hence the name "counterbrands."

Counterbrands have one essential advantage, in that they are able to multiply at will in the same store. As markets become more and more segmented, the retailer can slip in a counterbrand wherever he wishes, a freedom which would be denied him with his own corporate brand.

The own-label tactic is simple. First, take a major brand to be targeted. Then choose a brand name, type of packaging, outer design, and color which are as close to those of the targeted brand as possible. Pop it on the same shelf, and no one can tell the difference. As a result of its close imitation and reduced price, the own-brand then reaps the fruits of the major brand's investment in research and development, quality performance, and marketing. In fact, the simplest way of reducing costs and risk is to closely imitate the ready-made marketing strategy employed by the successful manufacturer's brand. There is a fine division between counterbrand and counterfeit, and several retailers have overstepped the mark, but the law can do little about this. Moreover, many manufacturers are reluctant to take legal steps on the grounds of unfair competition, for fear of seeing other of their products thrown off the retailers' shelves.

We can thus see that, in spite of a difference in terminology, there is a link between the brand strategies examined in this chapter and the concepts involved in retailer branding (Table 7.2). They are, however, widely separated on two counts. In the first place, counterfeiting being illegal, manufacturers cannot imitate each other as closely as they are copied by retailers' counterbrands. Manufacturers will sue each other at the drop of a hat. Second, except in those rare cases where retailers have direct involvement in the production side, no mention is made of the manufacturer, where retailer brands are concerned.

BREAKDOWNS IN THE BRAND–PRODUCT RELATIONSHIP: A FEW CLASSIC EXAMPLES

Brand–product relationship organization aims at optimally managing the image flows. Sometimes one wants to facilitate the descending flows; from the brand to the products, whenever their sales could be

Table 7.2

Retailers' and manufacturers' brands

	Brand Owner	
Brand's Main Purpose	Manufacturer	Retailer
To capture clientele of a targeted brand		Counterbrand
To personalize the product	Product brand	Own-label
To incorporate the product among others	Line brand Range brand	Own-label
To identify the product source	Umbrella brand Source brand Endorsing brand	(Banner brand) Retailer named brand
To indicate the manufacturer	Corporate branding	

increased by the application of a source-effect. Sometimes one wants to regenerate the brand thanks to a bottom-up image flow. Finally, horizontal flows between the products themselves can be a source of added value and may lead the consumer to try more products.

Not all brand–product architectures actually succeed in achieving their initial goals, however. We now turn to some classic cases of failure.

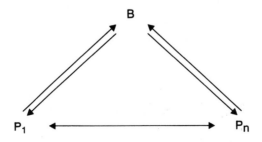

The most frequent case is that of a brand disappearing behind one of its products. Little by little, the parent brand becomes an empty name, lacking in content and substance. This is a real problem when future products were to be named by that parent brand, once strong but now weakened.

This problem arises when one product of the brand's range achieves unforeseen success. The success of Anais-Anais has made Cacharel's identity identical to that of its best product, a perfume for young and romantic girls. Such an identity does not help much in selling ready-to-wear clothes to older women. The same misfortune happened to Nina Ricci, which was shadowed by the image of its best-selling perfume, l'Air du Temps. In the computer industry, although Honeywell left the computer business in 1986, most consumers still think of Honeywell as a computer company. Because it made heavy use of advertising, the branding of the corporate name by the computer division gained much visibility and recall.

The second problem is that of brand–product disconnection. Many will have heard of Varilux, a revolutionary system which has changed the life of many long-sighted persons. But who has heard of Essilor? Not many indeed, throughout the world, despite the fact that Essilor is the number one manufacturer of lenses in the world and Varilux is in fact one of its products. Essilor has no significance as far as the public is concerned. Since it prefers to remain in the background, the Essilor name cannot constitute an endorsing brand. Today Essilor feels powerless faced with the arrival of brands such as Seiko and Nikon. Would you prefer your glasses with Seiko, Nikon, or Essilor lenses? The first two names have already accumulated a worldwide brand awareness founded, in Seiko's case, on the meticulous precision and high technology of its watches, to which Nikon has added mastery in the field of optics.

Brand–product disconnection also affects Corning. Though the company is scarcely known, it owns Pyrex, Vision, and Sunsitive. The public does not think of Pyrex as a brand, but as a type of ware. Again, since they are not formally associated with Corning, they do not contribute to the Corning name. The Corning image therefore is not nurtured by its best-selling products and cannot act as an endorsement brand on other products. The company may well be strong, but the Corning brand is not.

Many brands make a systematic and excessive use of product names, creating a brand name for each of their products. It certainly endows them with a precise identity and fosters their sales in the specific segment they are aimed at. However, all these names create a screen between the brand itself and the consumers: its meaning does not get through. From parent brand or source brand they become a mere endorsing brand, rather empty of values and core identity.

This is why all brands should choose specific products which they will sign alone, directly. These products must be those close to the core of the brand, the mirror of its identity, the vector of its values. The farther products are from the brand core, the more they will need a specific brand name, thus a double branding. For instance, perfumes such as Diorissimo, Miss Dior, and Diorella are close to the core Dior values, as their names indicate. To compete against Opium by Yves Saint Laurent, Dior had to create Poison, whose name is intended to convey specific meanings which are not the salient Dior values.

Kellogg's alternates its product-naming policy. Kellogg's directly signs health and nature products. Close to the core, they receive no brand name but are called by their generic name. The only brand is Kellogg's (e.g., Kellogg's All-Bran, Kellogg's Corn Flakes, etc.). As such they reveal what Kellogg's is. All products which are less health-oriented, with more fun and gimmicks (e.g., Choco Pops, Frosties) receive double branding.

As a rule, all brands should lay down their "brand map," i.e., the map of the organization, distance, and role of their products around them. The brand map views the brand–product relationship as a planetary system, the brand being at the center and the products being close or remote planets.

The more remote a product, the more it should rely on its own identity and strength. Being far from the brand's core project (or genetic program), it is autonomous and may have its own style and language. Products which directly express the brand's project or program, on the other hand, should obey the stylistic guidelines of the brand. As such, the brand map defines the rules for managing all the products of the brands.

Another classic problem arising within brand–product relationships is that of range disruption or breakage. In the case of a range brand, the products of the range must work in synergy and complementarity to fulfill the brand mission. It often happens that many products in a

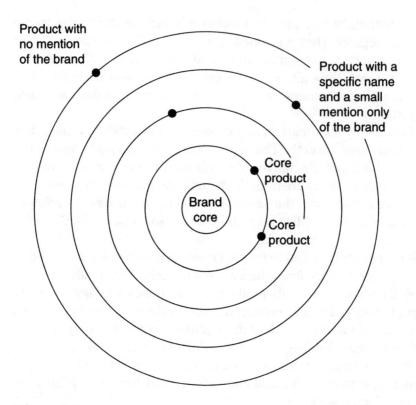

Figure 7.9

A "brand map" visual layout of brand–product relationships, distances, and structure

range have their separate lives, unexpected and even contradictory. A typical case is that of Johnnie Walker. This famous brand had seen its image deteriorate steadily since 1975. It was a range brand with two strong products: red-label whisky and a black-label whisky. Unfortunately, the black label had become a brand in itself and was living alone, with almost no reference to Johnnie Walker. This drift had been created, or at least encouraged, by the removal of the Johnnie Walker symbol from the bottle of the Black Label, and the dominance of the Black Label name over the brand name Johnnie Walker (unlike the red label, whereon the Johnnie Walker brand graphically dominated).

Unfortunately, at the same time the Red Label, now the pivotal product of the brand, was becoming the prototype of cheap, discounted whisky. Heavy sales promotion and rebates had killed its status. As a consequence, the Johnnie Walker brand was losing its equity. It was "covering" two products which were too different in status—a classic case of vertical disruption of the brand: a brand suffers when it signs both a basic, low-priced product and a top-class, premium-priced product. In any case, the Black Label was now detached and could no longer contribute to the brand with its positive image.

To reposition the brand, a range had to be recreated. This meant:

- Establishing a new equilibrium between the Johnnie Walker name and the Black Label name on the bottle itself. The brand was made to dominate again, as it did on the Red Label bottle.
- The introduction of new products in the range, beyond the Black Label: the 15 years Gold Label and the Premier.
- A real federating role for the Johnnie Walker symbol. The walking man is now prominent at the bottom of all bottles, the upper part of the bottle receiving a royal emblem or seal.

The final breakdown of a brand–product relationship can arise through the insistence on certain accounting methods, which sometimes conflicts with the processes of brand reasoning. This is illustrated in the case of Playtex. The Playtex communication architecture consists in theory of constructing the brand's meaning by way of its products. The brand relies on specific product lines such as Cross Your Heart and Super Look bras, together with 18 Hour girdles, etc. The idea was that by communicating along these lines, Playtex would acquire its own meaning in the eyes of its customers (as indicated in Figure 7.10(a)) and that individual lines could then be supported without advertising. Reality, however, is another matter, and the intended plan did not materialize. Making each product line financially accountable leads to communication on only one or two lines. The Playtex identity no longer enjoyed the rich benefits of its entire product range, and was supported only by the specific characteristics of those lines which were advertised (in this instance, only Cross Your Heart). In this way, Playtex acquired a harsh, functional connotation (associated with the Cross Your Heart positioning).

Moreover, since the other product lines did not receive any advertising, they inherited the same overall image—not from Playtex itself but from Cross Your Heart. The practice of self-accountability not

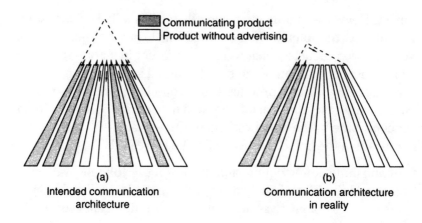

Figure 7.10

A classic effect of accounting procedures

only causes the brand meaning to be suppressed but also allows it to be overshadowed by the image of those few products which are capable of generating the financial resources necessary for communication. In order to extricate itself, Playtex Europe overturned a taboo in company policy by launching specific brand campaigns to make it more attractive and up-to-date.

8

The Brand Portfolio

The question of how many brands to retain per market is of interest to every senior marketing professional. The fact is that most firms find themselves loaded with a bulging portfolio of brands of every shape and size, most of which are legacies of the past. As firms have grown, they have naturally tended to create new brands each time they wished to penetrate new segments or retail channels without at the same time hurting their position among the former ones. Again, company mergers and takeovers have brought with them the usual job lot of brands which management was reluctant to throw out or merge with others. Brand portfolios have grown and grown.

Times have changed, however, and today's call is for a rapid slimming-down. Given the cost of supporting a brand, any attempt to finance too many would create a scattered effect and prohibit the rise of any singular brand. A brand's purpose is not simply to put its name on a product, but to acquire a significance, which must be communicated. Since communication expenditures are soaring in all sectors, to achieve a significant share of voice has become more and more expensive.

Mergers have led to a reduction in the number of retailers, and sometimes even a suppression of certain retail channels and small businesses. Brands which previously sold through specialized channels of distribution may end up being handled by a single wholesaler or purchasing group. The concentration of distribution leads to mega-retailers able to invest proportionately far greater sums on their own advertising than those spent on individual brands. In addition, most retailers have created their own private label or own-brands. If shelf space is restricted, these own-brands will further reduce the space allowed to other brands—another factor pointing to a necessary reduction in the number of manufacturers' brands.

Production methods have also become concentrated. The importance of productivity factors and competitive costs on the international scene has led to regrouping of factories, production units, and research and development activity. There is little justification in expansive brand portfolios when the products, however varied, come from the same factories.

Consumers still have the last say. One of the features they find most irritating is the confusion caused by too many brands, particularly when one considers that one of a brand's normal aims is to segment and structure the market. Too many dummy brands were created in the sixties and seventies, selling the same product under different guises.

On this point, it seems a topsy-turvy world when, at the very moment manufacturers are cutting out imitative brands in order to clarify the market, retailer brands are going in the reverse direction, selling their own-label products, often from a common supplier.

The last, but by no means least, point concerns brand internationalization. In many areas today, national barriers have lost their meaning. Class, lifestyle, and expectations are no longer exclusive to a single country but must relate to a European or world plane. The luxury trade has long been targeted at the world market, as indeed has most major industry. Not all brands are suited to the international arena, however. The investment required in establishing a significant presence at global level requires firms to retain only a small number of brands to enable a multibrand approach—or just a single one for a monobrand strategy such as that of Philips, Siemens, IBM, or Alcatel.

How many brands, therefore, should, be carried? It is obvious at this stage that there exists no magic formula or number. A major determining factor is the strategic role and status of individual brands. In keeping just a single brand, we are assuming that it is able to act as an umbrella brand in the intended market. For decades, the Philips name covered both brown and white products, but they got rid of the latter in 1988, selling them to the American company Whirlpool. Taking the opposite approach, an increase in the number of brands is more conducive to a product-brand or even range-brand strategy. Before deciding on the number of brands, there is therefore a need to analyze the brand's purpose in a particular market. Every market can be segmented by product, customer expectation, or type of clientele. Nevertheless, a market divided into six sections, for example, does not necessarily call for six brands. This depends on their function— will they be endorsing brands, or umbrella, source, or product brands? It is also influenced by long-term corporate objectives and intensity of competition. For instance, small and medium-sized companies may decide to support fewer brands than normally considered necessary. In so doing they are able to remain family-owned; otherwise, they would be obliged to look for the financial support of a larger company. The appropriate number of brands results from a multistage, multicriteria decision process, whereby various scenarios are evaluated. The hotel activities of the Wagons–Lits International Company provide a good example.

BRAND PORTFOLIOS AND MARKET SEGMENTATION

In 1988, the Wagons–Lits International Company drew the following conclusions on the international status of their three hotel chains.

- Since these chains were the result of purchases, there was considerable crossover among all three. Far from defining separate areas of activity, the brands overlapped.
- There was too much variance within individual brands. PLM, for example, ranged from bush stopovers in Africa to the St. Jacques hotel in Paris.
- Frantel was scarcely known outside of France. The name gave a vision of France—fine from a gastronomic point of view, but not so good where hotel service was concerned.
- Etap had made its mark in Turkey and was well-known in Hol-

land. In France, they were looked on as a two-star hotel, or a motel.

The company decided to rationalized their brands and to launch a chain of prestige international hotels located in capital cities, with four-star status just below that of the Hilton or Sheraton. This created a dual problem. On the one hand they had to determine the number of brands needed to cover the three- or four-star hotel market on an international level. They also had to choose names which would tie in with their present portfolio. In the hotel world—particularly at the international level—reputation is gauged on quantity. A brand must therefore cover a respectable number of hotels—in itself an argument favoring a reduction in the number of brands. Commercial and advertising costs discourage multiplicity of brands. Bearing in mind the presence of two different categories of traveller—business and leisure—there were eight possible brand patterns for Wagons–Lits to adopt (see Figure 8.1): a single brand (1), four brands (2), two patterns with two brands (3 and 5), two with two brands and a qualifier (4 and 6) and two patterns with three brands (7 and 8).

A primary concern when creating a new luxury chain is to avoid risk or any false step which might slow the gradual progress toward a powerful overall image. While Hilton, with no competition, can put its name on both business and leisure hotels, Wagons–Lits International had to avoid this during the early years of the new chain's existence. They could keep a close watch on things in Vienna, London, and Prague, but Nouakchott, Dakar, and Lagos were a little out of reach. They had to begin with a level of service which they were able to maintain.

They also had to be certain that the prestige chain would remain credible if its name was used for the three-star level also, by using a special qualification (X Comfort, for example). After all, Holiday Inn covers a wide variety of specifications, too. To cope with any vagueness in the expected service, they add product names such as Holiday Inn Express, when the hotel does not provide the full-service facilities, or Garden Court for full-service hotels at a value price. Any risk of association with the lowest level had to be excluded for a new international prestige name in its early infancy. The X name should only cover those few hotels offering a standard expected by senior management types on flying business visits.

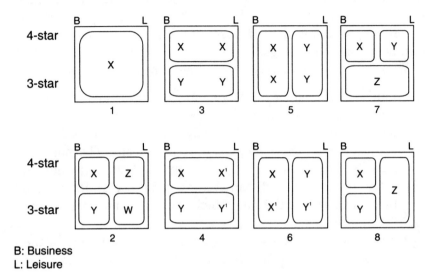

B: Business
L: Leisure

Figure 8.1

Options for a brand portfolio in the hotel industry

In targeting this type of clientele, the brand must be carefully defined. It becomes a product brand associated with a very precise level of service. On a two-day stay in Ankara or Munich, the guest expects minimal problems and has to be certain of finding all he requires (24-hour service, air conditioning, information desk, etc.). All these features are identified in the brand, which is the only source of information for the consumer. There should be no deviation from one hotel to another. On the other hand, there can be individual variations in the surroundings, to avoid a monotonous repetition of identical hotel layouts in every city. This could lead to the X name being supported by a suffix indicating some personal touch in line with the city.

The holiday guest is a different situation. His information is gained from brochures giving every hotel detail. The brand name therefore has a less pronounced role than previously. In this case the guest wants to languish away from it all. The hotel needs an evocative name to add to the appeal of its photographs (e.g., the Oriental, the Saint-Tropez Beach). Is there a need for a common brand name—or even several—for the holiday segment? In this case, the brand is only needed as a guarantee of quality and efficiency. It simply indicates that the hotel is under its control. Here the brand has only an endorsing function, and as such could support hotels of different types. Such differences would no longer pose a problem, since they are to be clearly seen in the catalogs.

With these considerations in mind, the company chose pattern 8:

- Pullman as brand for the new up-market chain, limited to business hotels. There are a few possible exceptions, as in the instance of a leisure hotel already recognized for its de luxe standard (e.g., the Hotel Cataract in Aswan). The nominal identity takes the form X-p, the suffix p indicating the hotel's actual name (e.g., Pullman–Astoria in Brussels). Pullman is the leader name, the one which gives the information and does the selling.
- A second brand, endorsing the vast range of hotels in the Caribbean, Morocco, and North Africa. Each of these hotels is known by an evocative name, followed by the endorsing brand.
- A third brand designating a three-star business hotel in a regional metropolis.

To manage this brand reorganization, the Wagons–Lits International Company changed the brand name in every hotel on the same day— 25 March 1987. A transitional program was devised to preserve the reputation of the Etap brand in Turkey.

This case illustrates certain guidelines in deciding brand numbers. The first applies to market segmentation. It demonstrates that there is no strict parallelism between product policy and brand policy. Products can be present in a variety of sectors without the need for as many brands. There is one Coke for many product segments.

MULTIBRAND STRATEGY

At the beginning of this chapter, we looked at the practical reasons why the number of brands should be reduced, even sometimes to a single brand. They all indicate a company strategy whereby costs should be allocated where they will gain the greatest competitive advantage. While recognizing market segmentation, it has been decided not to relate them to the brand itself, but to consider them only in product terms.

Multibrand entry is based on a process of differentiation. As such it removes the dominance of the cost factor in view of reduced production levels, technical specialization, and specific sales networks and advertising investment. Nevertheless, with the exception of exclusive luxury brands, price is a controlling factor where competition is concerned. In order to take advantage of further productivity gains, there is a reluctance to upset the production chain in the cause of differentiation until the last possible moment, thus exploiting the benefits of the experience curve.

With the apparent advantages of the monobrand policy, what necessitates a market presence supported by several brands? In the first place, market development. No single brand can develop a market on its own. Even if it forms the sole presence at the outset, once the brand has created the market, its development passes into the hands of other participants. The collective presence of a number of contributors helps to promote such a market. Differences apart, their combined advertising accentuates the common advantages of the product category. This is why certain markets do not develop. A multiple presence is necessary to support the market as a whole. It would not be in Philips' interest to see the other electric-razor manufacturers disappear. Taking the market in its entirety, this would bring about a decrease in the number of messages vaunting the merits of electric razors, which could only be to the benefit of Gillette and Wilkinson Sword. Whatever brands Philips may acquire, they are well advised to make an active contribution to the overall market in order to maintain them as brands. In the pharmaceutical industry, a laboratory discovering a new formula could profit from joint marketing with other laboratories in order to accelerate its impact. An example of this is found in the case of aspartame. This classical practice is called co-marketing.

Multiple brands allow for optimum market coverage. No single brand can cover a market on its own. As the market matures, consumer needs diverge and the market becomes segmented. Just as an adjective cannot signify two qualities at once, a brand cannot satisfy several different aims without running the risk of losing its own meaning. This is why Holiday Inn had to create product brands, each one corresponding to a segment of the middle market. On the other hand, purchasers and retailers themselves present an obstacle to further brand ascendancy. This dual process is illustrated by the case of Rossignol. The company, Skis Rossignol, follows a dual-brand policy:

- A monobrand multiproduct policy under the Rossignol name. This is how Rossignol is able to put its name on skis, ski suits, and also ski boots—formerly under the little-known Le Trappeur brand, which they bought and renamed.
- A multibrand monoproduct policy, with the Dynastar name on skis, Kerma on sticks, and Lange covering boots.

Rossignol is the world's leading ski manufacturer, with 20 percent of the market. Their share in the up-market ski sector is thought to be even greater—on the order of 40 percent or more. This is the area where they should not offend people's susceptibilities by expecting them to dress from head to toe in Rossignol products. If the world leader wants to grow even bigger, it is for him rather than for his competitors to open up the choice. In this particular market, the retail side is still handled by a large number of small independents. They fear the rise of a single retailer supplying everything—sticks, skis, boots, and ski pants. This is why each company brand has its own sales force. The Rossignol company has established a presence in the United States with two separate companies, Dynastar Inc. and Rossignol Inc.

Multiple brands offer a tactical flexibility which allows limitation of a competitor's extension possibilities. Delsey, the leading European luggage manufacturer, caught Samsonite in a pincer movement by creating another brand, Visa. Not only did it vie with Samsonite on price, but Delsey was able to restrain Samsonite's aspirations toward the up-market area.

Multiple brands are essential to defend a main brand against price war. Launching of a flanker brand allows a rapid counterattack on price from this small brand to exhaust the brand which started the price war. Meanwhile, the brand leader's margins are not decreased. The brand leader being responsible for the profitability of the whole product category, it must be preserved. Once decreased, the unit margins cannot increase: the retailers would refuse it.

Multiple brands are a must when it is necessary to protect the main-brand image—a major brand should not be put at risk by linking it with an innovation which is not guaranteed to succeed. This policy of defending the brand's equity partly explains why the Disney Corp. uses a number of brands in film production—e.g., Buena Vista and

Touchstone—to allow them to produce films of every type without the risk of damaging the revered Disney name.

The retail system also has a bearing on brand multiplicity. Each form of retail outlet has its own particular purpose, and is geared to a clientele who shop there simply because they do not wish to go elsewhere. Those who frequent specialist suppliers do so because the atmosphere is in keeping with their self-image, unlike that of larger stores. These retail channels are also identified by the products specific to each. Each brand will be positioned on different markets and distribution channels.

Finally, international brands are sometimes required to have their local counterpart, as a result of political or cultural sensitivity. This is a common feature in industry. Thus, the electric equipment leader Merlin–Gerin kept the famous brand name Yorkshire Switchgear after it bought that company. Maintaining the name allows Merlin–Gerin to capture more than 40 or 50 percent of market share in the U.K. Similarly, Facom bought and maintained Britool in the U.K., SK in the U.S., and USAG in Italy.

MULTIBRAND LIMITATIONS

A multibrand portfolio has no meaning unless, in the long term, the brands have their own territory. This does not always happen. Admittedly, if one digs deep into any collection of related brands, the odd difference in image will always emerge, but this alone does not justify a hodgepodge of brands. Each brand must have its own meaning. This calls for a disciplined approach in handing out to collective brands innovations among the brands of the same firm.

A multibrand policy has its own set path. The meaning of each brand should automatically pass to the ranges it covers and to the innovations which it promotes. If an innovation is conferred on every brand, the brand most capable of exploiting it will not have the resources to profit from it, since the innovation itself is shared by many. It is also illusory to think that an innovation will suit any brand whatsoever. Certain innovations are meant to be served by certain brands. Weak brands are not credible enough to market strong innovations. A further point is that the retailer does not take full ranges, but only selects part. The manufacturer therefore has only to look in the store to see which brand is selected to represent the innovation. To a manufacturer, conducting a brand policy means making this selection himself by awarding the innovation voluntarily on the merits of individual brand meaning.

The second constraint is linked with cost management. Even though multibrand reasoning is not directed principally at competitive price structure but at better adaptation to specific market needs, the price factor still acts as a general pointer. Productivity research is a constant necessity. To achieve the maximum overall saving, in spite of brand differences, manufacturers incorporate identical features in their brands as far as is desirable. "Desirable" is preferable to "possible" in this respect. There have been too many dummy brands which have differed only in terms of their outer packaging, destroying the notion of clear-cut brand confidence. Similarity between products should not reach the point where it endangers the perceived difference among brands. The car example confirms this.

The Peugeot Group decided that the market would be better covered by two brands. Not all motorists tending toward a specific price category have the same motivation, personality, or style. The Peugeot Group offers two brands with totally differing ideologies—Citroën and Peugeot. Nevertheless, they incorporate many common parts in an effort to hold down manufacturing costs and peg prices, while still allowing specialization.

While the Peugeot Group sells two full ranges of cars, VAG on the other hand handles three specialist makes—Seat, Volkswagen, and Audi—each at different points in the range. Peugeot's reasoning was that you can only cover the complete possible range by using two brands. In fact, to encompass every segment from the bottom of the range to the top necessitates cars having variations from one segment to another. This limits the inclusion of common parts and also overall saving. They therefore needed a larger number of cars in each segment, which they could only obtain with at least two brands. In fact, the Peugeot Group started with three brands—Citroën, Peugeot, and Talbot, the last of which was later abandoned.

Marketing processes impose a third constraint on a multibrand portfolio. The public must be made aware of the meaning of each brand by means of permanent advertising investments. This requires a long-term communication budget for each brand—which, in certain sectors, may be prohibitive or beyond a firm's means (if it wants to avoid being acquired or merged).

Major retailers do not suffer these constraints. Answerable to no one, they have no need to pay to achieve placement in their stores or on their shelves. Their private brands profit from the company endorsement, either explicitly on the packaging or as implied by the reputation of the store. Finally, since these often are tactical counterbrands, territorial bounds do not exist. The packaging and content of each counterbrand will have already been defined by the manufacturer-named brand. All that has to be done is to copy as closely as possible, and to hijack the customer with a cloned version of a known brand (Brodbeck and Mongibeaux, 1990). It is an effective ploy—detailed studies reveal high levels of confusion. For instance, when a Fortini bottle was shown to them, 42 percent of those questioned declared that they had seen the Martini bottle (Kapferer, Thoenig, *et al.*, 1992).

THE CASE OF RETAILERS' BRANDS

It is possible to apply the same concepts, criteria, and methods relating to brands, to the question of the number of store names which one multiple retailer should manage. There is, however, an associated problem to be considered—the size of individual stores. It is difficult for a single retailer to cover outlets in varying sizes. This is because the store name is associated more with a service than a product offer. The retailer does not set out to offer products, but to promise a service including products. The same service cannot, however, be provided in varying localities—in the center of the town and on its outskirts, for example, or in small stores and in large stores.

To maximize synergy, the retailer known as Casino uses its single name on a wide range of stores from the town-center minimarket to the outlying super-market. For logistical reasons (transport, split delivery, etc.), Casino minimarkets are necessarily costlier than the hypermarkets. This inevitably leads to the overall impression that Casino stores are pricey—a notion which is detrimental to their hypermarkets. Carrefour was well aware of the problem; their town-center stores are called Ed.

A large DIY retailer would be taking a risk if it applied its name to small town-center stores. They would be unable to provide the same comprehensive selection normally found in the larger stores. They would lack the range and depth of choice, advisory service, clear display and opportunity to browse—not to mention the favorable price—available in a less central location.

MERGING TWO BRANDS

We are now in an era of brand mergers. In the UK, Munchies became Brekkies in 1988; Mr. Dog became Cesar in 1989. In the USA, Kalkan Cat Food and Grave merged into the new Whiskas; Kalkan dog food and Mealtime became Pedigree; etc. Company takeovers and mergers have long been a fact of life, but not so with brands. Everyone is seeking to rationalize his brand portfolio. With an eye to satisfying the specific requirements of different countries, multinational firms have until now developed varying policies accompanied by different brands. Shell's oil is named Helix in the U.K., the Netherlands, and Italy, but Power 5 or Power 7 in France. Johnson markets the same product under the name Pledge in Great Britain, Pliz in France, and Pronto in Italy and Switzerland.

Brand mergers also result from the sale of a company. Whirlpool, who took control of the Philips white products, was allowed to use the Philips name for a maximum of ten years, but with a royalty rate increasing in time to make that period shorter. Whirlpool has little time to make the consumer and the retailer accustomed to this new brand.

The difficulty arises since, when a brand has a true meaning, a brand change is, to a certain extent, a change in meaning. This is most pertinent in the case of service brands. When a restaurant displays the sign "Under New Management," do we take this in the managerial sense (i.e., a change of owner) or in the type of management (i.e., change of approach and level of service)? Certain brand changes can get away without loss of customers, while others result in a partial loss of the market due to a change in attitude on the part of the consumer, or even the retailer. It is therefore important to distinguish two levels in managing such a transition. The first concerns its direct application to products and brand, while the second concerns business-to-business relationships, trade goodwill, and commercial negotiations. The General Electric/Black & Decker and

Chambourcy/La Roche-aux-Fées examples illustrate the process of brand change.

In April 1984, the Black & Decker Manufacturing Company bought the entire small domestic-appliance division of General Electric for $300m. At that time, General Electric was not only the market leader, but a well-known name going back many years—almost an American cultural institution. In buying the GE electrical-appliance division, Black & Decker realized the dream of every market competitor—the elimination of No. 1. General Electric sold because the division no longer held any strategic interest and did little for their corporate image. From Black & Decker's point of view, having seen its cordless vacuum cleaner take off, this presented a good opportunity to branch out beyond electrical tools, taking in equipment in general, including small domestic electrical appliances.

Black & Decker found themselves with a range of 150 products under the General Electric brand. However, time was not on their side—the company could use the GE name only until 1 April 1987. The brand merger had to be completed within three years. In this short time, they had to:

- Establish a new positioning and a new identity for Black and Decker.
- Keep all of General Electric's former customers.
- Retain the brand's capital assets in its initial lifeblood area—electrical tools.

This posed several fundamental questions from an operational point of view:

- What name would be used to replace GE? Should the Black & Decker brand—which had been very specialized until then—be extended, or should it be protected by launching a new brand?
- What should be done about the inherited General Electric image and reputation during the three-year transition period? Should it be given prominence, or pushed into the background?
- What timetable should be followed to allow transition within the appointed period?

- Should they make an immediate clean break, or proceed in gradual stages?
- With 150 products to handle, should the brand be changed for the whole lot simultaneously, one category at a time, or product-by-product?

To avoid losing the equity gained through the GE name, and to eliminate any confusion in customers' minds, Black & Decker decided to hasten the process by finalizing the entire transition in less than three years. The Black & Decker brand was retained for domestic electrical appliances. It was felt that the name already enjoyed a wide reputation and that its image was as strong as that of GE on two counts—quality and reliability. On the other hand, Black & Decker was not considered as innovative as General Electric.

A $1 million far-ranging advertising plan was immediately effected in order to establish the brand's awareness in this new segment, and thus to transfer its positioning. The Black & Decker Manufacturing Company became the Black & Decker Corporation. Its brand slogan was "Ideas that work"—enhancing its image as an innovative force both outside and inside the home.

As for the products, each underwent the name-change in a total of 140 stages, using phased planning. The first wave of brand mergers affected:

- GE products which had a real edge over the competition, together with new products
- products which did not rely too heavily on the brand—those where a brand name did not make all that much difference. (For example, similar products were sometimes featured on separate television commercials, the one under the GE name, the other Black & Decker)
- products with their own name, thus their own identity, under the egis of a product or range brand. (Here the General Electric name had only acted as an endorsement. Thus the new advertisement featuring the Spacemaker range ended with the words "Spacemaker, now by Black & Decker.")

The second wave of brand mergers dealt with those products where the brand was of real significance. For example, the name of General

Electric irons had passed down from mother to daughter. The strength of their reputation could not be ignored, and there was no way the Black & Decker brand could be slipped in on the quiet. Thus, while pointing to their new product features, their commercials ended in the qualifying words: "Its predecessors bore the General Electric name. My mother told me not to buy anything unless it was General Electric—this is why I bought Black & Decker."

So, to give credibility to the brand change, the company relied largely on a frontal policy using new products and services.

Black & Decker relaunched practically all the 150 products as though they were new—introducing changes in color and hand-hold, and more major innovations. Furthermore, the company extended the guarantee from the one year offered by General Electric to two years.

Black & Decker was no less vigorous in its approach to the trade. General Electric had always been treated favorably in this respect and had enjoyed regular shelf prominence. In retailers' eyes Black & Decker did not present such a good company image, as a result of their inflexible approach and poor service record. With the competition taking the opportunity to bombard retailers with promotions and special offers, it was vital for Black & Decker to protect their marginal products. They introduced promotional offers on their most threatened lines without, as such, having to concede on price.* In addition, the company launched a "service plus" program whereby retailers who participated in promotional events could see their names appear in the commercials.

The Chambourcy–La Roche-aux-Fées case illustrates the problems arising when two complete ranges merge. In 1985, Nestlé bought out Unilever's European activities in the chilled-foods sector. Nestlé had been synonymous with milk worldwide, but knew little about refrigerated dairy products. The buyout presented a particular problem in France, due to the coexistence of two brands—Chambourcy (Nestlé) and La Roche-aux-Fées (formerly Unilever). They both enjoyed an equal share of the market (11 percent). Like Chambourcy, La Roche-aux-Fées was a range brand. The two brands each covered numerous

---

*In the United States there is a balanced relationship between retailers, manufacturers, and consumers which permits such an approach.

market segments by means of a complete range—99 items in the case of La Roche-aux-Fées and 74 for Chambourcy.

Having considered the capital and potential of these two names, together with that of Nestlé itself, they decided to retain Chambourcy as the sole brand for Europe. Having done this, they had to look to each market segment, choosing a single product instead of the previous two which could represent them without serious loss of tonnage. This involved more detailed questions on name, taste, container format, packaging, and price structure. The difficulty lay in the contrasting regional popularity associated with these two brands. If the 5,000 tons of La Roche-aux-Fées "Bulgarian yogurt" were stopped in favor of Chambourcy's 12,000 tons of "Kremly," it would risk the immediate loss of the 5,000 tons in regions where Kremly was little-known. In fact these were absorbed by competitors' brands: Dannon and Yoplait. Since retailers allocated shelf space on a brand-for-brand basis, some loss could not be prevented if one brand were to disappear. In this particular sector, market share depends vastly on shelf prominence.

Nestlé succeeded in minimizing the loss whenever products that had two names—a product name (e.g., Hippopotamouss) and the brand name, using a fade-in/fade-out process. When a product has its own identity, a change of source brand is made easier. This happened in one segment where Créola from La Roche-aux-Fées and Chamby from Chambourcy had the same output of 6,000 tons each. It was decided to allow the two ranges to run parallel for the time being, allowing a gradual merger which would not alienate consumers who favored one or the other. The process is illustrated in Figure 8.2.

Children who have a preference for either Créola or Chamby associated the product through its name and visual identity—Créola carried the picture of a parrot, and Chamby the faces of two children. They had to fade out Chamby in a gradual manner, first amalgamating its visual identity with that of Créola. To do this they replaced the two children with the parrot. As for Créola, it immediately lost the La Roche-aux-Fées logotype and visual identity symbol, taking on that of Chambourcy, with a transitional reminder of the La Roche-aux-Fées name below. The final product had the original Créola container format, the best recipes (Chambourcy's vanilla, and La Roche-aux-Fées' chocolate and caramel), the more popular name (Créola), the Créola

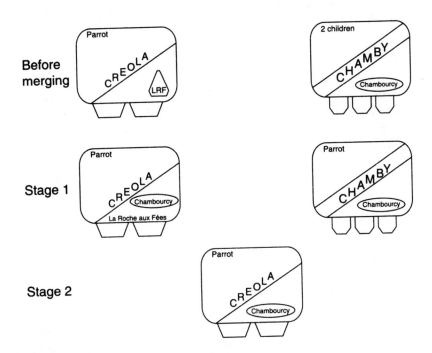

Figure 8.2

Merging of brands and product concepts

design and, of course, the Chambourcy brand. No tonnage was lost in this segment, and, in overall terms, the operation was a success. In spite of the fact that the merging of these two ranges led to the loss of a third of the units—from the total of 173 for the two ranges combined, to 111 at the end—the company lost only 13 percent of its volume in 1986, which it regained the following year.

The Black & Decker and Chambourcy cases illustrate two different approaches to undertaking brand change. There are others, some of which we might now investigate. As we have already seen, the key determining factor is the number of brand levels. Brands which operate with multiple branding (product name and brand name) are more flexible and can be dealt with in a more straightforward manner. In the case of two-tiered brands (endorsing brand and source brand), the normal procedure is to simply replace one with the other, without any transition process. The product name remains the same—this happens when well-known individual hotels are sold by one group to another:

$$Ax \longrightarrow Ay$$

The Créola and Chamby example illustrates a fade-in/fade-out process making use of the different symbols which go to make up the brand—name, logotype, and visual emblem. The process could be denoted thus:

A   A   A
x   →   (x)   →   (y)
B   B
(y)   (y)

When the French biscuit brand Lu went European, this same fade-in/fade-out process was used in Belgium, where the products were marketed under the endorsing brand De Beukelaer. To smooth the transition to the Lu name, they accustomed the purchaser to these products by way of the Lu logo. Gradual integration of logos, packaging, and color codes is a frequent practice when two industrial brands are to merge. Shell followed this path to standardize its motor-oil brands in Europe.

The third graphic process consists of reversing the order of importance of the two brands. This is what Valéo did when it first appeared, in order to prevent famous names such as Marchal, Cibie, and Ferodo from disappearing.

A → X
x   a

There is a fourth method, whereby each of the brands is given a prefix or suffix. Then, after a period, the brands disappear and only the prefix or suffix is left.

A   A-X
B   B-X
     →   → X
C   C-X
D   D-X

This is how Schlumberger resolved the problem of its myriad unknown brands, giving them the interim name Flonic–Schlumberger, Enertec–Schlumberger, etc. Alcatel is in the process of combining such brands as Telic–Alcatel and Opus–Alcatel before acting as a worldwide single corporate brand. When the Wagons–Lits International Company decided to rename its hotels, it had to hold fire in Turkey, where the Etap name was famous. They therefore prefixed it provisionally with the name of the brand-to-be (e.g., Pullman Etap).

When a brand has only one tier, the transition naturally becomes more apparent. Datsun's move to the Nissan name could not pass unnoticed. One way around this sort of fix is to create an extra brand tier, launching, for example, a new product whose name is precisely that of the future brand.

$$A \longrightarrow \text{A brings out x} \longrightarrow \text{X from A} \longrightarrow X$$

The Mars Corporation took this step when they wished to endow their brands—and more particularly their nominal identity—with a pan-European quality. The brand known in Continental Europe as Pal appears as Pedigree in the UK. In order to gradually do away with Pal, in 1989 the company brought out a new product under the Pal name: Pedigree. The initial campaign was fought under the name Pal Pedigree. A few months later, it changed to Pedigree Pal. A variation consists of making the first brand an endorsing brand for the new product.

$$A \longrightarrow Xa \longrightarrow X$$

Such a variation was used by ICI. This company had bought the leading French paint brand, Valentine; soon it appeared in new packaging as ICI Dulux Valentine. Brand-awareness tracking studies will tell when to drop the Valentine brand.

When an extra brand level is not possible, the classic system of overcoming this is that of dual branding at the same level. For instance, a few months after Whirlpool bought part of the Philips domestic appliance division in 1989, both the products and their advertising campaign bore the dual brand Philips–Whirlpool. Similarly, Siemens–Nixdorf will eventually become Siemens.

$$X \longrightarrow X\text{-}A \longrightarrow A$$

The final and simplest means of bringing about the change is to abruptly substitute one brand with another. This is how, on 28 October 1979, the internal American airline Allegheny, stifled by the local connotations of its name, became USAir. Every reference to its former name—including that on its planes—vanished overnight. In the chemical industry, AKU and KZO became AKZO, a world leader. On 18 September 1989 CGEE Alsthom became Cegelec, just as Sperry and Burroughs had changed to Unisys, and C2II Honeywell Bull had reverted to Bull, retaining the visual symbol of the tree. Soon most Pullman hotels will have been changed to Sofitel, the leading hotel brand of the ACCOR Group, which bought them in 1991. In management terms, the more clear-cut the change, the more it requires advance notice and credibility. Adopting a new name must not simply amount to a change in symbol—the name itself should symbolize the change. This means, for example:

- Warning consumers and retailers in advance. Jour et Nuit coffee did this by indicating on their packets that they were to become Night and Day—assuming the English translation to give the brand a European feel.
- Explaining its internal implications, especially when brand name and company name are identical. If this is not done, negative rumors may suggest that the change has resulted from problems. A new company name does not in itself create a change within the firm, but it can symbolize it and can even accelerate it. Organizing a referendum on the choice of company name is not desirable in case there should be divided opinion.
- Seizing upon the opportunity to announce that the change in name signals a resurgence of the brand. This calls for a campaign involving public relations, press relations and, above all, advertising.
- Reassuring clients, especially in business-to-business marketing, that the men will still be there as before. Maintaining trade goodwill is vital.

Adverse consequences of brand mergers have resulted from the too-rapid disappearance of consumers' recognition cues. The consumer is lost, literally. For instance, in Europe, Treets became M&Ms. This was not simply a name change (as with Raider becoming Twix), but a complete product change. Instead of a monoproduct in a yellow pack, M&Ms came in two packagings with different products. Nothing was similar before and after. To advertise M&Ms as coming from the makers of Treets was insufficient. The shelf recognition was lost, and sales dropped by 20 percent during the first year. Heavy shelf merchandising helped to restore the market share.

In many markets, the best merging process is that of gradual fade-in/fade-out. For instance, many consumers associate their car-oil brand with its specific packaging. If these packagings differ from one country to another, along with the oil name, a gradual habituation is necessary if one wants to retain one's customers in countries where customers do not buy their oil at gas stations, but in supermarkets or general stores.

In Europe, Shell is moving towards a unified packaging and a single name (Helix) for its car-oil line. Country by country, consumers will have to forget their former local name, the former typical colors of each grade, and the recognizable design of their packaging. The process is risky and will take two years.

The only problem with gradual fade-in/fade-out is when it takes too long. The management gets mixed up with double branding (i.e., Pal Pedigree) and looses the feeling of urgency. What was to be a transitory phase becomes a permanent stage. This is why the Mars group changed Raider to Twix in fifteen days, spending two weeks the equivalent of two years of advertising budget.

9

Going International

Geographical extension is built into the brand concept. On it depend the brand's growth and its ability to explore fresh avenues and to sustain its competitive edge in terms of economics of scale and productivity. Given this, marketing directors are no longer preoccupied with the principles involved in international expansion, but with the means by which this can be accomplished. They need to ask themselves:

- Where should we go? Do we traverse the single European market and enter the world arena?
- What balance do we maintain between a global brand which shuns linguistic and national frontiers, and one which makes provision for local requirements?
- What aspects of the brand policy can be adapted to global use, and which must remain more flexible?
- Which brands are destined to have global significance, and which should remain on a national footing?
- How do we condense the present multitude of national brands into a small number of global brands?

Reappraisal of the brand portfolio in this context will cause the necessary demise of a large number of national brands which have their identical counterparts in other countries. Any such transition must be carefully administered, as we have just seen in the preceding chapter.

GEOGRAPHICAL EXPANSION: A NECESSITY

A sound understanding of a brand's functioning leads to a permanent search for new openings. A brand can survive only if the product is kept permanently on its toes. Far from representing a source of unearned income, the brand is an obligation for perpetual endeavor. Customers quickly grow accustomed to the latest in techniques and performance. In order to survive, and to honor its implied contract with the customer, a brand must strive constantly for better performance from the products which it embraces. If Ariel wishes to hold its positioning as a state-of-the-art detergent, it must incorporate every latest chemical innovation and adapt itself to new washing processes in the modern-day household. Apple—the brand which changed the man–computer relationship—cannot rest on its laurels. Having established new standards, it has led IBM, Atari, and Amstrad to achieve new heights themselves.

Research and development are therefore the mainstays in brand achievement. L'Oreal is supported by over 1,000 researchers, and 3M by more than 3,000, while Unilever's R&D division tops 4,000. When an innovation seems promising, considerable financial investment is required before it can reach the production stage. Today it is no longer possible to delay the full effect of an innovation by initially offering it to a minority at a high price, and then gradually extending its market. If the brand is to remain competitive, the innovation must be offered immediately to all, at the lowest possible price. The marginal cost of each progressive feature rises day by day. Industrial investment and research costs must now be set against very low unit margins. Using the awareness and public confidence which it has acquired, the brand provides the firm with access to outlets on an ever-widening scale. Without these, such investments could not be economically justified. The manufacturer's brand opens the way to progress and, at the same time, makes it available for all.

With this in mind, economies of scale provide a competitive lever in that they contribute to a penetration price level. A company designing a car with worldwide market potential in mind has a competitive advantage over the manufacturer who only sets his sights locally. Even though the latter may produce a car which better reflects the tastes of his own country, the difference in price from that of a foreign car suiting global requirements will naturally make even the most patriotic motorist hesitate.

No matter what innovations it achieves, the nationalistic firm has no other way of overcoming the price handicap than to extend its outlets or markets. Geographical extension is an essential condition in the race for survival. It was true in the past—most top-ranking national brands started as regional small brands. It will be true for the future.

To summarize thus far: Globalization particularly affects products by allowing overall savings and rises in the experience curve. The same product can, however, be marketed under different brand names according to country—Ariel in England is Tide in the U.S.A., Cheer in Japan, and Dash in Italy. Ricoh photocopiers are called Savin in the United States, and Nashua in Europe. Each of these brands has acquired a national reputation which in itself commands sustained economic investment in R&D and production. But a global product does not necessarily signify a global brand. The transition from global product to global brand—in other words, to a single symbol—needs further discussion on the subject of economy of symbols.

GLOBAL BRANDS: A SOURCE OF OPPORTUNITIES

In certain market areas, the single brand is a necessity, whereas in many other cases it is a means of exploiting and taking advantage of new opportunities in communication.

The single brand is a necessity whenever the clients themselves are already operating worldwide. Firms using IBM or Bull in London would see no sense in having the same equipment in their Bogota or Kuala Lumpur offices under a different name. The same applies to most technological industries. Caterpillar, Sumitomo, Schlumberger, Technip, and Alcatel are of necessity world brands—quite apart from the fact that they are global enterprises.

It is also necessary to retain a single brand when the brand itself corresponds to the signature or griffe of its individual creator. Take the luxury trade—Pierre Cardin is Pierre Cardin wherever he goes, just as Yves Saint Laurent is Yves Saint Laurent. Their creations are bought throughout the world because the signature bears witness to the values of their creator. Whether or not the creator lives on in body or in spirit does not change the rule: from a single source comes a single name.

These cases apart, the single brand permits a product to adapt to new international opportunities. As tourism develops, for instance, there is a definite advantage to standardization. If Nashua's advertising is seen by American managers traveling in Europe, it will not benefit Savin's brand awareness and reputation in the United States, even though they sell the same products. A traveler from continental Europe visiting Britain might see Pledge advertised on television, without realizing that it is the same as Pliz in France, or Pronto in Italy. If Johnson had adopted a single brand name, its international significance would have gotten through. Many brands acquire further credibility when they prove to have international appeal. This is why, in 1989, Ariel brought out the first advertising commercial featuring testimony from housewives from different European countries.

The more the international media develop, the greater the opportunities they provide for the single brand. This has long been the case with traditional media. For instance, the French-speaking population of Belgium, Switzerland, and North Africa watch French television channels and therefore see French commercials. This has obliged brands with differing marketing mixes in these countries to avoid making use of TV advertising, so as not to pollute one area by the commercials made for another area. Global television channels such as Sky, aimed directly at an international audience, are also on the increase. However, the language factor—particularly where the English are concerned—has resulted in hitherto moderate audience ratings for such channels.

The real opportunities for worldwide coverage are provided by such sporting or cultural events as Euro Disney, the Wimbledon tennis tournament, the America's Cup, the Olympic Games, Formula 1, etc. Through its sponsorship of the Roland Garros tournament, the BNP is known in California, where they speak of the tournament as the "BNP tournament," in just the same way as it is where one hears of the "Volvo Grand Prix." These programs reach a world audience and therefore, in practical terms, exclude on-the-spot local brands, since the costs involved in appealing to only part of the audience would be prohibitive. Movie stars, rock stars, and sports stars are now international. Their endorsement of a brand is financially sounder when the brand name is international.

When a brand goes international, it can further benefit from the international services of certain retailers—brought about either by their own international extension of outlets or by agreements made by them with foreign retailers. Thus the Safeway brand will now be found outside of the U.K., in a number of local foreign stores.

Finally, the single international brand is linked with easing the process of brand extension involving a variety of products. The worldwide single brand allows the firm to capitalize on its name sooner than normal, since the name acquires a wider international presence and awareness, and—if the products or services make an impact—a corresponding reputation. The goodwill thus achieved by the single name on a world scale provides a lever for entering other markets and other areas. This conforms with the typical Japanese approach. They invest in awareness and reputation over the long term and on a global scale, without regard for the short-term effects or for any immediate return on investments in communication. Using one particular sector as a launch pad, they allow this reputation to permeate a public who are not interested in that sector alone.

FROM NATIONAL NAME TO WORLD BRAND

How far do we push the global idea? To what extent do we continue to make marketing decisions on a national level? Should we globalize positionings, creative concepts, and even the products themselves? The fact is that though no one denies that a single name often is an advantage, there is some dispute over the brand strategy to be adopted, together with the form it should take. For some, the essence of marketing policy is to stick close to the markets, while for others, the advantages offered by homogeneous marketing on a global scale leave no alternative.

Before dealing with the respective arguments, it is important to be precise about the terms used. Global marketing implies the wish to extend a single marketing mix to a particular region (e.g., Europe, Asia), or even throughout the world. It also denotes a situation in which a firm's competitive position in one country can be significantly affected by its position in other countries. The global approach sees the role of individual countries as only part of a wider competitive action. Marketing objectives applying to each country are no longer formulated by the resident subsidiary, but are determined in the light of global competition. Thus, whereas national subsidiaries have traditionally planned their activities on the basis of their own resources and the domestic market, when it is a question of a global strategy:

- Certain countries have the task of developing a marketing mix for a new product, testing its capabilities in their home markets before its extension to other countries. This therefore constitutes a test—not of the best marketing mix on single national lines, but of a global marketing mix prior to extension. As a consequence, nowadays it is insufficient to keep an eye on the competition in one country alone—every country should be included.
- Certain countries are assigned to develop a know-how on a particular brand or type of product so that they can act as a precursor and coordinator for others.
- Advertising spending decisions by country will be made at the corporate level. No advertising may be the decision for a brand in Spain, France, and Italy, for instance, in order to increase the brand's budget in Germany and eliminate competition.

In contrast to the global approach, many multinational firms follow a "multilocal" philosophy, preferring to follow specific trends in each country's market. Not only will the same brand differ from one market to the next, both in positioning and in price level, but it will also be supported by its own specific advertising campaign. Coca-Cola follows a global marketing policy, while Nestlé prefers multilocal marketing. Thus Maggi ready-snacks were launched:

- In Germany in 1981, under the name "Maggi, 5-minuten terrine," positioned as a practical nutritious food for men and women between thirty and forty.

- In France under its own name, "Bolino" (with "Maggi" in small print), positioned as an instant snack for the single person.
- In Switzerland under another name, "Quick Lunch," positioned as a quick meal approved by mothers.

In all three countries, the product achieved its sales objectives. Comparisons should therefore not be made between global and multilocal policies in terms of either customer appreciation or sales. However, a company's ultimate aim is not to achieve maximum sales—it seeks profitability.

Global marketing can contribute to this end. In the first place, it cuts out duplicated tasks. For example, instead of bringing out different TV advertising for each country, the firm can use a single film (TV ad) for the region in mind. Bearing in mind the high cost of producing these films, the potential for savings is considerable. The McCann–Erickson agency is proud of the fact that it had saved Coca-Cola $90m in production costs over a period of twenty years, thanks to producing TV ads with world appeal.

By launching a product in several countries simultaneously, one eliminates the problem arising when a new product appears at staggered intervals from one country to the next, depending on the local situation. This has the drawback of allowing competitors time to preempt certain ideas in one country which they have already seen in another. More and more companies favor a "rake" model of international expansion. Procter & Gamble launched Ariel micro all at once in Europe: laundry habits are now close enough between countries. In the past, this was not the case: it took McDonald's 22 years to expand internationally.

Globalization allows a firm to exploit good ideas wherever they come from. Since good ideas are rare, they must be made maximum use of. By getting representatives in several countries to put their minds to a particular question, there is a better chance of coming up with a strong idea which can be used on a global plane. This is how the creative idea, "Put a tiger in your tank," came to be used around the world. The IBM Charlie Chaplin PC campaign originated in Switzerland.

A global policy allows a firm to slip the stranglehold of the major retailer, whose commercial demands are closer to a systematic toll

(Yon, 1989) than to a payment for real services to the producer. A national brand may have few means of extricating itself; such is the intensity of the distribution concentration that it has to use a small number of major retailers in order to reach the consumer. The global brand is fortunately less susceptible to local pressures.

Arguments against globalization point to the specific nature of each market and the differences in the brand's life cycle, depending on the product. In fact, there are plenty of examples of failure resulting from undue haste in adopting a global marketing policy without certain pre-cautions.

For example, in January 1984, Procter & Gamble launched the anti-dandruff shampoo Head and Shoulders in France, relying on exactly the same marketing mix and positioning which had led to its success in the UK and in Holland. At the end of 1989, Head and Shoulders still had only around 1 percent of this market. The problem was that they had not taken sufficient account of a feature peculiar to the French market and not present elsewhere. Consumers either buy antidan-druff shampoos in a chemist's, should they require a course of treat-ment, or they pick up the appropriate variant of their usual brand in the hypermarket (Palmolive antidandruff shampoo, etc.), for quick results. Between these two segments, there is scarcely room for a brand, positioned as a treatment, sold in hypermarkets and much dearer than usual brands' line extensions. The communication mix which had been adopted did not help the situation at all:

- Procter & Gamble had decided not to translate the name, on the evidence that it had been well accepted in Holland as it stood. However, when one considers that, outside the U.K., Holland is the EC country where they speak English best, there is considerable inherent risk in extending a policy tested in Holland to a country such as France. Since Head and Shoul-ders is a descriptive name, it should have been translated to deliver its meaning.
- For its launch, Procter & Gamble used their British film ad showing a face divided in two, whereby one could visualize the results. The punch line was "Dandruff talks behind your back." In France, however, dandruff is seen as a social prob-lem—one should not point the finger, blaming the person, but

sympathize with their problem. The tone adopted in the British approach was perhaps in keeping with Dutch levels of sensitivity, but scarcely applicable to the French.

Head and Shoulders illustrates the harsh realities of different levels of sensitivity and competitive force in the marketplace, both of which make a monolithic global policy a perilous strategy. Difference in life cycle can also bring about failures in over-hasty global policies. Polaroid, for instance, decided to enter the French market using the popular Swinger—the first Polaroid camera sold in the United States for under $20, and introduced in France at less than 100 francs (£10). With a global policy in mind, they used the same advertisements for the Polaroid Swinger as they had adopted in the United States—"The Polaroid system now at only 99 francs!" It was a commercial failure. Though the Polaroid system was already well-known in the United States and in the UK, it was not in France. The Polaroid company should therefore have first set out to educate the public in the finer points of the instant Polaroid system before concentrating on the Swinger's price.

Such reverses do not, as such, amount to a rebuttal of global policy, since we have such universal successes as those of Marlboro, Coca-Cola, and Mars. The idea of global marketing has an inescapable draw, even though its progress has been seen to vary considerably according to the markets, the public, and companies themselves, and in spite of the fact that certain idiosyncratic brands are destined to remain on a local footing. If we look at consumer habits, we can see the reasons for this drawing power and identify the conditions which favor the global brand, together with those which impose limits.

GLOBALIZATION: THE CONSUMER PERSPECTIVE

The global brand results from management reasoning, and not from market demand. Most often the consumer is not looking for a global brand *per se*, but for a particular brand which suits their specific needs. Even when it is global, the brand is purchased on its own merits. The consumer buying Cajoline fabric softener in France is doing so because they prefer it to other brands. It never springs to their mind that there may be a Cajoline in some other country, enjoying the same positioning and promising the same softness, love, and security (as symbolized by its Teddy Bear). The consumer is well aware of its properties and of the brand personality, as are purchasers of Snuggles in the U.K. or the U.S.A. When it is therefore seen that purchasers in several countries appreciate the same qualities and have the same expectations, the opportunity arises for a global brand. People have rightly spoken of "coincidence of globalism," referring to the fact that globalism expresses a corporate view, from above, whereas at the consumer's level, in spite of so-called similar needs, their choice remains individualistic and egocentric (Buzzell and Quelch, 1988).

Examples of the coincidence of globalism are constantly arising in Europe. Studies point to converging lifestyles. There are fewer differences between German and Italian management groups than between management and employees within Italy. Increasing awareness of this feature is apparent in all countries, though to differing extents. We are not yet at the stage of the Euro-consumer, though there is a representative number in every country. It would therefore be preferable to speak of Euro-segments or Euro-types. We could also extend the analysis to North America.

The existence of Euro-segments is not sufficient justification for a global brand policy promoted in each country using the same name, positioning, and advertising material. The competition must be studied at national level—as we saw, Procter & Gamble underestimated the market structure in France, so Head and Shoulders was squeezed out. Apart from this factor, psycholinguistic and cultural differences have a real bearing. From one country to the next, any given symbol does not necessarily have the same symbolism, and vice versa. Language differences are another major obstacle to the use of global names, even within Europe. For instance, in 1991 Glaxo Laboratories produced a revolutionary drug, intending it to be the first worldwide pharmaceutical product. They had, in fact, just finished developing a new formula, known as Sumatriptan, a treatment for migraine attacks—until then still a major medical problem. The international brand name chosen was "Imigran." However, the name had to be slightly changed in France, where there was an outcry among the medical fraternity since immigration was a sensitive subject.

Descriptive names are nonstarters on the international scene, since they lose their meaning and impact in other countries, are sometimes unpronounceable, and smack of importation. Unless you speak English, you get only 50 percent of the meaning of Pampers. Few Europeans can both pronounce Safeguard and understand it. This Procter & Gamble deodorant soap was never a success. Hence the growing preference for nonsemantic names with no implications. It still has to be verified that they have not been previously registered in any country, and the necessary formalities have to be complied with. Even in Europe, this involves an extremely long and costly process. There is no single procedure. It can take more than sixteen months to complete the necessary searches, checks, and registration procedures required in establishing a European brand. At the end of all this, there is still a fair chance of finding that the brand has been registered elsewhere. The concept of an "international brand" is not yet a legal reality.

Depending on the country, ideas must also be expressed in different ways. The consequent paradox of this is that using the same product name from one country to the next does not necessarily imply that the brand's original concept will be transmitted the same in every case. Just as a rooster cries "cock-a-doodle-doo" to an English-sounding ear, while it sounds like "cocorico" to a Frenchman, the idea behind the French Cif cleanser name is better expressed in German as Viss.

You can only change an indigenous name to a global one when the former has no intrinsic meaning which encapsulates the precise concept which the product conveys—otherwise it disrupts the product's basic identity. Variations in name allow a closer adaptation to the consumers in each particular market. This is why Playtex has a variable policy. Although Playtex is a world brand, the company adapts its product names in relation to the market. In fact, all new Playtex products are promoted internationally. Their marketing strategy is standardized in large geographical zones. Thus their "Cross Your Heart" has the same positioning, the same customer advantages, the same advertising theme and execution, in every country. In order to adapt to national requirements, modifications are made in terms of material (for example, they include more cotton in Italy), and packaging (to allow for differences in retail networks). As for the name itself, it is "Coeur Croise" in France and "Crusado Magico" in Spain. In their persistent desire to convey the common concept, Playtex does not hesitate to change its product names where necessary, thus:

- Their line of wireless bras is called "WOW!" in the United States ("without wire"), but "Armagiques" in France.
- Their line of girdles offering lasting comfort is called "18-Hour," which can be translated in any country.
- They call another line of bras "SuperLook," which can remain untranslated in most countries.

Cultural differences in perception are another factor affecting global choice. This is why Procter & Gamble varies the examples of their Mr. Proper liquid detergent effectiveness according to country, while still insisting on its common aim in achieving a brilliant finish. Different cultures have, in fact, different notions of brilliance. In France it is expressed in the idea of a mirror ("You can see yourself in it"), while in the United States the emphasis is on still, humid-looking ground ("Is it water? No, it's the shine!"). Throughout the world, Camay is the soap which implies "seduction." This is the line which Procter & Gamble has always taken. However, though consumer habits and expectations are the same the world over, where soap is concerned, cultural blocs call for different approaches when speaking to a woman of her intimate moments.

- In France, the seductive power was portrayed for a full twenty years by a woman beautifying herself in her bath for her husband, who entered the bathroom at the end of the commercial. However, this scenario caused fury when the advertisement was screened in Japan. There, it is considered an insult for a man to enter the bathroom while his wife is performing her ablutions.
- In Italy, they preferred to show a fawning wife and her macho man.
- The Austrians just use Paris as a backdrop to signify seduction.
- In Greece, they added a more sensual note, bringing on the proverbial vamp.

Flexibility at the creative stage not only satisfies local cultural requirements, but also allows Camay to establish its own status in different countries. In France, Camay heads its market segment, with 10 percent of the whole market. The nucleus of its faithful clientele is made up of fifty- to sixty-year-olds who have been using the soap since their younger days in 1958. The aim is to regain a younger clientele without losing its ever-faithful. The brand has only recently appeared in Greece, and does not have the backing of an identity or a traditional clientele gathered over the years.

Ethnocentrism being what it is, French consumers cannot imagine that Camay's advertising could possibly be different elsewhere. They expect global communication to be a straightforward extension of that depicted in the commercial they see. This imagined global process constitutes an elevation of their own national system of values.

From an operational point of view, although a commercial may be made for a global audience, it should not give the impression of having been "imported." Whether he is sitting in front of his TV set in Munich, Glasgow, or Barcelona, the consumer must be made to feel that the commercial has been specially prepared for him. This is why we are not aware of the global nature of Coca-Cola commercials, whereas Martini's or Kellogg's advertisements seem to have been imported straight from the United States. Having been devised with everyone in mind, they do not manage to involve each consumer.

CONDITIONS FAVORING GLOBAL BRANDS

Certain situations make global brand communication easier. They are either those where the brand impresses its own system of values, or where the brand seeks its own source of inspiration in the collective subconscious of world consumers.

Social and cultural changes provide a favorable platform for global brands. In this environment, part of the market no longer recognizes long-established local values and is seeking new models on which to build its identity. Turning its back on prevailing national values, it is open to outside influence from abroad. In drinking Coca-Cola, we are drinking in the American myth—in other words, the fresh, open, bubbling, young, and dynamic all-American images. Youngsters form a target in search of identity and in need of their own reference points. In an effort to stand out from the rest, they draw their sources of identity from media-personified cultural models. Levi's are linked with a mythical image of breaking away down the long, lonely road— an image part-Dean, part-Kerouac. Benetton takes up the universal desires of youth, turning away from national confines of race and culture. In many countries, women are becoming a more emancipated clientele. Dim could see in the free, independent, and seductive Parisian woman an incentive for its own globalization. Brands which serve new eating habits (e.g., Gayelord Hauser, Mars bars, Kellogg's, Dannon) should forcefully impose their own vision of the world in order to rally consumers in search of change. In this way the brand is seen as a new flag-waver.

New, unexplored sectors have not, by definition, inherited a system of values. Everything is there for the making, and it is the brand's duty to do it. This is why there is nothing to prevent global marketing of high-tech, computer, photographic, electronic, and telecommunication brands. The brands themselves organize and segment these markets. Neither should the service sector lag behind. Hertz, Avis, and Europcar are international names catering for the stereotyped non-stop businessman. These companies operate in the knowledge that an Italian businessman wishes to be identified more as a businessman than as an Italian.

The world has seen a standardization of techniques. Products are no longer manufactured according to national traditions, but form part of an era. They are a materialization of the knowledge of our times, and as such are free from national traditions which hinder global advancement. This is why new products are easier to globalize.

In general terms, globalization is possible—and indeed desirable— in markets where the insistence is on mobility. This applies to the hotel industry, car rentals, airlines, and also the film industry. When the brand is perceived as being international, its authority and expertise are automatically accepted. Again, brands have a clear opportunity to organize and structure those market sectors which symbolize the disappearance of time-and-space constraints.

Products chosen for their "exotic" or "unusual" appeal virtually standardize themselves. Food habits are linked with traditional tastes; linked to old times and a specific territory. However, this is less true where coffee is concerned. It does not specifically belong to any European country, but is seen everywhere as an import. Its collective image reflects the imagined traditions of South America and Africa.

Globalization is therefore possible when the brand is a total cultural stereotype. AEG, Bosch, Siemens, Mercedes, and BMW rest secure in the "Made in Germany" label, which opens up the global market, since the stereotype invoked is a collective symbol breaking national bounds. It conjures a meaning of robust performance in any country. The Barilla name is another stereotype, built on the classic Italian image of tomato sauce, pasta, and a carefree way of life—as Heinz means America, and Uncle Ben's the Deep South.

Finally, certain brands represent archetypes. Snuggles fabric softener not only arouses the same notion in every country—that of gentleness (which is not in itself original)—but also the same image of reliance, love, and security as in one's childhood, as symbolized by the teddy bear. This is why, in order to express the notion of "snuggling, caressing, cajoling," the brand name is translated as Cajoline in France, Kuchelweib in Germany, Yumos in Turkey, Mimosin in Spain, and Cocolino in Italy. La Vache qui Rit, which corresponds to the archetype of the providing mother, is likewise translated (Die Lächende Kuhe, or The Laughing Cow). Marlboro embodies the archetype of the Rousseauist man—alone and protected, yet modernized and popularized worldwide in Western sagas of the conquest of America. Drakkar Noir is machismo wherever you see it. Brands endowed with a potent symbol are easier to globalize. The deep meaning of a shell is the same all around the world: even those who do not speak English will associate the shell brand with its motherlike virtues.

Several of the above factors explain why luxury brands and griffes have gained worldwide appeal. In the first place, they bear a message—each creator is expressing his own personal values. They were not conceived as a result of any market study or consumer analysis from one country to the next. It is the creator's identity and his desire to express his own values which form the automatic basis of the brand's identity, in no matter what part of the world. Secondly, behind every luxury brand there is a guiding standard—sometimes even an archetype. Cacharel and Nina Ricci represent the dawning of femininity, a dawn tinted with shyness and modesty. Yves Saint Laurent stands for female independence, even rebellion. Finally, the "Made in France" label and the myth of Paris imbue these brands with definitive cultural undertones. All these are reasons why such brands are able to impose their own vision of the world on national outlooks. Like any religion, brands which set out to convert must believe in their message and spread it unerringly among the multitude. Nike and Reebok do this, as does Benetton.

BARRIERS TO GLOBALIZATION

These come from two sources—external and internal. We have already examined the difficulties arising from differences in market structure, and their application to individual countries. It must also be accepted that the price of goods sold abroad is rarely that prevailing in their country of origin. This leads to differences in communication, as illustrated in the Perrier approach in Europe and in the United States. The high price per bottle in America—a country scarcely used to paying for water—completely changes the Perrier status compared with that in France.

Moreover, the "Made in France" connotation accentuates the fact that it is an import. The same situation arises with Evian. Barilla is a popular brand in Italy, a medium-range one. Outside Italy, it is becoming the symbol of the best Italian food. Many obstacles to global branding do, however, arise within the company itself. Globalization is a voluntary step. It was Theodore Levitt who said, "I know that the world is round, but from a practical point of view I prefer to think of it as flat" (1983). The global approach tends to concentrate more on similarities of behavior among countries, rather than to exploit their pertinent differences (see Table 9.3). It is therefore understandable why certain companies either favor or reject the global attitude, depending on their backgrounds and internal organization.

As we shall see below, some cultures are predisposed to a headstrong globalizing policy. One-man firms are more easily suited to global marketing, as we see in creators such as the Mars brothers and S. Benetton. Whatever the country, the physical and spiritual message of the brand's father-figure is always the same. We can understand why Mars is a global brand—the Mars family hold complete sway. They are Mars, and all decisions emanate from this one central source. The brand's singular position reflects the singularity of thought in its decision-makers. This was never more apparent than when Treets were replaced by M&Ms. The Mars brothers have in mind to make M&Ms the premier chocolate brand in the world. They disregarded all the arguments concerning Treets' past success, awareness, and value at national market level, in favor of their own resolute desire.

At the other end of the scale, firms whose power lies within their subsidiaries are less capable of brand globalization. The difficulty is that the ideal pursued by a subsidiary company lies in its ability to be self-managing, concentrating on the specific requirements of a particular market territory covered by a wide range of products. The global ideal is opposite—based on expertise in one product and one brand at transnational level. Decentralized organizations rely on their specific, ethnocentric attitude backed by the well-known byword "Not invented here." Such an attitude is above all an automatic means of defense on the part of organizations and does not always reflect reality where individual countries are concerned. In 1987, the Toshiba Corporation asked its French subsidiaries to include the world brand slogan "In touch with tomorrow" in all their communication. The answer came back that, since France was specific, such a slogan may not readily apply. With their expert knowledge of brands, the local advertising agency was asked by Toshiba to come up with other possible brand slogans. In all, around forty slogans were tested. The one which received unanimous acclaim among French dealers, company personnel, and consumers alike was the slogan "Toshiba, l'empreinte de demain." This was, in fact, almost the exact translation of "In touch with tomorrow." The above ethnocentric attitude had therefore revealed the relevance of the worldwide slogan when applied at the national level!

Shaping the Organization

The very least effect of globalization is a change in decision processes and general organizational setup. As shown by the extreme case of Mars, who dispenses with the duties of a local marketing director, the profit-responsible business unit is now a global brand CEO at the regional level (e.g., Europe). Unlike R&D, planning, and finance, marketing was a function hitherto dealt with on a decentralized plane at a country level. In the future course of events, subsidiaries will focus on sales, distribution, product promotion, and local adaptation of brand communication. To counterbalance the negative effects of this situation on the motivation of local managers, firms having global brands develop international personal-career plans. The aim is to dilute the ethnocentric nature of national administration. This is brought about by international recruitment, and relocation from one country to another. There is also a preference for recruiting fresh marketing personnel with no previous marketing training background. The latter trains the individual to focus more on demands and wants of specific consumers than on transnational resemblance. Where budget is concerned, an important part is left to local responsibility in order to maintain professional interest.

What types of international coordination are developing now in Europe? Our 1992 survey indicated that (on the basis of 210 European brands):

- 4 percent had full decentralization of decisions, with little or no coordination between decentralized units, which remained fully autonomous. However, 28 percent of the Japanese brands in the sample fell in this group.
- 45 per cent maintained the autonomy of their subsidiaries but developed some form of coordination by headquarters; 57 percent of the German brands adopted this approach.
- 31 percent adopted an approach whereby all strategic decisions were taken by a European steering committee. This management style is typical of U.S. and U.K. brands (respectively 48.5 percent and 58 percent).
- 6 percent had European decisions made by a lead country.
- 13.5 percent had pan-European brand directors. Local managers still existed but with limited responsibility. There is full central control. This is typically the Mars case.

Global advertising calls for a unique network. It facilitates creative homogeneity, interchange of men and ideas, and consensus of know-how. As for the working procedures, this will vary according to individual companies. In certain cases, every agency is requested to forward a campaign based on a similar strategy. The best are then tested in each country, in order to arrive at a global campaign. This is then either "imposed" or suggested, bearing in mind that a subsidiary can always refuse. As for its realization, it is either centralized—

allowing for maximum saving, as in the case of Coca-Cola—or decentralized. Brands which rely on international stars to convey their message naturally centralize their production. Those using only national figures do not.

Other companies may nominate a single agency in a particular network to be the leading agency. In all cases, globalization requires a basic structure and basic processes of information, persuasion, coordination, and approval. European advertising networks coordinate the managers of each individual brand in multinational teams under a leader. It must not be forgotten that brand globalization is not motivated solely by economic reasons, but seeks to further the best ideas in one country by exploiting them in all the others. The idea of comparing the protein value of Petit Gervais aux Fruits with that of a steak was first hit upon in Brazil and then passed on to Europe. Globalization of brands should not imply a weakening of their original values. In considering the impact of the single market on communication, a large proportion of European brand administrators share this fear—46 percent of managers interviewed in the following study considered that "If campaigns are unified throughout Europe, the best creative ideas are in danger of being lost." A healthy form of global branding seeks the reverse—to promote and spread these ideas and to overcome the "Not invented here" syndrome.

IMPACT OF THE SINGLE EUROPEAN MARKET

We are all expecting the single European market to bring about a number of changes in product and service sectors throughout the EC. What will be their extent, and how are we to prepare for the change? Moreover, what will be the principal effects on brands, marketing, and communication?

This was the subject of the pan-European study carried out in 1990 by this writer and G. Laurent in conjunction with the Lintas network, in which international directors and managers, general managers, and marketing directors of the main European corporations were sampled. Five hundred questionnaires were sent out throughout Europe, including Scandinavia, in English, French, German, Spanish, Finnish, Dutch, or Italian, depending on country. A total of 147 completed questionnaires—just under 30 percent—were returned, testifying to the interest in the subject involved. European managers had been asked to give their views on each of 23 suggestions concerning the probable impact of the Single Market on advertising and brand management. For each suggestion (for example, "1992 will bring about the disappearance of numerous small national brands"), each person replying was asked to indicate:

- if he agreed with the suggestion
- if he was personally concerned for his own company

In what areas did European marketing and advertising managers expect to see changes after 1992? In Table 9.1 we list each of the questions, ordered according to response in decreasing order of anticipated impact from 1992 on. As we have established, in the first place nearly all companies (more than 80 percent) expected to see the emergence of a new environment and a new framework of marketing activities. The greatest changes will affect legal status. Some rulings remind us that many brands will cease to be protected by restrictive national laws which impede the influx of competitors from other European countries. Such legal protection will no longer prevent the entry of foreign brands. Transborder influence will again be made easier, since media coverage regularly overspills political boundaries. According to those questioned, this state of affairs is expected to increase—another reason for rationalization of brand portfolios.

Companies see as a result of the single European market an inevitable standardization of decision-making and communication. Nevertheless, not all aspects of marketing strategy need to be condensed to the same degree. Few denied the near necessity for firms to take on a single corporate identity (86 percent)—no longer should companies change their name from one country to the next. The classic argument whereby industrial enterprises hid their international identity behind a Spanish name in Spain, a German name in Germany, or a French name in France no longer applies. To a lesser degree (78 percent), 1992 should lead to standardization of brand names themselves. It would be incongruous to have Pledge in Britain, Pliz in France, and Pronto in Italy. There was a further feeling (72 percent) that brands would tend to adopt the same positioning in all countries, and that a single packaging format would apply (69 percent). In the long run, this means, for instance, that Johnson's Pouss Mouss liquid soap cannot retain its positioning aimed at children in France while,

Table 9.1

Impact of the single European market (Basis: N = 147)

Do you expect to see (certainly or probably):	
1 A single "corporate" identity for your company throughout Europe	86%
2 A legal structure whereby anything permitted in the country of origin will be permitted in all other EC countries	85%
3 The establishment of numerous new pan-European regulations in your sector	83%
4 Increase in media "overlap" between neighboring countries	82%
5 A single brand name for your products throughout Europe	78%
6 A tendency toward unified product positioning throughout Europe	72%
7 A need to invest more in advertising, to maintain one's appropriate share of voice	70%
8 Standardized multilingual packaging and labels for your products throughout Europe	69%
9 Standardization of advertising campaigns through-out Europe	65%
10 Centralized production of TV advertisements	64%
11 Many more competitive brands per country in your market sector	64%
12 Extra competition reducing profitability and in-creasing expenses in marketing your brands	64%
13 Advertising agencies ready to face the new pano-rama in 1993	62%
14 The disappearance of numerous small national brands	60%

Table 9.1 (*continued*)

Impact of the single European market (Basis: N = 147)

Do you expect to see (certainly or probably):	
15 An increase in promotional activities (sales promotions and retail subsidies)	60%
16 Centralized media space purchasing for the whole of Europe	60%
17 A single European department within your company to approve advertising creation	60%
18 Retailers engaged in cross-border import of your brands outside your control	56%
19 Changes in your company organization as a result of 1992	54%
20 A single agency, in a given country, developing the entire European campaign	52%
21 A single advertising network for each of your brands throughout Europe	51%
22 Greater benefits for your company in the medium term, with the opening of the European market	50%
23 Good creative ideas in danger of being lost if campaigns are unified throughout Europe	46%

Source: Pan European Survey, Lintas-Kapferer-Laurent, 1992

named Douss Douss, it is targeted at women in Italy. Likewise, Camay's positioning in the UK—soft to the skin—should move more in line with its global positioning of seduction. This is a further argument in favor of universal advertising campaigns throughout Europe (65 percent). While we can therefore determine a trend toward standardization, it should not eliminate the ability to adapt to each country as companies begin to feel their feet.

There was a general feeling that competition would intensify—that it would require a greater financial outlay to make one's voice heard (70 percent). The advent of new brands (64 percent), was expected to reduce the profitability of certain others (64 percent). This could prove fatal for small national brands (60 percent), and could bring about a fierce territorial battle, fought with sweeteners to retailers and consumers alike (60 percent). It is understandable why only half the companies questioned were optimistic that the European market would bring greater benefits. We shall nevertheless see in a moment that the pessimistic view is held mainly in particular countries.

To a lesser degree, the single market should influence the logistical approach. Probabilities which spring to mind are centralized production of TV commercials (64 percent) and a single media-buying agency (50 percent). Finally, only one in two firms considered that the single market would lead brands to select a single advertising network or agency. These prognoses have been proved right—in 1992, 48 percent of the European brands surveyed had adopted a single network.

GLOBALIZING BRANDS IN EUROPE

The classical examples of global brands, the monolithic Marlboro and Mars, are of little relevance to most European brands. These examples concern monoproducts, whereas most brands are multiproducts: the difference is that a brand may then be present through some of its products in the U.K. and through some other products in Germany, or in Italy. Even if brand management necessitates a headstrong process, such realities cannot just be forgotten. Globalization for most brands will be done through a modulated progressive harmonization, not in an all-or-nothing fashion. A process of convergence has certainty started, but its speed will depend on company cultures and on product categories. In 1992, together with the Eurocom advertising network, we undertook a survey of all major international brands operating in Europe. In all, 210 international advertising coordinators answered a questionnaire on the current status of globalization within their company, and concerning their specific brands. As expected, 81 percent of the sample admitted that they were heading toward homogenization and standardization in Europe. Interestingly, there was a significant difference in response according to the country of origin. Ninety-five percent of German brand managers said they pursued globalization,

Table 9.2

Country of origin and globalization policy

	We leave freedom to each local subsidiary (%)	We push towards homogenization and standardization (%)
Italy	30	60
France	24	69
Switzerland	20	80
USA	5.5	77
Japan	0	85.5
UK	5.3	94.5
Germany	4.5	95.5
Total (base 210)	13	81

Source: Eurocom/Kapferer Pan European Survey 1992

as opposed to 69 percent of French and Italian brand coordinators. Due to the sample size, a possible confusion exists with product category, since some countries are more closely linked to one or two specific categories. Examination of globalizing tendencies within product categories reveals significant differences, too. The highest homogenizing and standardizing tendencies are found in the beauty/cosmetics sector (95.5 percent), home appliances (92 percent), hi-fi and video (87.5 percent), and detergents (85 percent). The rate is only 70 percent in the food industry and 56 percent in the textile sector. Finally, heavy use of television is shown to act as an impetus toward standardization: 85 percent as opposed to 70 percent among those brands making no use of TV.

Interestingly, although 41 percent of all brands have the same marketing mix all over Europe, and only 25 percent follow locally specific marketing policies, 34 percent of the brands divide Europe into two or three zones, each having a specific marketing mix: the classic lines of segmentation are cultural (North versus South, Anglo–Saxon countries versus Latin countries), or linked to con-

Table 9.3

What differences between countries would compel you to adapt the marketing mix of the brand?

Type of Difference	Necessary Adaptation (%)
Legal differences	55
Competition	47
Consumption habits	41
Distribution structure	39
Brand awareness	38
Brand distribution level	37
Media audience	37
Marketing program success	34
Consumers' needs	33
Media availability	32
Brand images	30.5
Norms for products manufacturing	27.5
Brand history	25.2
Lifestyle differences	25
Cultural differences	25
Subsidiary sales	23
Consumers' buying power	22
Consumers' age differences	12

sumption habits (heavy beer-drinking countries versus wine-drinking countries, butter-oriented versus margarine-oriented countries, etc.). This clustering into zones typifies the food-industry brands (50 percent), whereas a global unified approach is more typical of luxury brands (60 percent), or cosmetics and beauty brands (61 percent).

Finally, the results show that, although their existence is acknowledged, differences between countries are considered less and less to require a local approach. Table 9.3 reveals that only one item leads a majority of the international brand managers to consider the necessity of adapting the marketing mix: legal differences. These legal differences will tend to disappear soon within the EC, indicating that the majority of managers feel no necessity to adapt the market mix to suit existing differences.

Differences in consumers' characteristics now represent the weakest reasons for refusing to standardize and homogenize brand policy, indicating that globalization is largely a question of managerial will and conviction.

HOW GLOBAL ARE GLOBAL BRANDS?

Although the trend is toward brand Europeanization, not all the facets of the brand will be equally open to standardization across countries. When we speak of brand management, this refers to at least eighteen specific areas of decision-making, from brand-naming decisions to advertising positioning and sponsoring activities. The survey of the 210 major brands reveals which facets are already global and which are purposely differentiated. The underlying philosophy seems to be, "Think global, sell local."

The facets of brand management which are least globalized are short-term response variables such as direct marketing (60 percent of the interviewees differentiated from country to country) and sales promotion (80 percent). Then come two decisions linked to local competitive forces: brand pricing *vis-à-vis* competition (67 percent) and the below-the-line/above-the-line ratio (50 percent). This ratio measures the need to locally defend market shares by trade and consumer promotions. The vectors of brand-selling messages are also most often adapted: thus the media mix was differentiated by 57 percent of the major brands in Europe, as was the final touch and style of advertisements.

At the other end of the spectrum, globalization is greatest for the logo (95 percent are global), the symbolic character representing the brand (91 percent), and the brand name (88.5 percent). As to this last facet, differences in name most often are the result of history: for instance, Procter & Gamble's Ariel is sold under the Dash name in Italy. Brand target definitions are quite global (73 percent), as are brand positioning and promise. Because of legal and cultural differences, the physical characteristics of the product itself cannot be fully standardized (73 percent): local tastes and norms require certain necessary adaptation.

These are average responses across the sample of the 210 major brands operating in Europe. One can identify different types of brand behavior, by means of cluster analysis.

One group of brands changes the many facets of brand management as little as possible. Everything is homogenized, except for tactical decisions (local direct marketing and the media mix). A quarter of the European brands belong to this globalizing type: they represent the luxury market and the beauty/cosmetics sector, as well as such brands as Mars, Twix, Milka, and Orangina.

A second group (27 percent) practices a maximum of tactical adaptations: they differentiate most of the direct-response facets of the marketing mix. The car industry represents a prototype of this behavior. It is a "glocal" type. The advertising global concept may be the same, but everything else is different (creation, production).

A third group (16 percent) is the least global of all. This "differentiating" group changes major aspects of the product and packaging, even names and logos or brand basic positioning. This type represents the behavior of many food and detergent brands. But it is a historical type. New detergents would be more likely to be launched globally (as was Procter & Gamble's Vizir).

A fourth group (35 percent) comprises those brands whose marketing is determined by the trade and distribution structure. Since there are wide differences in distribution structure between countries, their globalization is hampered. This affects, for instance, the home-appliance industry, as well as hi-fi and video-camera products.

Interestingly, the strong brands were little represented in the first group. Brands in the sample were indexed to account for the number of countries where they operated, and their relative market share in each of these countries. Each brand received a weighted brand-strength index. The strongest brands were found in the second group: they think global and sell local. Coca-Cola is such an instance.

Table 9.4

Globalizing the marketing mix

Which adaptations are most frequent from one country to another?	(%)
Sales promotions	80
Relative pricing	67
Direct marketing	60
Media mix	57
Advertising execution	57
Below/above the line ratio	49.5
Sponsoring	38.5
Packaging	36
Creative idea	34
Distribution channels	33
Brand slogan	31
Brand positioning promise	27.5
Product features	27.5
Target market	27
Brand name	11.5
Brand symbol and emblem	9.5
Trademark, logo	5

(Base: 210 European brands, 1992)

Source: Eurocom/Kapferer Pan European Survey 1992

THE PATH TO CONSISTENCY

Adopting a standard form of communication for a product such as a Mars bar or Pliz polishing spray is one thing. It presents a different problem when promoting the international image of multiproduct, multimarket umbrella brands like Kodak, IBM, Dannon, and Alcatel. The same applies to range brands covering a number of models, each having its own personality—as in the automobile industry. Many of these brands have already standardized their communication framework, following laid-down principles regarding type, logo, color codes, and media coverage. It is certainly a step in the right direction where a universal image is concerned, but it does not get to the heart of the standardization process.

As the foregoing tables have shown, firms can follow different courses of action when seeking to portray a basic consistency in their brands. The first takes the form of centrally-chosen brand campaigns which extend over many countries. In order to cater to national variations, AT&T suggests to each country several options for the same advertising campaign (several print advertisements, for example). The national subsidiary can then take its choice from among these.

When a brand communicates solely through its products, the brand meaning must be instilled in the product or service communication. At the very least, systematic presence of the brand slogan is required. For instance, every form of Toshiba advertising throughout the world is accompanied by the slogan "In touch with tomorrow" (or its translation). Apart from this, subsidiaries are allowed every freedom. Others turn to the well-worn "brand communication handbook," with its do's and don'ts. The "do's" give guidance on key words to be used, and the main communication paths to be followed, together with recommendations on style. As for the "don'ts," certain brands prefer not to write them down. This is why advertising proposals for every Porsche model are first scrutinized at brand HQ in Stuttgart. They can sometimes be rejected as not in keeping with the Porsche idea of Porsche. Rather than distribute a negative list of verboten, which may be either too short or too long, they prefer their objections to remain implied. It is only when a finalized ad is thrown out that the basis for such rejection becomes apparent.

GSI has adopted an original approach in order to achieve coherent brand communication. Rather than provide their various divisions worldwide with a verbal index of key words, GSI supplies them with a picture bank, depicting people, places, offices, monitors, symbols, decor, etc., all linked by a distinctive common style. Each division or subsidiary is free to formulate whatever campaign it wishes, on condition that it makes use of these visual aids.

There is an important difference between a written manual and a picture bank. The former is often considered as a constraint, in that it specifies the words to be used in conveying the brand's personality and culture. On the other hand, the picture bank allows an additional freedom. The GSI subsidiary has only to draw on this bank in order to convey the desired theme and message. The words can be chosen freely, but the visual part must emanate from a common source available to every division throughout the world. The images which form the basis of the visual bank are not chosen at random—they express the brand's identity.

With its greater centralization—partly through its nature and partly through necessity as a result of crisis—Bull has no other option than to make full use of its brand's presence on a global scale. To this end, the visual brand symbolism—the tree—is always prominent. It serves not only as a means of recognition, but also as a supporting link in every campaign, whether it is promoting the brand, its products, or the markets themselves. The tree may take on all forms and shapes in different countries, but it must remain the coordinating feature in every campaign. No matter which approach is adopted in harmonizing international communication, it must be compatible with the normal management style of the firm involved.

Finally, the best path to homogeneous brand identity is to lay down what the brand identity is. Instead of focusing on creation itself and trying to make it uniform, it is better to start by creating a consensus around the brand charter, its values, its mission, its program, and its identity prism.

HANDLING THE NAME TRANSITION

Until now, most companies have adhered to a plurilocal policy. They find themselves in charge of a confused patchwork of national brands. Unilever, for instance, has a frozen-food brand in France called Captain Igloo, corresponding to Birds Eye in the U.K.; in Italy, Unilever use the name Findus, which, everywhere else, belongs to Nestlé, Unilever's main competitor in this market! Likewise, Nestlé markets Gervais ice cream in France, whereas elsewhere Gervais is the top brand of its competitor BSN. Such confusion is bound to cease. The advent of the single brand signifies the ultimate demise of dozens of well-known national brands. Pedigree, for example, is to replace Pal, Dulux is taking over the Valentine name, Nuit et Jour became Night and Day in June 1988, Treets disappeared in favor of M&Ms, and Raider has given way to Twix.

What criteria are used in deciding which brand should remain and which should go? When each enjoys a high level of awareness at the national level, firms have to appraise the international potential of each name, and the risks involved locally in abandoning one particular name in favor of a hitherto unknown brand. In the domestic-appliances market, the Italian group Merloni has preferred to concentrate its efforts on its brand Indesit, well-known but having a poorer image than Ariston, its other brand, which has a very good image but is hardly known. The costs of increasing brand awareness are too high since Whirlpool's entry into the market.

In general terms, descriptive names in a particular language do not readily lend themselves to internationalization—Procter & Gamble, for instance, had to withdraw its Safeguard deodorant soap in France. Not only was the name unpronounceable as such to the average consumer, but it was moreover untranslatable. Americans like the direct name, expressing the product's advantage in straight terms. We saw this with Head and Shoulders antidandruff shampoo, and find it again in Safeguard. Where Latin countries are concerned, however, one has to resort to allusion in approaching the problem. In the international arena, there is a natural advantage in names which have no exact meaning (e.g., Ariel, Dash, Skip, Kodak, Agfa) or whose original meaning has disappeared (e.g., Bull, Tide, IBM). Names which have a descriptive force in one language also have a "foreign" air when exported, which does not always go down well with customers in other countries. This is why Mr. Clean had to be translated to Mr. Proper. On the other hand, in France the coffee called Nuit et Jour changed to Night and Day without any problem, since coffee is considered a foreign product in every country.

Decisions which lead to a brand's being suppressed are not always rational. Pal had higher sales in Europe than had Pedigree in the U.K. It was nevertheless decided to retain only the British brand, even though it was unknown in Europe. Is this a result of ethnocentrism? One could also argue that Pedigree has an international meaning understood by every dog owner, and that the name is intimately linked with its original concept as the favorite product used by pedigree dog breeders. It makes one wonder which of the three brand names Pledge, Pliz, or Pronto will be chosen by Johnson as the European brand name for its spray polish. Whatever the decision, the problem of transition will arise. No matter how a brand is to be changed, it must retain its national reputation and share of the market. Three types of strategy have until now been employed: fade-in/fade-out, transparent forewarning, and summary axing.

The first approach consists, for instance, of introducing the future single brand under a new product name. Over a period of time, the product gains prominence and the former brand is faded out. For example, in 1989 Pedigree was introduced in France as Pedigree by Pal. During a transitional period, Pedigree received all the advertising, with Pal acting as an endorsing brand. Other examples of surreptitious transition have already been referred to (see page 198). It is ideal when consumers use multiple anchors to recognize their product: one can be changed after the other.

The example of Night and Day is a good illustration of the way in which one brand forewarns its consumers that it will change. It can be described in detail. Mr. Jacobs, the majority shareholder of the Jacobs–Suchard company, launched a new decaffeinated coffee in several countries, adapting its name as appropriate—Nacht und Tag in Germany, Austria, and Switzerland, and Night and Day in the United States and Canada. It had been test-marketed successfully as Nuit et Jour in France. In each country, the product was endorsed by a national brand. Then, at the beginning of 1987, Mr. Jacobs decided to create an up-market international brand of coffee under its own Jacobs name. He turned to the product leaders among the original local brands. Mr. Jacobs decided upon "Night and Day" as the world name and, as the first product of the new Jacobs brand, placed it in the hands of an advertising agency with offices in forty countries. The launch was to center upon a change in the decaffeination process. The transition was made in the countries where the coffee name was not in English, in two communication stages:

- Prior to June 1988, all packaging carried a label announcing the forthcoming change ("Soon, Nuit et Jour will be called Night and Day").
- After June, an explanatory note was included on the back of temporary packets: "Your Nuit et Jour decaffeinated coffee is now called Night and Day. We have changed its name to reach out and captivate decaffeinated-coffee drinkers throughout Europe who, like you, will be able to savor its wholesome, satisfying taste. With its caffeine removed through the natural action of clear water, Night and Day has all the aroma and richness of a great coffee."
- In further support, a series of commercials on radio during July 1988 informed of the change: "Here comes Night, meaning Nuit, and Day . . . ah yes, that means Jour. Night and Day from Jacobs: the decaffeinated coffee to enjoy day and night. What a formidable challenge for the Europe of tomorrow."

Mars went about a similar name change in a totally different way. There was no advance warning when Treets disappeared in December 1986. M&Ms was launched almost as a new product, keeping the famous Treets' slogan, "Melts in your mouth, not in your hand." They scarcely capitalized on the former brand, simply including the words "by the makers of Treets" on the packet and in the TV commercial. Three years on, profits were still low. The failure of the move is explained in the historical liking for Treets on the part of adults. The downfall would not have come about if the change involved only children, since their attachment to the historical Treets was nil.

Learning from this mistake, the change from Raider to Twix made use of extensive forewarning. In addition, the TV commercials explained "Now Raider becomes Twix, for it is Twix everywhere in the world." The international extension of the Twix name boosted the status of this name change and actually significantly increased the sales in Europe.

III

The Brand in Perspective

10

Brand, Products, Enterprise, and Institution

The brand is not the only mouthpiece of an enterprise. This is apparent by the increasing number of agencies and consultants offering communication advice, be it "corporate," company, institutional, global, financial, or in the recruitment field. In terms of reaching the outside world, the emergence of these new forms of service—distinct from the traditional advertising agency—drives home the message that company communications derive from more than one source. The brand is among these, but is not alone.

This new supply of communication advice and services creates a dual problem relating to concepts and practice. The notional problem arises from the confusing terminology which these new forms of communication have brought with them. Many managers, having just grasped the difference between brand and product, are now bewildered by the vague ideas implied in the words "corporate," "institutional," "global," and "company" communications, together with their sometimes tenuous relationship with brand communication.

The confusion springs from three sources. In the first place, all concepts actually and implicitly express a certain vision of communication, a vision which may differ from those held so far by those managers who now feel they have to use them. For instance, "corporate" communication seems to refer to all that is not product-oriented communication. As such this view overlooks the fact that brand communication also is distinct from product communication; their respective fields of activity need to be defined. There are other terms for corporate communication: we also talk of institutional or company communication.

A second source of confusion lies in the fact that brand, product, and firm often have the same name! Henkel or Procter & Gamble have little difficulty in distinguishing the specific functions and territory embraced by corporate and brand communication respectively. Procter & Gamble is the body—Dove, Camay, Ariel, Pampers, etc., are the brands. Likewise, Dulux and Valentine are two ICI brands among many. The same does not apply to IBM, Bull, Renault, Coca-Cola, or Nestlé, however. IBM puts its own name on all its products—an increasing practice called corporate branding. Japanese firms, too, have dropped their own name in favor of that of their leading brand, turning to what actually amounts to "brand corporating." For example, Tokyo Tsuhin Kogyo (Tokyo Telecommunications Industry Co.) became Sony Inc., with the Sony brand assuming global responsibility (Yoshimori, 1989). In France, CGE changed its name on 1 January 1991 to that of its two main brands, Alcatel–Alsthom. From now on brand, product, and firm will often have the same name, as in the case of Canon, Shell, and Sainsbury (whose name is also on certain of its products). Name identity makes it even more important to have a clear mental picture of the various forms of communication, their aim, *raison d'être*, and means of application.

There is just as great a need in the service sector, where brand or product concepts often are unknown. In the service industry the product is ethereal, invisible, and intangible. If we compare Apple with Arthur Andersen, Apple sells the Macintosh, while Arthur Andersen sells an accounting service and man-hours. Again, the service industry has always worked under the identity of its corporate name—Marriott's, Barclays Bank, or Lloyd's. They have therefore spontaneously thought of communication as dual: institutional and service. They are now discovering that their names are taking on the role of brands. This is why B. Thiolon (1990), Managing Director of Crédit Lyonnais, wrote that "The bank seems to be in the infant stages of becoming a brand."

This chapter seeks not only to clarify the concepts, but also to supply the necessary groundwork, for a practical strategy. The communication sector is split into different types of communication. Side-by-side with advertising agencies, historically charged with brand and product communication, are the emergent corporate, institutional, company, and global communication agencies. The problem now is in deciding what ails one in order to know which specialist to consult. Making the wrong choice could lead to a diagnosis which is nothing more than the specialist's own partial vision of the world. This is what happened to Essilor, the world leader in optical lenses, in mid-1990. Faced with significant market changes affecting both retailers and consumers—and imminent newcomers on the competitive scene—Essilor felt the need to communicate on its own name and not, as previously, on that of its products, such as Varilux. However, each specialist consulted offered a different diagnosis. The "Doctor of Institutional Communication" recommended that they communicate on Essilor's contribution to humanity, so that they might reach out to the world around them through the medium of sight. The "Doctor of Company Communication" suggested a campaign highlighting Essilor's position as the world's number one in optics. As for the "Doctor of Brands," he advocated a brand campaign with a "high-tech" theme. Whom were they to believe? Firms now need to have an overall knowledge themselves, in order to determine which communication doctor to consult. It is up to them to carry out their own diagnosis, and to this end they require an understanding of each type of communication, and the interrelationships thereof.

DISTINGUISHING THE LEVELS OF COMMUNICATION

There are four distinct levels of communication—enterprise, institutional, brand, and product—each having its own specific purpose, target, content and style.

So-called enterprise (or company) communication seeks to make the firm more transparent to the outsider. It reveals the firm's physique and its human, technological, and financial means. It highlights the company goals as an economic agent, and points out the means by which these will be achieved. As such, its content is both factual and economic (Krief, 1986; Schwebig, 1988), formulated on a desire for exactitude and truth. This does not mean, as so many believe, that its style should be drab or intellectual. Every enterprise has its own personality which is apparent in its communication. Communication of this first type is mainly targeted at company personnel, shareholders, outside suppliers, leaders of public opinion, and economic, financial, and social analysts. However, it could well be directed at the users themselves, since consumers will be more content in the knowledge that, behind a brand name, there are firms in good economic health. When Renault and IBM announce their profits, they are communicating on the company, but are also reinforcing the brand status.

Certain firms are sadly lacking when it comes to communication. We know virtually nothing about them—or, in any case, not enough. Apart from their own personnel and financial analysts, who is aware that the world leader in optical lens research is Essilor? Their thoughts should go beyond any self-admiration or chauvinistic ideal. With the world competition on its doorstep in the form of high-performance Japanese and German companies, such as Nikon, Seiko, and Zeiss, there is no advantage to be gained in concealing from the wider public the scope of Essilor's established capabilities. This does not imply a massive advertising campaign on the subject—advertising is, in fact, only one of the media available in the "communication mix." In any case, it might be more appropriate to target just the trade—opticians, ophthalmologists, and optometrists—throughout the world, to boost the company status.

Communication referred to as "institutional" points to a firm's wider values. It is the voice of the company heart, expressing its calling. The fact that this type of communication is on the increase is not surprising, since the public looks to major firms to prove that their operations are legitimate. Economic and financial prowess itself is insufficient—firms should make clear their social justification. The more a firm carries weight—whether it be at national or international level—the more it should look to its "institutional" standing: its contribution to society, and its civic and moral value in the wider sense. Institutional communication announces the firm's contribution to society. It is no longer a question of addressing the financier, employee, consumer, or supplier, but of appealing to the citizen in each of them. Institutional communication has a moral, political, and philosophical content. When the chemical company Rhône–Poulenc uses the words "Welcome to a better world," showing a newborn baby, it is

pointing to the fact that Rhône–Poulenc is an institution—an important actor in the cause of human progress.

Here again, advertising is only one vehicle of institutional communication. The chairman speaks for the institution, declaring its values
and aims in credible terms. Social consciousness stems from the very
heart of the company. This is why, as soon as the public becomes
aware of a firm's activities, the latter should be aware of the institutional implications. On this point, there is no doubting why companies
producing chemicals (e.g., Bayer, ICI, Rhône–Poulenc, etc.), petrole-
um products (e.g., Shell, Elf, etc.), and pharmaceuticals were the first
to turn to institutional communication. They operate in technologically high-risk sectors—some time in the future there is going to be
another Seveso, another Bhopal, another Amoco Cadiz. It is therefore
important—quite apart from the stringent security measures
employed onsite—that firms in these sectors whose image is at risk
should take the precaution of conveying their fundamental legitimacy
and sincerity to the outside world. This they now do on a wide scale.

When a small or medium-sized firm gains the status of a dominant
local economic actor, institutional problems can again arise, since its
importance has a social effect in that it leads to constraints and subor-
dination. When this happens, local sponsorship and patronage serve
to restore smoother relations and bring about social integration.

In 1990 Toshiba, like other Japanese firms dominating certain markets, realized the urgent need for institutional communication in
Europe. Until then, Toshiba had relied only on brand communication
("In touch with tomorrow") and product communication (e.g.,
portable microcomputers, televisions, etc.). Despite having sponsored
a French team in the Tour de France cycle race, Toshiba was becoming tarnished with the same negative image of overbearing aggressiveness associated with other Japanese groups in the U.S.A. and
Europe. Toshiba decided it was high time they concentrated on their
institutional approach internationally.

As we have seen, brand communication expresses the meaning of a
brand's products. The brand injects its own values into the product,
and thus transforms its status. It endows it with qualities which correspond with the brand's original aim. Brand communication seeks to
portray the brand concept and its identity. When Coca-Cola declared
throughout the world "Coca-Cola is it," they were using brand com-

munication in an effort to convey the rich significance of "it," with a symbolic embodiment of unsullied joy. Likewise, when Renault expresses its identity and notional values in the slogan "Cars for living," it too is using brand communication. Each of its models personifies this concept, and has been specifically designed as such. In a desire for brevity and thrust, brand language often is symbolic. When creating a product or service, the brand can indicate its ideal, its fantasy and source of inspiration, in the most concise phrase. Brand communication is aimed at the consumer not yet engaged in the precise comparison of alternative products. As we saw in Chapter 7, the brand can be promoted either directly by means of a campaign pointing to its specific values, or by way of products specifically chosen to convey the brand's meaning. Benetton is communicating at brand level in its campaign "United Colors of Benetton"—although its symbolic reference to friendship among the peoples of the world also has institutional overtones. We see brand communication again in Vuitton's "The art of traveling" campaigns, and in the Bull advertisements in *Time, Newsweek, Der Spiegel, and Kapital*, where they use the tree as a symbol of life. Bull is expressing quite openly what it is trying to inject into the services covered by its brand.

Finally, product and service communication is targeted straight at the consumer or client trying to make a decision. It concentrates on those deliberating over product attributes and price. When Coca-Cola communicates in the United States on Diet Coke, caffeine-free, New Coke, or Classic Coke, it is direct product communication—though, in this instance, surreptitiously backed by the tone of the brand itself. Volkswagen has never used its brand name to communicate "direct," but does so through the medium of its cars.

Table 10.1 illustrates the four communication levels. As the Renault example shows, communication is sometimes affected by events outside the company's control. For example, each time a factory goes on strike, this rebounds against the company's image. Again, when the Renault Managing Director, Georges Besse, was assassinated by terrorists, that highlighted Renault's institutional dimension as an arm of state capitalism, bringing home the fact that the Renault management is answerable as much to the Prime Minister or the Industry Minister as to their own state-appointed Managing Director.

Even though each level of communication has its own territory,

Table 10.1

The four communication levels

	Coca-Cola	Renault	Nestlé
Institution	Jewel of triumphant capitalism Coca-Cola in Beijing and Moscow	State owned National social laboratory and premier French exporter Formula 1 winner	Archetype of the multinational company. Ethical problems in the Third World
Enterprise	Atlanta, turnover, worldwide presence	Strikes Strong trade unions Financial results	Multiactivity groups Headquarters in Vevey Leaders in food Secretive
Brand	"Coca-Cola is "it'" or "the feeling's called Coke."	"Cars for living"	Maternal nourishing
Product or service	Bottle of Coca-Cola Diet Coke Caffeine-free Coke Classic Coke	Clio, Safrane, R5 to R25 Espace, Alpine	Babies' milk Cornflakes Chocolate Coffee, etc

communication sometimes intentionally straddles several levels. For instance, Benetton deliberately allows the institutional influence to permeate its brand communication. In showing a white woman breast-feeding a colored baby, it is adopting a political and philosophical form of communication. It is in phase with the internationalist ideal of their young clientele, and echoes the emphasis on ethnic color in relation to Benetton products.

MANAGING INTEGRATED COMMUNICATION

Having four different communication levels offers the advantage of diagnosing problems and relating them to the required treatment. Such a diagnosis will allow Essilor to determine which facet of its image is least likely to sustain the increased competition in a world market. They have to ask themselves:

- Is the Essilor enterprise insufficiently known, and are its investments in research and production not fully appreciated?
- Has the Essilor institution been silent for too long, and has it failed to show a significant contribution to the collective sphere?
- Is the Essilor brand on a lens or frame just a series of letters with no particular meaning for the user—having no physique, no reflection, no personality, no culture?
- Are the products unknown, or are they not attributed to Essilor—who, until now, has hidden behind such product names as Varilux?

We prefer this distinct four-way split, rather than a somewhat hodge-podge idea of "corporate" communication which does not differentiate between brand and product, and between institutional and enterprise communication.

It would nevertheless be a mistake to see these four communication levels as separate strata, even though, in a graphic sense, Figure 10.1 indicates this form. What we must remember is that the consumer cannot be compartmentalized in this way—part of him does listen to the institution, while another relates to the brand. When purchasing, the consumer is not preoccupied with brand and products, but is also influenced to some extent by the efficiency and economic results of the company, and the institution's social responsibility.

The consumer's ability to incorporate all these factors in a single choice emphasizes the fact that these four communication types should not be thought of as being in watertight compartments—each with its own different aim—but should be treated as units in an integrated communication plan. All four levels can be used at the same time without concealing their individual aims. The four communication levels should be interwoven. One can, for example, mix the brand and institutional levels (Benetton). Certain food brands show their civic responsibility by participating in humanitarian causes, which they publicize on their labels or packaging. Firms now like to see their names on their brands. For instance, ICI, a world giant in the chemical industry, puts its name on the Dulux painting brand. In so doing, it adds an image of its own technology to the brand. Many firms now prefer the simplicity of a single name for both company and brand. They either use their company name as that of the brand, or adopt the name of their leading brand and its accompanying reputation. The process referred to as "corporate branding" combines all the features associated with institution, enterprise, brand, and products.

When institution, enterprise, brand, and products bear the same name, all four merge in the mind of the consumer, overlapping to such an extent that one could speak of the institutional features of the company or brand. When we see Toshiba entering into cultural patronage, we might ask ourselves whether it is the company or the brand which emerges as the more philanthropic. When all is said and done, however, this notional question concerns the practice of sound management, but has scarcely any relevance for the consumer.

IMBALANCE IN INTEGRATED COMMUNICATION

Having established the four types of communication, we now have the framework which allows us to diagnose problems and decide on the appropriate communication strategy. In order to further study the relationship between these levels of communication, it is better to adopt the system illustrated in Figure 10.1, rather than the descriptive classification seen in Table 10.1. In any communication strategy one needs to decide which of the B,I,P,E levels—brand, institution, products, and enterprise is/are to receive the heaviest investment. One then has to look at their synergies and differences, bearing in mind, for example, that communication aimed at the institution or enterprise can possibly affect the brand. Figure 10.2 illustrates the network of image flows resulting from Renault's overall communication. The Renault brand image was inferior in terms of finish, quality, and reliability, compared to the Peugeot brand. Does this mean that the contrasting brand images stemmed in reality from an image of the products themselves? Historically, perhaps, certain models have tended to leave their mark on the brand image—Citroën, for example, still suffers the legacy of an image associated with the 2CV, Dyane, Ami 6, and Visa. In Renault's case, however, the brand image—gauged by the opinions of non–Renault owners—was largely influenced by its institutional facet. This came to the fore each time the Finance Minister

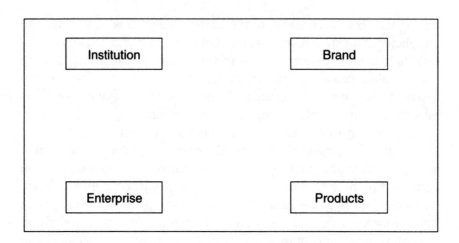

Figure 10.1

The BIPE framework for communication decisions

reminded us that Renault is state-owned, or the trade unions called for a strike, emphasizing the fact that, as a public enterprise, it was governed by other values than those of efficiency and competitiveness. The fact is that an image of quality finish normally originates at shop-floor level, in the factory. However, on the rare occasions when the Renault factory hit the headlines, it was either with news of strikes and demonstrations, or of ditherings on the part of its directorate regarding its continued public status. This is the kiss of death for any decent brand image. It also earmarks it as a popular brand— the Renault owner does not seek individuality. Behind the Renault brand there lies a mood of egalitarianism emanating from the Renault institution. This is reflected both in its products and in its target public. It is therefore not surprising that, in spite of its favorable price and the undeniable intrinsic quality of the car, Renault sold only a few dozen of their R25 deluxe Limousine version. The Renault–Volvo agreement fits in with this diagnosis.

Clearly, a flow of image from products to brand scarcely occurred in this case. With names such as Renault 5, 21, or 25, the brand dominated the products: the flow was top-down. Fortunately, the company had a well-established commercial setup, with a wide range of main dealers, agents, and local outlets delivering an efficient marketing push. This gave them a fair share of the market. What major changes

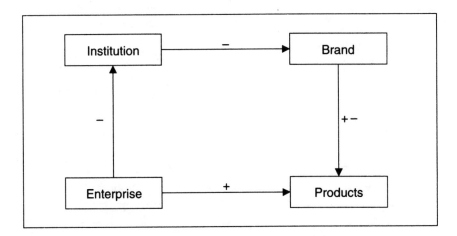

Figure 10.2

The BIPE diagnosis applied to Renault's communications

of communication did Renault therefore adopt? Given that the brand influences its models, but that the products do not reciprocate by contributing to the brand image, Renault gave their models greater autonomy and a source of identity in the form of specific names, such as the Espace and Clio. Its presence in Formula 1 racing has also contributed to the enterprise's international reputation. This imbues its products with a vitality which is not included in its normal brand program—the slogan "Cars for living" does not naturally evoke an idea of high engine performance. In one respect, Formula 1 gives the brand greater freedom, by allowing it to pursue its concept of living to the extreme. As we see, the BIPE framework allows us to identify abnormalities of image flows within various communication systems. We shall consider a few examples.

When Brand Communication is Lacking

Salomon is the world leader in bindings, alpine skis and shoes, and hiking shoes. It operates in the U.S.A., Japan, and Europe. Paradoxically, Salomon as "brand" has rarely communicated throughout its history. Its communication system worked well with three sources only. The founder of the company, Georges Salomon, was himself

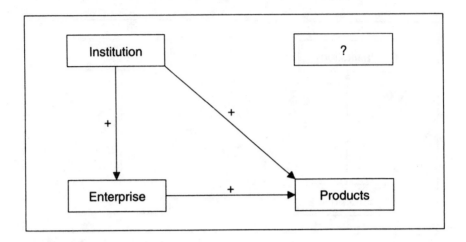

Figure 10.3

The BIPE diagnosis of Salomon communications worldwide until 1992

something of an institution in the skiing world. Permanently traveling around the world, he was known for his ideals and his ethics, and he was the ambassador of the Salomon company. The latter, led by a strong corporate culture and their boss, had growing profits and confidence. The Salomon spirit was shared by its trade channels. Salomon's products were known for their innovation and excellence. When it comes to bindings—i.e., security—there is no room for halfway measures.

Starting in 1990, the economic situation changed drastically. A lack of snow created a crisis in the ski business. Inventories were high, and retailers were reluctant to push new products. Financial difficulties affected the Salomon company, although it had diversified its risks by taking control of the American Taylor Made golf equipment company. Georges Salomon had to step down, and the whole communication system became imbalanced. What previously had not been a problem was now an obstacle to recovery. The company founder was no longer there, the company was undertaking reorganizations, and its products were becoming more diversified. It was high time for the Salomon "brand" to speak, to replace its former communication sources which had played a major role so far, and to endow added values to the products it signed. This was all the more necessary, as the brand was endangered by both product and international diversity. Today, Salomon signs bindings, alpine and hiking shoes, and top-class skis. So far its subsidiaries have managed their local communications autonomously. A specific program of brand communication was needed to reinforce the brand's status as reference brand in the alpine skiing world. This entailed a prior investigation on brand identity which out of lack of necessity, had never been undertaken. Salomon as a brand has a specific image in Japan, America, Germany, Austria, Sweden, and France. Brand communication cannot stem from so many mirrors. The brand has to proclaim internationally its own personal values. To know them, image studies were not enough, nor were the classical corporate culture studies. (Actually, it is not often realized that brand identity is not the same as corporate identity, although both are necessarily related—see page 77.)

One byproduct of investigating their brand identity was that it created *de facto* convergence in Salomon's previously unrelated Japanese, American, and European campaigns.

Having established the Salomon brand identity prism and its identity charter, the company was able to instill these into its local product communications. The common adoption of a brand identity platform was a first step toward homogeneity of the source. Throughout the world, ads will still be different, but the source will be recognized as unitary, and led by the same values. This is in line with Salomon's corporate culture, which is to give autonomy to its subsidiaries and personnel in general.

Stepping Down from Institution to Brand

Moët et Chandon is the best selling-champagne in the world. It is naturally first in terms of brand awareness. Even so, a Japanese importer visiting Paris will not necessarily be served Moët et Chandon in his own hotel, even a five-star one. Even at the Presidential Elysée Palace, Moët et Chandon is no longer the official champagne.

Moët et Chandon has not communicated well enough to counterbalance a negative flow of image arising from its wide distribution network and its rising sales. While certainly not a problem in terms of its immediate profits, the slow deterioration of its brand image has

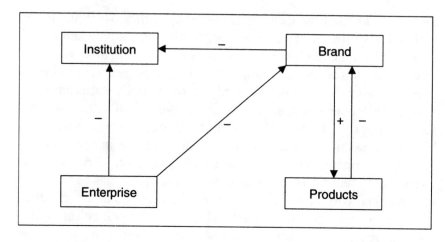

Figure 10.4

Moët et Chandon communication diagnosis

become a real problem for the institutional status of this champagne in its home country. Moët et Chandon is no longer considered the qualitative reference point.

Most of the communications concerning Moët et Chandon derive from its sponsoring activities, whereby the brand wishes to be associated with success. Each Formula 1 car race ends with the ritual bottle of Moët et Chandon being poured on the ground by the winning team. It is not good for a luxury brand to be associated solely with images where the liquid itself is not drunk but is considered as a mere commodity whose bubbling physical properties count for more than its organoleptic ones. It is not the Formula 1 sponsorship which is the problem (its worldwide audience is remarkable) but Moët et Chandon's progressive neglect of all that a real institution has to do to deserve its status.

Being a market share leader is not in itself sufficient. Moët et Chandon had forgotten its mission as an institution for the whole champagne category. It relied solely on brand communication and allowed the quantitative connotations of its sales and distribution to overcome the qualitative connotations one is entitled to expect of a good champagne.

Vuitton and Cartier have carefully avoided that risk so far, by putting a necessarily strong emphasis on institutional communication.

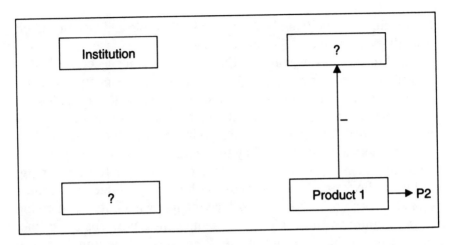

Figure 10.5
Nina Ricci in 1988 (BIPE diagnosis)

When the Product Absorbs the Brand

This is a classic instance of a brand losing all its meaning when it takes on that of one of its products. In doing so, it can no longer function as a source brand. This happened in the case of the Nina Ricci brand, which was taken over by G. Fuchs in 1988 after the death of M. Robert Ricci, the founder's son.

Nina Ricci no longer existed as a brand. It was true that sales were increasing throughout the world, but for other reasons. Nina Ricci continued to be an institution, where haute couture was concerned. The House of Ricci participated in the ritual presentation of new collections, and its fantastic evening gowns still gave notice of its affiliation to the exclusive "griffes de Paris" club. Though Ricci remains a prestigious name, it is several steps behind Dior, Chanel, and Yves Saint Laurent—closer in its unfashionable, reserved style to Balmain, Balenciaga, or Lanvin. The Nina Ricci brand had no substance—or at least this was found only in its top product, L'Air du Temps, the world's favorite perfume with young girls and nostalgic oldies. Just as Anais-Anais had engulfed the Cacharel identity, L'Air du Temps had given its identity to parent brand Nina Ricci. They had tried to give the brand space by launching a new perfume, Nina. However, since its advertising—like that of L'Air du Temps'—displayed the David Hamilton touch, Nina could not both undertake this role and distance itself from the star product. L'Air du Temps was still too close to Nina, and seemed to smother it (whereas Cacharel's Loulou succeeded in distinguishing itself from Anais-Anais, while still respecting certain codes). Such a situation was prejudicial to Nina Ricci's plans for developing new products. L'Air du Temps was, for example, an inappropriate basis for a cosmetic line having in mind the young girl on the threshold of femininity. They therefore had to give the Nina Ricci name an autonomy through increased direct access to its meaning, either in the form of accessories—with the same effect as Hermès scarves—or in fact with a "Nina" having its own identity and giving new meaning to the brand, or in launching a new cosmetic line, directly under the Nina Ricci name, to convey its long-forgotten core meaning. Cacharel did the same to revitalize its source brand. They relaunched Cacharel Ready To Wear for women, and a line of underwear, closely tied to the brand's original core values.

HANDLING THE IMAGE CRISIS

The brand image can sometimes burn out. There are very few sectors whose brands are shielded from possible crisis. The most exposed sectors are those in which the technological risk can never be nullified—food, household products, pharmaceuticals, transport, cars, gasoline, chemicals, etc. Since the citizen is also a consumer, and vice versa, facts relating to the firm itself can have an adverse effect on the public's attitude toward its products. Thus when sales of Nestlé baby milk to mothers in the Third World were criticized, quiet but disturbing questions concerning the motives of the Swiss institution were provoked, leading to boycotts of Nestlé products in the United States and throughout Europe—although these never attained significant proportions, since the Nestlé brand image is so well developed. While in their case this image, which is linked to motherhood, served to protect their products, any other company with a poorer brand image would have suffered greatly from such a crisis. The effects of a company crisis usually penetrate through to its products. This is why Procter & Gamble envelops its products within a safety zone.

Like Henkel or Unilever, Procter & Gamble does not practice corporate branding—brand names are totally dissociated from that of the company, which only appears minutely on their packaging. Again, Procter & Gamble follows a product-brand policy. While a common brand and company name provide the advantage of combined capitalization, the single identity runs the risk of allowing company reverses to affect the brand, and vice versa. This is why, in reappraising communication after a crisis, it is important to carefully choose its focus in the BIPE system. It will not necessarily be the same as that giving birth to the crisis, as can be seen from the example of Chaumet jewelers.

The Chaumet affair hit the news in May 1987, when investigations revealed that the prestigious jewelry firm—internationally known for the past two hundred years—had liabilities of £200 million, resulting from illegal activities and fraudulent practices. The company bosses, Messrs. Jacques and Pierre Chaumet, were prosecuted for bankruptcy, fraud, breach of trust, and illegal means of obtaining credit. On 3 November 1987 the ailing company changed hands. The investment bankers Investcorp provided capital of £9.3 million. Apart from rights to the lease and to the workshops, the payment represented the capital value of the Chaumet and Breguet brands—stock was negotiated separately. A new director was named. The question now was where to focus their communication—on the new company, the products, the brand or institution.

The situation was easy to diagnose. In a certain way the company crisis provided an opportunity for Chaumet to develop, and to throw off the adverse image from which it had suffered before the crisis. The point was that, before the affair, Chaumet seemed weighed down by the notion of being too traditional and elitist, and somewhat immovable from its lofty perch in the jewelry world. In 1988 the ground was prepared for a complete break with the precrisis image. Those who had taken over Chaumet had done so to bring about change, and not to recreate an inferior version of the former image. If Chaumet were to carry on, its original style could not be imitated. It was therefore the ideal moment for product innovation and communication thereon. Nevertheless, such innovation should not lead to any loss of identity, whereby Chaumet would become just a name—an empty shell with no legitimate substance—as has happened to Rover, to some extent. We know that organizations focus their identity on one of three poles—a person, a management principle, or a product or skill. The removal of the Chaumet brothers meant that the new focus of communication could be none other than the product. It could therefore be said that product innovation was doubly necessary.

The more Chaumet developed, in both management and product terms, the more important was the need to consolidate the trust on the part of its followers in the Chaumet tradition—still regarded as an institution in the Place Vendôme. The international campaign, "Chaumet will always be Chaumet," proudly proclaimed its steadfast institutional standing, permanently rooted in the traditions of high-class jewelry. Such a stance would give credence to their new collection, even if it were unconventional—in fact, especially if this were so. Its declared affiliation to the permanence of the luxury trade had a double implication for their target public. It answered the sceptics—those ready to believe the rumor that Chaumet was no more. With its indirect reference to the scandal, it had faced up to the past and silenced it once and for all. In addition, however, the words "Chaumet will always be Chaumet" were the selling point for the new creations, so far as the majority of the international public—those unaware of the crisis—were concerned. They rekindled the sense of commitment and deep-seated identity which distinguishes Chaumet from creators with no tradition. The greater the creative qualities of the collection, the more the need to render them acceptable by recalling institutional values.

11
Financial Evaluation of Brands

The fact that the brand is a firm's capital asset scarcely needs emphasizing. In certain sectors, in fact, it forms the very lifeblood of the firm. Though factories and manpower may disappear, firms still retain a name whose public reputation is one of enduring asset value.

Until recently, awareness of the brand's importance was qualitative. It was a ritual slogan within marketing circles, which marketing managers used to ask for more advertising money. Their insatiable demands for brand support were not backed by a short-term view, but envisaged the long-term effects of such investment in creating a true brand equity.

It is common knowledge that massive sums spent on advertising are not always justified by short-term sales (Broadbent, 1983; Channon, 1987). Advertising investment can be quantified in monetary terms quite easily, but there is only a verbal promise of its long-term influence on brand value. The return on this investment is translated into another, less tangible, currency—brand awareness, brand image, attitudes. This subtle switch of currencies used to evaluate the inputs of the investment in brand equity, and its output, was for long a cause of incredulity among hard-headed financiers.

263

Ironically, it was the financial brains of hostile raiders which first revealed the monetary value of a firm's brands. These were not everyday financiers but those employed by companies having a firm intent on taking over another, or eager to purchase companies showing modest net results, or even those showing losses as a result of accumulated debts. From 1985 onward, in fact, there was an increasing number of mergers and acquisitions, for sums reaching previously unheard-of levels. Until then, price levels had been gauged on the financial results of the targeted company. The sum involved was on average eight to ten times its profits (coefficients known as the "multiple"). If the company included brands, these were considered as part of the assets.

In July 1983, for example, it cost Bernard Tapie 1 franc to take control of a 66 percent share in Look–a company famous in the world of skiing, with a turnover of £13.3m (millions) but with a deficit of £5.3m. Six years later, Bernard Tapie Finance sold Look to Ebel–Jellinek, an American–Swiss combine, for £25m, even though the company's latest balance sheet showed a loss of more than £4.1m and accumulated debts approaching £25m. Its turnover had, however, risen from £13.3m to £35m, thanks to successful diversification into automatic pedals and composite cycle frames sold internationally. To justify this high price in the light of their poor financial results, John Jellinek declared: "the brand has maintained a strong potential; we have our sights set on the boom in the U.S. cycling market." The future justified his price.

The case is not unique. In 1985, the Italian financier Carlo de Benedetti was about to buy the Buitoni company for less than £100m. The giant BSN, which had had its eyes on Buitoni for a few years, did not top the bid—the Buitoni company had a bad economic performance, with uncertain liability guarantees, while its products were considered of mediocre quality. Three years later, de Benedetti sold Buitoni to the Nestlé group for £800m—35 times its profits! In the interim period, de Benedetti had turned Buitoni into a truly European brand. It was a market leader in ready-cooked meals, and had expanded beyond its original Italian recipes. As an umbrella brand, Buitoni now covered couscous and paellas, as well as the typically French gratin dauphinois, in both canned and frozen form. In all, it embraced more than a hundred products worldwide, each with a common outlook—the same Buitoni logo which de Benedetti had conferred on all his subsidiary companies following its purchase.

De Benedetti had demonstrated his skill in basing the Buitoni purchase price on former averages calculated against the company's balance sheet, while being perfectly aware that Buitoni's true value was not represented in full measure in previous figures, but was available to anyone capable of exploiting the potential of the Buitoni brand name already implanted in all main European countries. This in fact he achieved by systematic recourse to brand extension and European globalization. In three years, Buitoni had grown from the seeds of possibility to become a brand leader, enjoying the privilege accorded to established European brands—a privilege whose possession was valued by Nestlé at £800 million, in view of the shortage of such brands on the market. In 1985, when other bidders were calculating their offers as if they were buying a company producing just canned foods and Italian pastas, de Benedetti knew that he was buying far more—a tremendous brand capital asking to be developed.

These are not two isolated cases. On the contrary, since 1986 there has been a frenzy of mergers and acquisitions in which brands have formed the real stakes—thus explaining the overbids and high multiples affecting takeover bids and raids. It is no longer rare to find offers at a multiple of more than 25 times company results—two or three times the share value. Nestlé, for example, bought Rowntree (maker of Kit-Kat, Polo, Quality Street, and After Eight) in April 1988 for £2.4bn, whereas its market value of equity was only £1bn. Nestlé was bid up to this figure by an initial offer by the Jacobs Suchard group on 13 April 1988, proposing 630 pence for each Rowntree share, then valued at 450 pence. On 26 April, Nestlé offered 890 pence. On 26 May Suchard raised its bid to 950 pence, which led Nestlé to offer 1075 pence per share.

This overbid was triggered by the necessity to gain a dominant foothold in the prospective European market. New brands stand no chance of rivaling the Mars group in the confectionary market. It is no longer an expanding market, and the older brands such as Mars, Nuts, Treets, and Kit Kat have their brand-loyal consumers. To create a brand from scratch would cost gigantic sums, take years, and probably result in failure. Suchard and Nestlé had no other choice than to expand externally. There were, however, few candidates throughout the world—Cadbury and Rowntree in the U.K., Hershey in the United States, or the Swiss competition. Faced with a restrictive market, it was natural for the two Swiss companies to keep raising the bidding in their own strategic interest. Even at such a high price, the world-established Rowntree brands represented better value than a possibly-futile attempt to promote their own brands. Apart from the instant access to an existing share of the market, the acquisition would afford considerable savings as a result of synergies and integration of activities. Such savings are part and parcel of any merger—a single headquarters instead of two, a single sales force, extra discounts from suppliers, and better cooperation with the retail trade.

The sums involved in these transactions provide an indication of the financial value of the brands—at least in the eyes of their purchasers. At the maximum, this value is equal to the difference between the price paid and the value of the net assets indicated on the company balance sheet (the purchased goodwill). In fact, this "overvaluation" does not necessarily correspond wholly to the value of the brand. Part of it often is the result of overbidding. For example, in June 1989, Hermès made an offer of £2.7m for the Saint-Louis Cristal company. Since the latter had no net assets, one can assume that this price reflected the estimated value of the Saint-Louis Cristal glass brand. Faced, however, with a competing offer from the American company Brown Forman, with its Jack Daniel's whiskey and Lenox porcelain, Hermès raised their bid to £6.8m. The difference between the two offers indicates the amount of overbid. The purchase price thus incorporates the cost of outbidding a competitor. Commenting on the price which BSN paid for Nabisco Europe ($2.5bn—a multiple of 27), the *Financial Times* indicated on 7 June 1989 that, like Nestlé, BSN were paying twice—once to obtain the brands, and a second time to prevent them ending up in a competitor's brand portfolio.

The specific value of purchased brands is isolated in consolidated accounts. In France, accounting rules stipulate that the overvaluation known as "goodwill" must be posted as an asset and written off over five years. At the same time, firms may allocate part of this goodwill to intangible assets such as patents, business capital, and brands. In charging part of the goodwill to brands, firms are able to write them off over a longer period, or even to refrain from depreciating their cost altogether—as in the case of BSN. In the U.K., it is customary for goodwill to be totally eliminated by deducting it from reserves the same year, thus preventing the burden of the depreciation from affecting annual results—though leading to a reduction in profits. This practice was overturned by Reckitt & Colman. Having bought the Airwick group (and its brands) from Ciba–Geigy, in March 1985, for £165 million—a record multiple of 41 times the profits—Reckitt & Colman decided to post £55.8m as assets, deeming this to be the value of the purchased brands. The difference between this amount and the price of £165m was the value of material assets such as buildings, machinery, and stock, together with the unassigned overvaluation or goodwill. They continued to deduct this unassigned goodwill from reserves. Reckitt & Colman was able, by means of this technical twist, to show a clear increase in company assets—resulting in this case from the acquisition of intangible assets in the form of well-known brands.

In 1988, Ranks Hovis McDougall went a step further, when they decided to post as assets an estimated value of the brands created and developed by themselves. Though not strictly taboo, it was the first salvo in a fierce battle over the capitalization of internally grown brands on the balance sheet. The debate provoked in the U.K. spread to Australia and Europe, where there was a cry for harmonization of accounting practices. The decision on the part of Ranks Hovis McDougall—followed by others in the U.K.—is contrary to European and American practices, which forbid the reevaluation of purchased intangible assets, and as a consequence the inclusion on the balance sheet of internally created assets.

Apart from the debate in accounting circles, the RHM action posed a fundamental problem. Whereas companies acquiring brands have a right to show them on the balance sheet, thus openly pronouncing their asset value, companies which prefer to develop their own brands do not have this facility, and are therefore unable to display their true asset figure. This inability to include one's own brands could lead to a weakening of the company structure, leaving it a prey to raiders. With the company undervalued on the market, share values would open the way for a low-price takeover bid, with almost guaranteed profits. The Rowntree affair really opened out this argument. Though the Rowntree market value of equity was just £1bn in

March 1988, Nestlé bought them out in July for £2.4bn. Was it a question of the market having undervalued the brands and their future potential? When threatened with a takeover bid, Ranks Hovis McDougall preferred to take the initiative by openly emphasizing the estimated value of their brands, thus swelling the company assets for the benefit of shareholders and investors.

The controversy surrounding the inclusion of all forms of brands—acquired or created—raises fundamental questions regarding accounting procedure. What goals should statements of accounts and annual reports pursue? Should they allow a very subjective appreciation of the company's real economic value, or should they incline toward prudence by including only objective details of actual completed transactions? Until now, every country has chosen the second option, allowing external brands to be entered. Since they were purchased, there is an objective transaction value. The inclusion of internal brands, though bowing to reality, places a question mark over the reliability and consistency of the accounting process. A balance sheet compiled according to inconsistent and sometimes subjective evaluation methods would lack credibility. Since an acquired brand constitutes a cost, its charge conforms with basic accounting principles. How, on the other hand, is one to evaluate one's own created brands? As we shall see, it is impracticable to use methods relying on historic or replacement costs. One can only base such evaluation on projected future revenue—a highly subjective approach. Such hypothetical figures in the balance sheet would introduce an element of uncertainty and discord which would be far from prudent, leading to permanent reappraisals, up and down, from one year to another.

We can thus draw our first conclusion concerning a brand's financial value. To be acceptable in both financial and accounting terms, the evaluation method should be applicable to both acquired and created brands. This, however, is not possible, since the notion of value depends firmly on one's point of view. As far as the Rowntree shareholders were concerned, the company was worth £1bn; to Nestlé, it was worth £2.4bn. The Midland Bank valued Lanvin at £40m; L'Oreal put it at £50m. A further point is that accounting methods are governed by principles of prudence, objectivity, and consistency. By definition, a predator forms a very different evaluation. Brand evaluation made in the context of a merger or acquisition is a specific one, aimed to fix a starting price based on the intentions and expectations of the prospective purchaser and the synergies he expects. Evaluation for accounting purposes has to respect other standards and be regarded from a different point of view. Taking the internal brand, for example, with no transaction on which to base its value, it would have to be valued according to its existing use, as opposed to an intended or potential use. This again will result in a necessary difference between the asset value of a purchased brand and that of a created brand. Also, if one's own brands are to have a legitimate place in the balance sheet, they need to be periodically revalued—up or down—in a rather subjective manner. Such fluctuations undermine the reliability of annual reports. One can understand why accountancy experts at the London Business School, when asked their opinions on the inclusion of every brand in the balance sheet, were against it (Barwise *et al.*, 1989).

Those who were happiest at the prospect of adding brand values to accounts were the marketing fraternity. They now had a means at their disposal—legitimized by accountants and financiers—by which the long-term effects of marketing decisions could be measured. Even though, as we recall, it is taken as granted that advertising has both short-term and long-term effects, brand accounting processes are governed by the short term. Product or brand managers have to produce positive annual running accounts and profit-and-loss balances. Evaluation and assessment are therefore necessarily carried out on an annual basis. This tends to favor all decisions which have advantageous short-term results. Accounting for brand value would allow marketing personnel to counter this short-term drift, which admittedly allows inflated annual returns but can sap the brand's equity. Such undermining can, for example, result from permanent promotions, and extensions which are too remote from the brand core—both of which afford rapid results, though with adverse effects in the long term. The pursuit of increased brand awareness at any price can eventually cease to provide any marginal increase in the brand's capital value, and the sums involved would have been better allocated elsewhere.

In more general terms, measuring a brand's value means identifying the sources of this value—in other words, measuring is understanding. Marketing bosses are therefore less interested in the final valuation figure than in the process by which it has been arrived at—

that is to say, their understanding of the brand's operation and expansion, and of its various fluctuations in value. It is a gradual understanding, calling for logical analysis and concentrated thought. As such it allows for deep interplay between such disciplines as marketing, finance, accounting, and law. For these reasons alone, in fact, even if inclusion of one's created brands in the balance sheet is not allowed, there is no reason why their value should not be measured, internally, for the firm's own purposes. Realistically speaking, even though mergers and acquisitions capture the media attention, they are comparatively rare. The movement by firms to take up battle stations in the run-up to 1992 was bound to slow. A brand should not be valued only on such occasions—the process is justified at any time by the benefits gained in management, decision-making, control, information systems, and the training of product or brand managers. The demands of presenting annual reports for the benefit of shareholders and investors are one thing—those required in systematic management control are another. The two should not be confused, since they share neither the same objectives nor the same constraints.

Thus in respecting the principle of prudence, company accountants only consider a good investment to be one which guarantees a future return—no matter how far off. With no such guarantee, advertising is termed an expense, and charged annually. Part of the advertising budget can certainly bring a short-term profit—advertising does lead to short-term but temporary behavioral shifts. However, the rest of the budget can still do its work in promoting the long-term awareness of the brand and its image. This second objective could, in fact, be set against the internal brand valuation, in so far as awareness and image are necessary contributors to a brand's value.

What conclusions may be drawn at this stage?

- Brand evaluation provides a unique opportunity for various company departments—marketing, financial, etc.—to put their heads together.
- It introduces the prospect of capitalizing in the long term, as opposed to the processes of annual evaluation.
- It reminds us that it is no longer land, buildings, or machines which constitute a firm's true wealth, but its intangible assets such as know-how, patents, and brands.

The debate over brand valuation is basically a matter of the appropriate accounting methods—which are soon to be regulated as a result of EC directives. Although it is important, this issue should not lead us to forget the main point: the importance of a brand's valuation in appraising marketing and advertising decisions—governed until now by the annual accounts system. Before entering into any detail on brand valuation methods themselves, it is important to remember that the very objective of an evaluation—takeovers, management control, or presentation of accounts—has a modifying influence on the criteria controlling these methods. With this objective in mind, one is made to choose between two scarcely compatible requirements—further validity or further reliability. In other words, one has to decide on a path of either greater subjectivity or greater objectivity.

THE PROBLEM OF BRAND SEPARABILITY

Whatever method is used to value a brand, the most difficult problem, and the least resolved, so far is that of brand demarcation—its separability from the rest of the company and from the other intangible assets such as patents, know-how, and business relationships. In a legal sense, the right to use a brand name can, of course, be transferred, or even sold. However, in buying the name, is one buying the brand? Though the name signifies a difference, it is only an echo of the underlying difference. The brand, on the other hand, accumulates its strength over a period of time as a result of combined know-how and communication. Through advertising, the brand can reach out to a wide clientele, justifying the risks in R&D and production which can offer a return on investment. The image and confidence so formed in the minds of a satisfied public allow the brand to conquer new product territories, and to take further risks in innovation. From the company's own point of view, the brand is a means of reassurance and a source of stability and confidence.

The established brand has true economic value—a firm having brands is worth more than one with no brands. Nevertheless, measuring the value of brands, and of their marginal benefits over other company assets—material and otherwise—is a delicate problem resulting from the difficulty in separating that part of the profits accrued by the brand from those applicable to other assets. There is certainly little problem in this respect in separating the brand from fixed assets. Yet how are we to sort out its share of the profits from that of other intangible assets? Was Zantac's success due to its brand or to its revolutionary formula, ranatidine? Is the value of a service brand separable from its managerial know-how, which, though intangible, is real in the sense of being a guiding force? If, for example, one buys an advertising agency—renowned though it may be—without its top managers, is it still the same brand? As we can guess, for accounting purposes it is almost impossible to isolate the specific economic value of the brand in the strictest sense. A brand's strength is composed of many contributory factors. The problem does not arise in the case of mergers or acquisitions, since more often than not the whole company is purchased, including all of its intangible assets. The brand's financial evaluation encompasses all these intangible assets, and is easily differentiated from the material assets, whose intrinsic value and appropriate cost can soon be established. Following the purchase, however, the problem of separability arises in determining that part of the overvaluation (or goodwill) to be apportioned to the brand. The figure will be influenced by accounting, financial outlook, and tax considerations. The near impossibility of separating the brand from the other intangible assets does not impede valuation for internal administration purposes, since in this case the brand's value is considered as the sum total of all its contributory factors.

Separability ceases to be an accounting or theoretical problem when the brand is sold separately from the firm. This happened when the Buitoni brand was bought in 1989 by Nestlé. The rest of the Buitoni company assets, such as factories and warehouses, were sold separately. Here it is important to examine whether those assets not sold with the brand constitute factors necessary for its success. The brand can only be separated if, in spite of its alienation from the rest of the company, it remains unchanged. This is not always the case.

Smirnoff Vodka is a brand which could be separated in this way, Mars rather less so, and IBM not at all. The reason is that there is little specific know-how required in producing vodka. Anyone purchasing only the exclusive ownership rights of the brand name, label, and bottle, but forsaking the factories, could still benefit from the brand's attraction for retailers and consumers alike. The Smirnoff reputation does not derive from any particular devotion to the company as such.

Vodka being vodka, the only differentiation lies in the brand image, whence the fact that it is only necessary to hold the rights of ownership to the brand images—bottle, symbol, label, name. Counterfeits and retailer counterbrands reinforce this point by the way in which they closely reproduce these images.

Would Mars still be Mars if the brand were sold separately from its factories? No, since the Mars-brand loyal consumers have become used to a very specific taste, and texture, which are part of the company know-how. Mars is a product with unique qualities—a brand–product, or "branduct" (Swiners, 1979). The know-how is part of the brand, and cannot be dissociated if the brand is to retain its equity.

Could Ricard pastas be sold as well by anyone other than Ricard? The brand undoubtedly enjoys a high degree of awareness, and is likely to be the first name to spring to mind when one thinks of pastas. It could, however, be debated that the strength of the brand is overestimated. Part of its sales are possibly due to the influence of the Pernod–Ricard group, which carries weight in persuading retailers to give the brand maximum presence on their shelves.

Wishing to get out of the diaper market, Colgate–Palmolive sold its Caline brand in France for a relatively small sum. Celatose, who bought it, went bankrupt a few years later. Caline's market share was not the mere result of its brand awareness and image; it had previously been created and nurtured by a permanent and costly emphasis on R&D with the corporate backing of the Colgate–Palmolive group. In purchasing Caline as a separate entity, Celatose had bought a homonym, but not really the same brand. This necessarily applies in any sector where technology counts, and where the brand signifies a real noticeable difference.

The promise of security implied in the IBM name cannot be disconnected from the company itself. An asset is something which promises likely future benefits as a result of previous transactions or undertakings on the part of the firm. In line with this definition, the brand is an asset, whether it be acquired or created by the firm. As the above examples show, the brand's asset cannot be isolated in the case of every company. Sometimes it is but the recipient of a combination of attributes exclusively linked to such other intangible assets as patents, know-how, and trade relations. An acquired brand has, by definition; a separable value, indicated in the transaction. On the other hand, it is difficult to isolate the value of an internally created brand, since it is often inseparable from a firm's other assets. One step in resolving this difficulty lies in an appreciation of the brand system and its interrelationship with other sources of product growth, together with its means of gaining a profitable share of the market.

Figure 11.1 indicates the two essential sources of brand value. Profits attributable to the brand derive either from an increment in demand compared to that of a generic product, or from reduced production and distribution costs resulting from overall savings and productivity gains based on the experience curve. Such productivity gains can serve to finance growing retailer demands, influencing the presence and prominence of the brand on the shelves. They can also allow a reduction in selling price, thus increasing the brand's competitive advantage and its quality/price ratio. This then results in customer loyalty, since each repurchase offers the same satisfaction—resulting from the product's performance, stability, price, and image. From the consumer's point of view, the brand distinguishes the offer, reduces risk, and saves on the effort of making a choice. The brand acquires its meaning through the communication and use of its products, and, in its familiar and reassuring nature, is regarded as a promise of performance, quality, convenience, service, style, and modernity.

Not all brand sales are necessarily attributable to the brand itself. Trial purchases may result from a high shelf visibility and an attractive penetration price. If satisfied with the product, the consumer will retain a visual memory of the brand or its position on the shelves, thus making it easier to find on the next occasion. On the other hand, no mental picture will be evoked if the brand does not have a specific quality or particular meaning. In such a case the brand is weak in spite of having a high share of the market. Many brands survive only because retailers want them to.

Figure 11.1 further emphasizes that many brands would not enjoy their share of the market without the corporate support and reputation. When a retailer orders a brand, he is influenced partly by the corporate weight. One could extend the argument to product brands whose sales reflect the influence of the endorsing or parent brand.

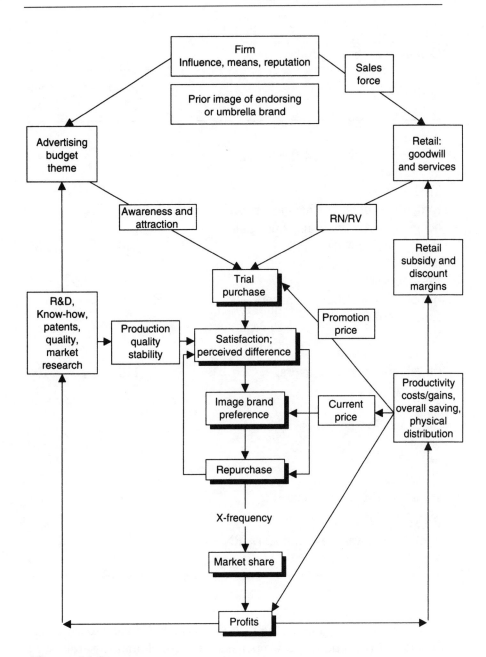

Figure 11.1

The brand system and the problem of separability.

Table 11.1

Comparative brand profiles

	Brand A	Brand B
Awareness (% of people who know the brand)	50	40
x		
Trial (proportion of people having already bought or used the brand among all those who know it)	40	35
x		
Re-purchase (proportion of initial purchasers who continue to use it)	20	40
x		
Level of purchase (in relation to market average)	110	100
x		
Availability (% of people who can easily find the brand)	70	20
=		
Use share (equivalent to market share)	3.1	1.1
Potential (with 100% awareness and 100% RN/RV availability)	8.8	14.0

Figure 11.1 also draws attention to the importance of knowing which factors contribute to the market share, with a view to assessing the brand's potential. As it happens, a measure of brand awareness or market share at a given moment can give a false idea of respective brand values. The following illustration demonstrates this. Compare the profiles of brands A and B, as shown in Table 11.1

On the face of it, the brand profile scores would lead us to believe that brand A is stronger than B (3.1 against 1.1). However, where potential is concerned, B is the more promising and less exploited in relation to its market share (14.0 against 8.8).

Any evaluation of a brand's long-term potential in a given market must incorporate the relative influences of generating factors linked solely with the brand, and should not be based on variables which, though coincident, would no longer apply if the brand were sold and became separated from the firm.

Potential in a segment = pure demand x pure offer x time x segment growth

By "pure demand," we are referring to that proportion of sales which can be guaranteed by the brand and its various attributes, as opposed to the proportion which would immediately pass to another brand having the same exterior characteristics sold at the same spot at the same price. This is calculated by measuring brand preferences. The "pure offer" is the level of retail numbers or value (RN/RV) attributable to the brand rather than to the influence of a group or endorsing brand. What, for example, would be the attitude of a retailer if the brand changed hands? The time factor measures the brand's ability to be less sensitive to circumstances and to maintain its competitive edge over a period:

- Will it avail itself of patents and specific know-how; and if so, for how long?
- Will it be capable of following up its efforts in R&D in order to achieve continuous product improvement?
- Will it have the means of maintaining its in-store awareness and presence?
- Is it prepared against new competition?
- Can it easily sway the preferences of consumers and retailers?
- Will the advantage be maintained in the face of retailer counterbrands?

Finally, one must take account of the anticipated expansion of the segment itself.

The above analysis is compiled within a market segment. It should be followed up by an examination of the potential in sectors or markets from which the brand is momentarily absent, but which it is capable of joining.

VALUATION IN TERMS OF COSTS

In determining a brand's value, one comes across difficulties arising from the very concept of value. There is not one value but several, depending on the point of view of the person making the valuation—the premise of value. Value is a subjective notion in that it is governed by the changeability of those who make the evaluation, and their specific goals. The process is therefore contrary to the principles governing accounting and financial information—those which call for substantiation, objectivity, and reason. From this point of view, the only acceptable methods are those based on historic or replacement costs. While not totally objective, they have the advantage of at least being semisubjective in the sense that independent valuations would arrive at roughly the same figures.

Valuation According to Historic Costs

The brand is an asset whose value springs from investments over a period of time—even though accountants do not strictly regard this as a true form of investment. The logical approach would therefore be to add together all the costs over a set period—development costs, marketing costs, advertising and general communication costs, etc. These costs can be determined objectively and will have been included in past income statements.

As we can see, such an approach overcomes the delicate problem of separability, by isolating the costs directly attributable to the brand and also by including a proportion of indirect costs, such as sales force and general expenses. Simple and logical though the principle may be, this method nevertheless presents the following practical difficulties, which reintroduce a certain subjectivity:

- Over what period should costs be taken into account? Numerous brands are very old, as we know—Coca-Cola goes back to 1887, Dannon to 1919, Bull to 1933, Yves Saint Laurent to 1958. Should we include costs right from their very beginnings? So many old brands are today very weak. The more realistic approach would be to determine to what extent the present market share can be attributed to past advertising.
- Which costs should be taken into account? Advertising investment has a double marketing purpose. One part provokes

extra sales, which can be measured immediately, while the other part reinforces the brand awareness and image, to the benefit of future sales. The practical difficulty is in estimating year-by-year the proportions of the two-way split. Again, when we speak of future sales, how far ahead are we looking? We need to look at the advertising wear-out curves over a given time. If—as shown in studies on the persistence of attitude changes—such effects decrease linearly over five years, for example, one can include expenses arising over the past five years, accepting only 20 percent of those for year n - 5.

- It is not simply a question of adding up the costs, but of taking into account an appropriate discounting rate which has to be determined.

In addition to the fairly subjective approach necessarily required in tackling the above difficulties, valuation by means of costs causes several basic problems resulting from a partial understanding of the brand.

- In creating a brand, a large part of the long-term investment does not involve a cash outlay, and therefore cannot be entered in accounts. These include stringent quality controls, accumulated know-how, specific expertise, personnel involvement, etc. All are essential in achieving continuous sales and enduring quality reputation.
- To create a strong brand, one of the major strategies consists in choosing a competitive launch price, even though one may be offering an upgraded product compared with that of the competition. Swatch was a typical example. They could have opted for a slight price differential, or price premium, to cover the costs of the innovation in their product. They decided, however, to set an attacking price equal to that of their competitors, thus maximizing the brand's quality/price ratio and enhancing its attractiveness. This was one of the pillars of the Swatch success. Unfortunately this noncash investment would not appear in a system where only cash outlay can be registered.
- The method therefore favors brands whose value results only from advertising and marketing, compensated by a large price differential. It would not apply to brands such as Rolls–Royce

or St. Michael, which rely much more on reputation. It could also be said that past expenditure is not a guarantee of present value. Several heavily advertised brands today show hardly any value, or indeed presence.

In strict accounting terms, the use of this method to include internal brands on the balance sheet—if it should gain recognition—would pose two considerable problems. On the one hand, one would be reentering costs which had already been posted at an earlier date as running expenses. More problematic is the choice of the point in time from which an internally created brand should be included in the balance sheet. As we have already said, the brand historically comes to light as a product name. During the early years, no distinction is made between brand and product. The point here is that only that part of the advertising aimed at furthering the brand should, in theory, be taken into account—and not the marketing costs involved in selling the product. Unfortunately, several years have to pass before we know if a real brand has been created—one capable of detaching itself from the initial product and of supporting other products in other markets. With no precise means of prediction, should we not, during these initial years, refrain from including the brand as any asset whatsoever, but enter its value all in one go at a time when the brand has revealed its ability?

It is obvious that the use of the historical costs approach requires many assumptions concerning the sources of the brand value. On the other hand, studies have shown that many brands which led their market in 1989 were doing so as far back as 1933—e.g., Colgate, Kodak, Gillette, Kellogg's, Hoover, etc. (Blackett, 1989). Other writers have shown that the best prediction of being today's leader is to have been so ten years ago (Jones, 1987). Communication and R&D during the interim period help to maintain the leadership, but cannot be considered as reasons for a brand's present leadership. Choosing a valid accounting period is, as we can see, very hit-and-miss.

Valuation According to Replacement Costs

To overcome the difficulties arising from the historical costs approach, it might be preferable to return to the present and to confront the problem by resorting to the classic alternative—as we cannot buy this brand, how much would it cost the firm to recreate it? With its total profile in mind—awareness, percentage of trial and repurchases, absolute and relative market share, distribution network, image and leadership—what would we have to spend, and over what period, to create an equivalent brand?

Could one remake Coca-Cola, Schweppes, Chanel, or Adidas? Probably not. Could one remake Benetton, Bang & Olufsen, or Amstrad? Probably so. For a certain number of brands, the question no longer arises, since they could not be recreated. There has been too great a change in context: they were born in an era when advertising investment was negligible, and were nurtured over the years by reputation. Today, the high cost of just a 1 percent share of voice confounds any hope of rapidly recreating a brand leader in unaided awareness. In any case, unaided awareness is a very restricted area (Laurent, Kapferer, and Roussel, 1987). In order to gain entrance, a competing brand must be ejected. There is no reason why today's well-known brands should allow themselves to be thrown out (see page 91).

It is not easy to imitate the performance level of brand leaders. Backed by research and development, and an intangible but nevertheless very real know-how, they enjoy a long-lasting competitive advantage which affords an image of stability. Any challenger is taking a risk. Unless he has access to the necessary technology, his chances of acquiring continuous sales and brand loyalty are zero.

Major retailers have now used their combined efforts to carve up the market. They give pride of place to their own brands, only keeping one or two national brands, the market leaders (Thil and Baroux, 1983).

Finally, when we look at the high failure rate of new product launches, we can grasp the uncertainty surrounding the benefits of the huge sums which need to be invested over a long period. As this price increases, one may as well buy certainty—hence the rash of takeover bids, incursions, mergers, and acquisitions of firms with strong brands which are already market leaders. On the other hand, when there are no such factors making up barriers to entry, the market is more accessible. The possibility of creating tomorrow's brand leaders from scratch ceases to be theoretical, even though the uncertainty and necessary time element might remain. If this happens, we shall probably see future Benettons arise—the franchise system allows wider penetration without admitting defeat at the hands of major retailers. Again, the fashion world is open to new ideas. In this domain, style is more important than technology. Computer services and the high-tech world in general are also crying out for innovation. Generally speaking, the future will see the emergence of new international brands, each settled in its own particular niche. As such they will cease to pursue global awareness, but will aspire to leadership of specific segments.

Brand valuation through replacement costs nevertheless remains very subjective. It requires the combined opinions of experts on somewhat ambiguous lines. Moreover, it should be remembered that the aim of the valuation process is not, in itself, to arrive at a figure for the sake of it, but to obtain a fair idea of the economic value of the asset in question—in this case the brand. Cost methods focus on the brand's input, whereas its economic value applies to its output—what it produces, and not what it absorbs.

VALUATION ACCORDING TO MARKET PRICE

In valuing a brand, why not use the value of similar brands up for purchase as a starting point? This is how property and second-hand cars are valued. Each dwelling or car is inspected and given a price above, equal to, or below the market average for its corresponding type.

Enticing though it is, this approach raises two major problems when applied to brands. The first is that a market does not effectively exist. Although such transactions hit the financial news, acquisitions and brand sales are relatively few and far between. Brands are not generally bought to be resold. In spite of this, the fact that the number of acquisitions since 1983 has given an idea of the multiples applying to a particular sector—from 25 to 30—could tempt anyone seeking a valuation to adopt such an approach. There is the further consideration that the housing market has a far wider scope than the present small brand market. Where housing is concerned, the purchaser has to take the price fixed by the market. Irrespective of the use he will make of the property, the price remains the same. In the case of brands, the purchaser sets the price. Each purchaser bases his valuation on his own views and future strategy. Why did Unilever pay £70m for Boursin, the prestigious cheese brand? It resulted from the pressing need on the part of the group to acquire major retailer shelf space in an area from which it had previously been absent. Having at its disposal an obligatory brand for such purposes, they saw a way of opening the door to other speciality products.

In abstract terms, the purchase price is therefore not that paid for the brand, but is the considered value of the purchaser's use of it. To use the price paid for a similar brand as a reference, without knowing the specific reasons behind that brand's purchase, would ignore the fact that an essential part of the price probably corresponded to the specific aims of the purchaser in question. Each purchaser has his own intentions and framework of ideas. Value cannot be determined by proxy. Furthermore, the published price is not always the real price: noncash or deferred advantages are kept secret. This is what basically differentiates the brand market from that of housing. In the latter case, the price is governed by certain standards which are independent of the purchaser's intentions. In spite of this, valuations in the luxury market frequently take account of recent transactions, and have been based on a multiple of the turnover (1.5 for Yves Saint Laurent, 2 for Lanvin and Balmain, 2.9 for Martell, and 2 for Benedictine).

Realizing the difficulties inherent in methods based on costs or on reference to a hypothetical market, prospective purchasers tend rather to consider the profits to be anticipated from brand ownership. Since this third type of approach relies on two major philosophies, we are devoting a special section to its study.

VALUATION ACCORDING TO POTENTIAL EARNINGS

Since the brand aspires to become an asset, we might begin by defining an asset. It is a factor bringing probable future gains. Valuation methods have, as such, been based on the anticipated returns relating to brand ownership. Naturally, these tie in fully with the purchaser's intentions. If he seeks to internationalize the brand, it will be of greater value to him than to a purchaser wishing to retain the brand on a local footing. Value gauged on expected profits is totally linked with the intentions of the future purchaser and his wide-ranging plans for the brand. It is for this reason that the stock-market value of a branded company will always be structurally lower than that seen by a predator. The former valuation is related to the existing business, arrived at through current facts and figures provided by the firm. The latter can be ascribed to the overvaluation created by the prospect of synergies, complementary marketing processes, and the attainment of strategic market positions.

There are two independent phases in the process of evaluating a brand's anticipated gains. The first is one of separation, the second that of prediction. In other words, the first task consists of isolating the net revenue attributable to the brand—and to it alone—while the second task is to estimate the future flow of such revenue and its present value.

Isolating the Brand's Net Revenue

What is a strong brand? It is one capable of bringing in revenue greater than that of an unbranded product. In other words, the "augmented product," designated by its brand name, should be a source of profits over and above those accruing from a simple, unbranded product. The "augmented product" idea reminds us that it is not simply a question of evaluating the brand name and symbolism—its associated tangible attributes should also be taken into account. If a firm allows its "augmented product" to pass under the guise of an unbranded product or retailer own-label, it will certainly boost its sales but will undermine the basic reasoning behind the brand (to indicate a difference) and trivialize the brand name. It thus destroys the brand's value. Marginal income, versus that of selling an unbranded product, has three sources: a higher demand (QB), a possibly higher price (PB), and a lower production and distribution cost (CB). From these must be subtracted the cost of marketing the brand, and also the cost of R&D and taxes on the excess income.

$$RB - R = QB(PB - CB) - Q(P - C) - MKTG - R\&D - TAX$$

The practical problem now lies in evaluating the excess profit due directly to the brand's influence. There are several possible methods.

THE PREMIUM-PRICING METHOD

This consists of taking the difference between the brand price and that of a generic or unbranded product, and multiplying it by the brand's volume of sales to obtain the turnover which is due to the brand. In the above equation, this frequent approach assumes that costs are identical (CB = C) and that there is an equal volume of sales from the unbranded product (QB = Q). Sometimes these hypotheses are well-founded, as in the evaluation of champagne brands. They use the premium-pricing method since, with champagne, the difference between the top and bottom range for one particular brand depends on the quality of grapes as a whole, the year, and the ripening period. The cost price is overall identical (C = CB). Again, with demand clearly outstripping production, there are no unsold products—and unknown champagne would sell just as well as a bottle of Veuve Clicquot (Q = QB), though certainly not at the same price (PB = 2P). In this case it is therefore easy to calculate the excess annual profit attributable to the brand, particularly since there are lower marketing budgets in this sector, and no R&D at all.

The problem with this method lies in its hypothetical nature, there being no guarantee of a generic product with which to compare. The appearance of generic colas is a recent market phenomenon. What is the generic equivalent of unique products such as Schweppes, Chanel, or Mars? The suggestion that generic features could be "notionally" reproduced is scarcely realistic. More serious is the fact that this valuation method implicitly assumes that all brands pursue a price premium strategy. This method overvalues the dearer small brand and undervalues major brands such as Swatch, which pursue an aggressive price policy and derive their benefits largely from added volume and increased productivity.

THE ROYALTIES METHOD

What annual royalties could the company hope to receive if it transferred the rights to use the brand under license? The answer to this question would form a means of directly measuring the brand's financial contribution in the strictest sense, and would also dispense with the problem of separability. The figure obtained could subsequently be used in calculating the discounted cash flows over several years (see below). Unfortunately, this is not a current practice in most markets. We find it in soft drinks—e.g., Coca-Cola—and in the service and luxury trades. In strictly notional terms, it is not certain that this method properly isolates the brand as a unit (Barwise, 1989). The fact is that licenses often are used by firms to cover countries where they have no presence. However, the royalty figure does not solely include the use of the brand. The brand owner also undertakes to supply a package of basic materials, know-how, and services which allow the licensee to maintain the brand's appropriate quality level.

THE BRAND-SENSITIVITY METHOD

In this case, the brand strength is not measured by the number of its purchasers but by the number of those who recognize the brand (Kapferer and Laurent, 1983). This line of reasoning stems from an acknowledged fact—a certain proportion of the purchasers of brand X do not buy it just because it is X. They would just as soon buy Y or Z, or even an unknown brand. Their behavior is ascribable either to price, or to the fact that it is the only commodity of its type in the store, or in its particular format, or is the most easily accessible, occupying major shelf space. For low-involvement products, the customer's behavior is greatly influenced by such situational factors, and scarcely by any attachment to the brand. This is how major retailers decide where to place their own labels and counter-brands. Though disappointed, the purchaser will not go away empty-handed.

A percentage of purchasers in any market are sensitive to certain brands. This brand sensitivity—an indirect pointer to the purchasing influence of the brand—can be measured (Kapferer and Laurent, 1988). Among those consumers who are brand-sensitive in general, only a certain number may know* a particular brand and can thus be influenced by it. Finally, a proportion of purchases depend on the ease with which one can find the brand in a retail outlet—an ease which could be less apparent if the brand were marketed by some other company than its current owner. The more a brand is autonomous from the firm, the smaller will be the influence of the brand's compa-

---

*Depending on the market, this constitutes either unaided or assisted awareness.

ny on retailers' attitudes. The formula applying to the turnover attributable to the brand itself is therefore:

$$QBPB = SB = SALES \times INFLUENCE \times AWARENESS \times AUTONOMY$$

We then have to subtract the turnover expected from the exploitation of a current unbranded product (QP), in the brand profit equation (see page 284). In many markets, this type of exploitation has now become impossible. Since major retailers only retain the strongest brands, the possibilities of persuading them to accept an unbranded product have become nil—unless the firm has undue influence, which is exceptional. The only way out is to supply retailer-named brands. In this case, we are forced to appreciate that the provision of retailer-named brands can lower the production costs as a result of full capacity, and vice versa.

SEPARATING SUPPLY EFFECTS FROM DEMAND EFFECTS

In today's consumer-goods markets, brand sales depend considerably more on the attitude of retailers than on that of customers. For low-involvement products, very few customers will change store if their brand is not present. This is why many retailers are able to dispense with national brands. They are safe in their attitude as a result of inertia on the part of the weekly shopper, who has no say in the matter.

How do we separate that part of a brand's gross sales due to the offer—its availability in the store and prominence on the shelves—from the proportion due to the brand? The brand-sensitivity approach relies on verbal replies to a questionnaire. By turning to panel data, it is possible to obtain a behavioral response to the above question.

The principle is simple. Suppose we take four brands, all at the same price, each having a 25 percent share of the total sales. The mathematical assumption is that the sales of each brand resulting from the offer are 25 percent of the total sales on the shelf. Any sales above or below this expected figure will result from the brand. Thanks to data banks, panels can measure the effect of the percentage of the shelf allotted to a brand on its sales, and the effect of price on demand—again in relation to the type of store (e.g., hypermarket, supermarket). It is this difference between gross sales (observed) and predicted sales—taking into account the brand's price, shelf share, etc.—which is the real measure of a brand's strength.

$$\text{Brand strength} = \frac{\text{Actual sales}}{\text{Sales due to the supply}}$$

The separation methods examined above allow us to come up with a figure specifically attributable to the brand—in the form of either excess profit or net cash flow. They need to be related to the business plan which justified its acquisition, or in any case to stimulate interest.

Valuation of future profitability therefore progresses in three stages:

1. A strategic evaluation of the brand using a multicriteria approach allowing us to appreciate its strengths, weaknesses, and potential.
2. Assessment of the revenue specifically attributable to the brand in considering its possible strategic extensions. Here the above separation methods are used.
3. Capitalization of the brand revenue. This is achieved either by applying a determined multiple to the present result, or by discounted cash flow. Both methods are often used together, since each relies on approximations.

Multicriteria Valuation of a Brand's Potential

A company acquiring a brand naturally seeks to profit from it. The brand is often assigned to products or markets from which it was hitherto excluded. Such ambitions for the brand must be realistic and must take account of its intrinsic potential. In practical terms, this requires auditing the brand according to a small number of criteria predicting its future potential, either within its own market or beyond. The brand's overall profile according to these criteria will indicate its strength.

Different authors or consulting agencies have put forward several criteria. The Interbrand Company marks the brand against seven factors and sums the total of the seven individual marks, balanced against the weightings of each factor. The resultant total gives a "brand strength score." What are the most pertinent factors in evaluation?

MARKET LEADERSHIP

Does the brand lead its market? We are now well aware of the link between market share and profitability, as well as the strategic advantage in having a dominant relative market share (Buzzell *et al.*, 1975; Porter, 1980; Jacobson and Aaker, 1985). This criterion becomes even more important in fast-moving consumer goods, where major retailers are inclined only to hang on to market leaders.

Although market share gives the appearance of being a simple, objective measure, we have to make a subjective judgment to define what is understood by "market." According to whether one has a narrow or broad notion of the market, the brand can be considered as either dominant or dominated. We know too well the dangers of a shortsighted attempt to assimilate product and market. Should After Eight be valued only against the similar-products market, or against the whole chocolate market which includes tablets as well? A further subjective feature is the weighting allotted to first, second, and third place—60 percent, 50 percent, and 40 percent, setting a value on the relative market share itself.

Analysis is not limited to an examination of current market share but also extends to the potential for expansion. Taking the comparison between brands A and B again (See Table 11.1), A clearly has a current market share superior to that of B, but B's level of loyalty (repurchase) is double that of A. Brand B has a strong lever for expansion, which should undoubtedly be exploited by investing in awareness and availability, in order to increase the brand's rate of penetration. Certain markets are more fluid—leadership can be contested, or new segments permanently appear (e.g., high-tech or fashion).

THE ESTABLISHED STATUS OF THE BRAND

This factor defines the basic stability of the brand. Older brands, which in the course of time have built a loyal, satisfied clientele, are now an integral part of the market, almost its very substance. In the United States, General Electric is practically a national emblem—an institution in the family home—as are Javel in France, Hoover and St. Michael in the U.K., and Bayer in Germany. We have a word to characterize this brand following—brand franchise. The term well describes the long and ever-renewed process by which a brand succeeds in creating a high level of loyalty. This it does by analyzing customer needs, investing in R&D, and developing its communication to give full meaning to the brand.

PROSPECTS FOR THE CURRENT MARKET

When a brand is valued, it has a presence in certain markets. The questions to be asked are:

- What are its intrinsic prospects?
- Are they stable, declining, or promising growth?
- Are newcomers expected?
- Can these new arrivals be warded off—e.g., with superior technology, economies of scale, retail networks, and advertising budget?
- Could the market be invaded by retailer own-labels?

BRAND EXTENSION POSSIBILITIES

This criterion relates to the brand's ability to diversify by entering markets other than its present ones. There are several measures of such potential—for example, the brand's existing awareness in markets where it has no presence, and the ability of certain features of its identity to support the products necessary for diversification. Seiko, for instance, is known everywhere. Its watchmaking prowess over the years has caused the Seiko name to be synonymous with precision, esthetic quality, and modern appeal. The basic concept of the brand lies in its intimate link with time. The brand is also accepted in the optical-lens market, since glasses are also intimately linked with time and aging. They are also objects of precision and esthetic quality—good looks conceal age. With its established awareness and image, it is ready for such an extension. Not all brands necessarily have such a basic concept allowing extension.

THE POTENTIAL TO BECOME INTERNATIONAL

Italian cuisine is appreciated everywhere. This is why Buitoni had strong potential in every European country. It was not simply a question of internationality—Buitoni was well-prepared for an attack on the pan-European market. This was the determining factor which drew Nestlé's interest to Buitoni, as it had to Rowntree. Legal factors must also be taken into account when evaluating international potential. Bearing in mind the legal disparities between different countries, it is important to check the power and extent of brand protection in the countries envisaged (Chanterac, 1989).

ADAPTATION TO TIME

Certain brands survive the passage of time better than others. Though they may be over a hundred years old, they can seem astonishingly contemporary and up-to-date. While their products have had to undergo continuous renewal to keep up with purchaser demands, the brand has managed to update its codes without any diminishment of its identity and basic concept. In evaluating this factor, we have to pay particular attention to trends and long-term developments in the brand's image and awareness.

CONTINUOUS BRAND INVESTMENTS

Those brands which have enjoyed continuous support are more valuable than those which have received intermittent, periodic investment without any long-term consistency. Advertising investment should be sufficient to achieve relative market prominence. Attainment thereof can be gauged in the richness and depth of the brand image, its clarity of identity, degree of awareness and recognition, and acceptance of its associated signs (e.g., colors, symbols, logos, personalities, slogans).

LEGAL PROTECTION

Since the brand is of economic value, it attracts not only predators but also counterfeiters. The latter are eager to profit from part of the cash flow created by the brand—as seen in its distinctive signs—resulting from the confidence acquired over a period of time. Brand legal protection seeks to limit this form of hijacking. Major risk areas in which counterfeiting is common need extra caution—where legally possible, one must register not only the name, but also all those distinguishing features associated with the brand (e.g., design, packaging, logo, codes). Thus Coca-Cola has registered its two names (Coca-Cola and Coke), together with its own particular graphic format, throughout the world. Wherever possible, the company has also sought to register the distinctive shape of its bottle. In cases where the brand name itself is difficult to protect, the presence of a distinguishing graphic identity gives further protection since it, too, can be registered.

POTENTIAL FOR SYNERGIES

In acquiring a brand, the motivation is often provided by the anticipated profits resulting from its synergetic effects on other brands. For instance, when an acquired brand already has a dominant share, it opens the door hitherto closed on some of the purchaser's other brands. This can lead not only to increased effectiveness, but also to considerable cost savings.

Calculating the Brand's Value

In practical terms, what can be achieved from a brand profile based on the above criteria? There are two opposing schools of thought. The first—that of financial analysts—uses the brand profile to establish its business plan and to predict future net cash flows, using the current brand market or new anticipated markets as a starting point. The brand profile is compared with that of other brands in a similar or closely-associated sector. Financial analysts use the brand profile as a means of diagnosing and estimating how realistic the predicted cash flows are. The second method relies on a weighted mark allocated to each factor in order to achieve an overall total which measures the brand strength. This combined mark allows one to calculate a suitable "multiple" to be applied in the brand's financial evaluation. Though neither system is totally inflexible, their differences point to two different philosophies in tackling the problems of evaluation—both necessarily producing different valuations. We shall first analyze the discounted cashflow approach, then the multiple method.

DISCOUNTED CASHFLOW

This is the classic approach to the financial evaluation of any investment, whether material or intangible. The analyst establishes the year-by-year revenue attributable to the brand over a period of five, eight, or ten years. The discounting rate is the weighted average capital cost, this being increased where necessary to take account of the risks arising from a weak brand—in other words, to reduce the weight of remote future revenues in the present value equation. Beyond this period, the residual value is estimated on the basis of a perpetual income, assuming that such revenue is constant or increases at a constant rate (Nussenbaum, 1990).

We thus have the formula:

$$\text{Value of the brand} = \sum_{t=1}^{N} \frac{RB_t}{(1+r)^t} + \frac{\text{residual value}}{(1+r)^N}$$

Where:

RBt = Anticipated revenue in year t, attributable to the brand
r   = discounting rate

$$\text{Residual value beyond year N} = \frac{RB_N}{r} \quad \text{or} \quad \frac{RB_N}{r-g}$$

g   = Rate of revenue growth

Even though analysts offer numerous variations, this is the model-type for evaluation by means of discounted net anticipated cash flows (Maugieres, 1990; Melin, 1990). Following this method, Hennessy Cognac was valued at £690m, based on a capitalization of its net results over 25 years at a rate of 6.5 percent (Blanc and Hoffstetter, 1990).

Skeptics of this methodology (Murphy, 1990; Ward, 1990) point to its three sources of fallibility: anticipation of cash flow, choice of period, and discounting rate.

Any prediction is, by definition, uncertain. This does not solely apply to the brand, but to any investment valuation—material or otherwise—which is calculated on the above lines. Where the brand is concerned, cash flow predictions could be ruined if a competitor launched a superior product which was not accounted for in one's calculations. However, this argument overlooks the fact that predictions were made following a solid diagnosis of the strengths and weaknesses of the brand—on the basis of the earlier criteria. It can be assumed that these were incorporated when calculating anticipated cash flow. In any case, the discounting rate precisely serves to take into account the anticipated risk factor.

A second criticism relates to the subjective nature of one's choice of discounting rate. However, on the one hand, valuers test the sensitivity of their findings against any variations in this rate, while on the other hand, the rate itself is fixed in accordance with stable company figures, such as average cost of capital, etc. The only subjective assessments apply to shifts in inflation or interest rates. Furthermore, from the purchaser's point of view, the risk is often zero, since he feels that he is buying with the certainty of success.

Finally, criticism has been aimed at the choice of period for calculating cash flow—in other words, why ten years, and not fifteen or twenty? What is the value of predictions made so far ahead? In the first place, the brand can disappear after just a few years, and secondly, in certain volatile sectors—microcomputers, for example—even three years is a long time. Hence the pragmatic and realistic view of certain valuers—that brand value should not be founded on calculations but on the certainty of its net revenue over the past three years. This is the basis of the multiple method. The value is arrived at by applying a multiple to the current brand profits.

THE MULTIPLE METHOD

We often judge a firm's financial position by its price/earnings (P/E) ratio, which links share capital with net profit. A high ratio signals shareholder confidence and optimism in increased future benefits. Though brand and firm may be separate, the same reasoning may still be applied.

$$\text{Firm}: \text{P/E} = \frac{\text{Market value of equity}}{\text{Known profits}}$$

$$\text{Brand Multiple} = \frac{\text{Brand equity}}{\text{Brand net profits}}$$

The only difference is that there are no pointers to a brand's share capital, since it doesn't exist. Yet some equivalent of this is precisely what we seek to determine. This notional share valorization is the price required to buy the brand—forgetting any overbid. To ascertain this, we must calculate M, the multiple equivalent to a ratio P/E in relation to the brand.

This approach is widely used in the U.K., particularly by the Interbrand Company. There are four stages:

1. Deciding the applicable net profit. Interbrand uses profits for the three previous years, thus avoiding a possibly atypical evaluation based upon a single year. These are discounted to take account of inflation. A weighted average of these three figures takes into

Table 11.2

A means of evaluating brand strength

Evaluation Factor	Maximum Score	Brand A	Brand B	Brand C
Leadership	25	19	19	10
Stability	15	12	9	7
Market	10	7	6	8
Internationality	25	18	5	2
Trend	10	7	5	7
Support	10	8	7	8
Protection	5	5	3	4
Brand strength	100	76	54	46

Source: J. Murphy, Brand Valuation, Hutchinson, 1990

account the most and the least representative years. This weighted average of post-tax net profits specifically attributable to the brand forms the basis of all calculations.

2. Assessing the brand's strength. To determine this, the brand receives an overall mark based upon a set of marketing and strategy criteria. Interbrand uses only seven of these factors to obtain its overall mark—i.e., a weighted sum of the individual marks for each factor, as in Table 11.2 (Penrose, 1990).

3. Deciding the multiple. There has to be a relation between the multiple—that gauge of confidence in the future—and brand strength. If this connection were known precisely, the multiple would then be indicated by the brand strength score. Interbrand has developed a chart known as the "S-curve," linking multiple with brand strength.

The chart is based on Interbrand's examination of multiples involved in numerous brand negotiations over the recent period—in sectors close to that studied. For want of such transactions, P/E ratio of companies with the closest comparable brands are used. Interbrand then located these companies' brand strength scores on the

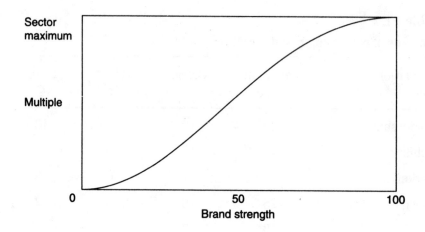

Figure 11.2

The Interbrand S-curve—Relation between brand strength and multiple

section, and related them to the multiples (or P/E) to form the S-curve.

4. Deciding the brand value. This is calculated by multiplying the applicable net brand profit by the relevant multiple. An actual case will illustrate this.

In 1988, Reckitt & Colman evaluated their following brands:

- household and hygiene, in which area they are brand leaders
- condiments, where they likewise head the field
- pharmaceuticals, having somewhat average success

Brands in the first group specifically enjoy:

- world leadership
- growing markets, with little chance of competition except from retailer-named brands
- unaided awareness (e.g., Airwick), particularly in the U.K., but less so in France
- customer loyalty
- strong quality-defined brand image
- low susceptibility to diversification

Reckitt & Colman estimated that 5 percent of profits on these brands came from sales under retailer-named brands. Interbrand regarded the remaining 95 percent as the brand gross profit. Brand net revenue was calculated by deducting the expected income from net assets. On this basis, after proper weighting and discounting the three-year figures, they recorded the following net revenue:

- household and hygiene: £53.8m
- comestibles: £24.7m
- pharmaceuticals: £17.1m

What multiple should be applied? They used the multiple in Reckitt & Colman's acquisition of Airwick in 1985 for the first group. A multiple of 17 for foods was based on transactions in parallel fields over the past few years. This included the BSN–Nabisco takeover bid. The final group was accorded a multiple of 20. Recent multiples in the pharmaceutical world had actually been closer to 30; the lower figure reflected Reckitt & Colman's relatively weak position in this sector. Applying these figures to the profit in each case, the estimated brand values were:

- household and hygiene: 53.8 x 20 = £1,076m
- comestibles: 24.7 x 17 = £420m
- pharmaceuticals: 17.1 x 20 = £342m

COMPARISON OF METHODS

The multiple method developed in Britain is becoming a standard. It was in fact used by such companies as Ranks Hovis McDougall, and Grand Metropolitan. Their decision to post brand values to their balance sheets caused a controversy which is still not settled. The simplicity of the method used is such that it is uncharacteristic of the stringent world of financial analysis. As such, however, is it valid?

In the first instance, the multiple concept is akin to the classic method of discounted cash flows. When a constant unlimited annual cash flow is anticipated, the current brand value is defined as:

$$\text{Current brand value} = \frac{RB}{(1+r)} + \frac{RB}{(1+r)^2} + \frac{RB}{(1+r)^3} + \cdots\cdots + \frac{RB}{(1+r)^\infty} = \frac{RB}{r}$$

As we see, the multiple is none other than the reverse of cost of capital adjusted for risk $(1/r)$. If a constant rate of increase (k) in annual revenue is expected, the multiple equals:

$$M = \frac{1}{(r-k)}$$

Equations aside, the point to remember is that we cannot reproach the discounted cashflows method for relying on hypotheses, since the multiple approach is itself a special case of this method, making itself an hypothesis, questionable but nonexplicit. It draws its apparent validity from the fact that all its calculations are based upon:

- net profits attributable to the brand over the previous three years (therefore, hard facts)
- marketing data and the subjective opinions of management regarding brand strength
- multiples duly based on recent deals in a similar field
- an S-curve, emanating from a data bank, linking these multiples (or P/E ratios) to brand strength scores

However, face validity does not mean validity *per se*. In its present form, the Interbrand method poses various problems.

Market multiples, serving as variables to form the S-curve, are not valid indicators of the strength of the brands which were the subject of these deals. Final transaction figures admittedly incorporate the estimated brand value, but also reflect an element of overbid—take the fight between Jacobs Suchard and Nestlé, in which the offer rose from 630 pence to a final price of 1,075 pence. Market prices include the result of overbid, and thus overvalue the brand. It is therefore a rather curious notion to try to link market multiples to a value for brand strength when that value ignores the effect of overbid. Use of this method to evaluate and post unacquired self-created company brands is therefore questionable. The declared asset exceeds the brand value and includes an unspecified overbid amount. The fact that companies may nevertheless have used this method to represent their brands as assets in no way validates the practice.

Even in a market free from overbid, the potential buyer measures the value of the brand in the multiple he proposes. It expresses his vision, his strategy, and his expected synergies. BSN did not buy Buitoni in 1985, in spite of its derisory price. There is no suggestion that Buitoni was worth little—rather, that it was of little worth to BSN. In 1988, Nestlé valued Buitoni at £ 800 millions. It again seems strange to attempt to link market multiples and brand strength totals, the one being under the close control of the purchaser, the other defined by an outsider and having no provision for the synergetic factor. This poses a particular problem when self-created brands are posted to the balance sheet. They are evaluated in the context of a "going business," valued according to their current benefit to the companies who own them. On the other hand, multiples coming from market transactions reflect quite different business plans thought of by the purchasers.

No illustrations of the S-curve to date allow for variance, thus ignoring the quality of the empirical relationship between the two variables. As it stands, the chart leads us to believe that there is nil variance. This is impossible. One single score probably corresponds to several multiples, or at least to highs and lows which the S-curve intercepts. Such uncertainty causes a problem. In reality, the slightest variation in the multiple can tilt the value of the brand significantly. Going back to the Reckitt & Colman household and hygiene range, a one-point variation in the multiple corresponded to £53.8m either way! A far cry from the principles of prudence, reliability, and rational certitude, watchwords in accounting practice and theory.

The very validity of the S-curve is questionable. Interbrand reasons that:

- A new brand grows slowly in its early stages.
- Passing from national to international recognition, its growth is exponential.
- On entering the world market, its progress slows once more.

The gap between the Buitoni purchase and resale prices indeed signaled the transition of a national brand to one of wide European standing.

Experience shows that brands are susceptible to strong threshold effects. They acquire their strength with customers and retailers in stages. Thus today a moderately-known brand may have scarcely any more value than a little-known one. Beyond a certain threshold, however, it bursts forth. Research on brand awareness (see page 91) has shown that, in the markets with intensive communication, a brand will only see its unaided awareness increase after having attained a high level of assisted awareness. Likewise, major retailers do not hesitate

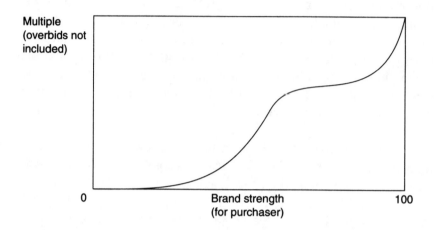

Figure 11.3

Stepped graph showing relationship between brand strength and multiple

to substitute their own products for medium sellers. The latter rely more on supply than on demand, and their sales would cease if the retailer replaced them with his own brand. Their future position is therefore tenuous. This leads one to suppose that the relation between brand strength and multiple—provided both are assessed by the same potential purchaser—should be defined by a stepped graph, as in Figure 11.3.

We may conclude by saying that the diffusion of the multiple method is not a proof of validity, as we have just seen, but testifies to its simplicity and handiness for nonspecialists—in short, its pedagogical value. A small variation in the chosen multiple leads to huge differences in brand evaluation. The present method of ascertaining the multiple is rather unsatisfactory, in terms both of the multiple itself and of the brand strength score.

Validity is impaired by the desire for simplicity. In spite of its claim to accuracy, the multiple method in its present form is just as subjective as that of discounted cash flows. To impose a hundred or so criteria instead of seven would change nothing. The more subjective one is, the clearer the method should be. A true audit of the brand has nothing to gain in being summarized by a single score, an overall score. It is better to look at the brand profile. This brand profile will be used to make a realistic, valid business plan, materializing in discounted cash flows. The choice is therefore between two methods—the one precisely false, the other vaguely precise.

BRANDS, BALANCE SHEETS, AND FINANCIAL INFORMATION

Having analyzed the various methods of evaluating the brand, we can now take a more realistic view of the question of posting brands to the balance sheet. The question was raised by British firms for two types of reason.

The first relates to the specific rules in the U.K. concerning the treatment of goodwill after a merger or acquisition.

Goodwill itself is the difference between the purchase price of the targeted firm and the value of its net assets. Though not obligatory, the normal procedure is to write off the entire goodwill against the reserves, thus eliminating the purchased brand(s) from the balance sheet. This allowed British firms to avoid the other accepted means of dealing with goodwill—capitalizing it as an intangible asset and depreciating it through the profit-and-loss account. The latter process has the disadvantage of depressing share earnings—an embarrassing outcome after a merger or acquisition. Time has shown that directly charging the overvaluation, or goodwill, to reserves produced a perverse effect. It certainly left profits untouched, much to the pleasure of shareholders, but it also gave an artificially low reading of the firm's financial status. By drawing on reserves—in other words, the firm's own funds—one was having an adverse effect on most of the financial ratios in which these sums play a part. For example, borrowing capacity is judged by comparing the ratio of debts against capital. The point is that, since brands are purchased for the precise reason of being developed, this in itself creates a need for extra financing to support further communication and marketing budgets. The firm therefore runs the risk of being unable to borrow to finance this development, due to the fact that its own capital has been drastically cut as a result of accounting methods. To overcome this problem, British firms have broken with tradition and opted for amortization of goodwill. In 1988, Ladbroke even went so far as to include the value of the Hilton International brand in its balance sheet, though the goodwill associated with its 1987 purchase had been set against reserves that year.

Firms which had not acquired any brands, but which possessed strong self-created ones, considered that they were receiving a raw deal. A purchased brand could be posted to the balance sheet, but not an internal brand. Firms which had created brands by their own efforts, but which were not authorized to include them in accounts, gave the impression of having net assets inferior to those of their counterparts. This could result in misleading information to shareholders, and attract the attention of predators. Nestlé's takeover bid for Rowntree, and the difference between the share value before the bid and the value paid by Nestlé, are often put forward as an example of market inefficiency. Since the Rowntree brands did not figure in their assets, shareholders would have underestimated the value of the company, and would thus have quickly accepted the Nestlé bid. To avoid the risk of such circumstances, Ranks Hovis McDougall decided to include in their balance sheet a value appropriate to their own self-created brands. Under the Companies Act of 1985, firms have the right to do so. Moreover, it is possible in the U.K. to reevaluate such intangible assets as brands whenever one wishes, whereas in other countries such as France the difference in the reevaluation figure would be immediately taxable.

The debate is now becoming international. Since methods of treating goodwill differ from country to country (see Table 11.3), there can be a disparity in the way companies present their accounts following a merger or acquisition. In France, for instance, the law compels companies to write off goodwill. However, the EC seventh directive accepts that goodwill can be posted as "identifiable assets." This ideally suits brands which cannot be written off, since their expected lifespan has no limits. The major French holding company BSN has taken full advantage of this practice. Following their 1989 transactions, the group decided to place a value on those brands included in the goodwill arising from recent acquisitions, and not to amortize them. In so doing they boosted their 1989 net results by 99 million francs (£9.9m). The decision not to amortize brands through a regular depreciation rate makes economic sense. Firms which have bought brands devote major communication budgets to their support. These

Table 11.3

Methods of treating goodwill

Methods	IASC (planned)	7th EC directive	France	Germany (1) (2)	Italy (1)	Spain (1) (2)	UK	USA	Japan
Positive Goodwill									
Deducted from reserves	NO	YES	NO(*)	YES	NO	NO	YES	NO	NO
Immobilized and written off	YES	YES	YES	YES	YES	YES	YES	YES	YES
Amortization limits	5 years	5 years	NO	4 years	5 years	5 years	NO	40 years	5 years
Negative Goodwill									
Added to reserves	YES	NO	NO	NO	YES	YES	YES	NO	NO
Deducted from acquired assets	YES	NO	NO	NO	YES	NO	NO	YES	NO
Posted to liabilities and written off	YES	YES	YES	YES	YES	YES	NO	YES	NO

(1) Seventh directive not yet in force.
(2) Based on the inception of the seventh directive scheduled for 1990
(*) No, apart from exceptional cases.
Source: Coopers & Lybrand Euromas

budgets have to be posted as debits, and thus reduce the final profit. It would be incongruous to further burden results by writing off brands whose advertising—among other things—is precisely aimed at maintaining their value. On the other hand, if the firm ceased to support the brand, the fact that it was not written off would be economically invalid. Fortunately, the law foresees the possibility of depreciating a brand as soon as any decrease in its value is anticipated.

In France, Article 12 of the Business Code, which forbids the reevaluation of intangible assets which are already tied up, opposes the inclusion of company-created brands in the balance sheet. We can also see that several British groups have differing attitudes toward the accounting methods applying to self-created brands. This international disparity must eventually disappear. World standards are needed, to suit a worldwide competitive arena. The IASC (International Accounting Standards Committee) is about to prohibit direct charging of goodwill to reserves. The problem of created brands is as yet unresolved.

THE CASE OF CREATED BRANDS

The question of the posting or nonposting of created brands provokes several thoughts, all showing the extent to which the recognition of the brand importance threatens to bring about deep changes in the presentation of financial information—both in its goals and in the criteria used.

The noninclusion of part of one's assets contravenes the notion of faithfulness and sincerity normally attached to financial statements (Gelle, 1990).

Since a brand represents a source of current and future revenue for the company which owns it, irrespective of whether it has been purchased or not, why is it possible, within the same firm, to recognize the value of acquired brands, and impossible to recognize that of created brands? If the value of created brands is not brought to public attention—by whatever means—it represents a practical distortion of information which could have grave consequences for companies who have chosen the path of internal growth (Gelle, 1990).

Acquired brands are posted at their purchase cost, which is assessed in line with anticipated profitability. In a quest for uniformity, created brands developed internally should also be evaluated in accordance with their expected profitability.

Ironically, by following the principle of homogeneity in treating the two types of brand, one creates heterogeneity in the balance sheet, since tangible assets are themselves evaluated on their historical cost. The homogeneity principle would require that internally created brands be evaluated on the basis of a portion of their historical costs, i.e., those which can be considered with a fair degree of confidence as being likely to be a source of future revenues. For instance, test-market costs would not satisfy this criterion. The difficult point will be to identify, for a new brand, at what point a "fair degree of confidence" begins. So many brands die after two or three years.

Apart from not knowing when to begin, the posting of internal brands would also introduce a high degree of uncertainty into the information provided in the balance sheet. It would lead to a relaxation of the principles of prudence and reasonable certainty. As we have seen, all valuation methods are extremely subjective and open to question. Considering the values placed on brands, the impact of such uncertainty on the reliability of financial information would be serious.

If it did become permissible to post created brands as assets, it would be inconsistent to forbid the inclusion of other intangible features, such as know-how and human capital. However, one would come up against the formidable problem of separability, since these other features often form an integral part of the brand's success. Under German law, the brand cannot be sold without its underlying tangible and intangible assets. This problem of impossible separability is already present in the question of attaching a portion of goodwill to brand value. It too remains subjective.

For all the above reasons, researchers at the London Business School have deemed it scarcely desirable for created brands to be included in the balance sheet (Barwise, 1989). If the main objective is to provide information for shareholders and analysts, other means exist. In France, accounting legislation on 30 April 1983 stated that "When any accounting item does not give a sufficiently true picture . . . supplementary information must be provided in the annex." The annex normally attached to annual accounts is intended to supplement the balance sheet and statement of results. We have to remember, however, that the amounts shown are only evaluations. Some believe that a dual accounting system is developing—the one being controlled and objective, though not reflecting reality, while the other is more valid, but freely subjective.

As we can see, the transition to an economy in which the capital asset no longer lies in land, buildings, or machines, but in intangible features, leads to conflicting adaptations of the system of relaying company information—a system conceived in an era when the invisible did not count.

Since, in accounting terms, the definition of what an asset is makes no reference whatsoever to its tangible or intangible nature, the difference in treatment between both types of assets has no legitimacy. To be consistent with accounting practices and to avoid yo-yo balance sheets, the historic cost is the only way to account for both acquired and created brands. For the latter, however, a clear view as to what costs to crystalize needs to be established. Out of these accounting objectives, brand valuation at the point of cession, merger, or acquisition will best be made on the basis of the expected earnings its possession should bring.

Conclusion

Over the past twenty years, there has been insistence by management on corporate planning, culture, and identity. They have been totally preoccupied with integration of human resources, mobilization thereof, and overall dynamization. Their attitude has either directly resulted from external expansion through the absorption of other firms, or from changes in identity arising from this expansion, the firm having progressed from its family status focusing on one man or on a single trade to that of a multiskilled group under a management body. The future beckons firms which not only appreciate the meaning of the brand but which are able to instill this meaning throughout every corner of the organization. Whereas a company's culture is internally directed, the brand meaning reminds us of the competitive priorities, and of the need for perpetual improvements in satisfying the market.

The meaning of the brand is not solely the concern of marketing management. Everyone, from the highest to the lowest echelons of the firm, must consider the brand in a professional light, becoming an active living support, and an integral part, of its functioning. This implies a constant stimulus and awareness of the brand's objectives on the part of all those involved in the production process, in both factories and laboratories. It also concerns the other end of the chain—retailers and after-sales services throughout the world.

The key word in brand management is now capitalization. This term encompasses both financial and marketing perspectives. To be able to acquire a financial value, the brand must be managed by marketers in a new way:

307

- Brand portfolios must be drastically reduced. One cannot capitalize on too many brands, each receiving insufficient support.
- Continuity is now preferable to permanent change. One should reward resistance to undue change.
- New products must be launched under existing brands to nurture them and make them long-living, if not eternal.
- Brands should be extended in product categories they can fruitfully and profitably segment.
- To manage brands with a long-term perspective, one needs brand identity charters.
- As a countereffect to management turnover, brand responsibility should no longer be in the hands of junior brand managers, but at a higher level in the organization.
- Brand management should not seek to be democratic, asking everyone what he/she thinks about the brand (customers from all countries, advertising agencies, etc.). Brand management must be dynamic—a kind of well-informed despotism.

Bibliography

Aaker, D (1991) *Managing Brand Equity*, The Free Press, New York.

Aaker, D and Biel, AL (1993) *Brand Equity and Advertising*. Lawrence Erlbaum & Associates, New Jersey.

Aaker, D and Keller, K L (1990) "Consumer Evaluations of Brand Extensions" *Journal of Marketing*, January, vol 54 (1), pp27–41.

Agefi (1990) "Le Goodwill, Objet de Controverse en Europe", 1 February.

Alba, J W and Chattopadhyay, A (1986) "Salience Effects in Brand Recall" *Journal of Marketing Research*, vol 23, p369.

Arnold, T (1989) "Accounting for the Value of Brands" *The Accountant's Magazine*, February, p12.

Baillot, J (1990) "La marque et l'automobile" *Humanisme et Entreprise*, 181, June, pp5–8.

Baldinger, A (1992) "What CEOs are Saying About Brand Equity", *Journal of Advertising Research*, July/August, 32(4), pp6–12.

Barwise, P (1989) *Accounting for Brands*, London Business School.

Berard, C (1990) "La marque: élément du patrimoine de l'entreprise" *Revue de l'E.N.A., 202, May, pp24–5.*

Berry, N C (1988) "Revitalizing Brands" Journal of Consumer Marketing, 5(summer), pp15–20.

Birkigt, K and Stadler, M M (1980) *Corporate Identity: Grundlagen, Funktionen, Fallbeispiele*, Verlag Moderne Industrie, Munich.

Birol, J and Kapferer, J N (1991) "Les campagnes collectives" Internal document, Agence Sicquier-Courcelles/HEC.

Blackett, T (1985) "The Role of Brand Valuation in Marketing Strategy" *Marketing and Research Today*, November, pp245–7.

Blackston, M (1992) "Building Brand Equity by Managing the Brand's

Relationships", *Journal of Advertising Research*, May/June, 32(3), pp79–83.

Blanc, C and Hoffstetter, P (1990) "L'évaluation des marques" Research paper, under the direction of Kapferer, J N, June, Jouy-en-Josas.

Boddewyn, J, Soehl, R and Picard, J (1986) "Standardization in International Marketing: Is Ted Levitt in Fact Right?" *Business Horizons*, pp69–75.

Bon, J, Michon, C and Ollivier, A (1981) "Etude empirique de la démographie des marques: le rôle de la publicité" Fondation Jours de France pour la recherche en publicité, Paris.

Botton, M and Cegarra, J J (1990) *Le nom de marque* McGraw-Hill, Paris.

Broadbent, S (1983) *Advertising Works 2*, Holt, Rinehart and Winston, London.

Brodbeck, D and Mongibeaux, J F (1990) *Chic et Toc: le vrai livre des contrefaçons* Balland, Paris.

Buchan, E and Brown, A (1989) "Mergers and Acquisitions" in *Brand Valuation*, ed. Murphy, J, Hutchinson Business Books, London. pp81–94.

Burgaud, D and Mourier, P (1989) "Europe: développement d'une marque" *MOCI*, 889, pp125–8.

Buzzell, R D (1968) "Can you Standardize Multinational Marketing?" *Harvard Business Review*, Nov–Dec.

Buzzell, R D, Gale, B T and Sultan, R G (1975) "Market Share—A Key to Profitability" *Harvard Business Review*, Jan–Feb, pp97–106.

Buzzell, R D and Quelch, J A (1988) *Multinational Marketing Management* Addison-Wesley, New York.

Buzzell, R D and Quelch, J A (1990) *The Marketing Challenge of 1992* Addison-Wesley, New York.

Cabat, O (1989) "Archéologie de la marque moderne" in *La marque* (eds Kapferer, J N and Thoening, J C) McGraw-Hill, Paris.

Carpenter, G and Nakamoto, K (1990) "Competitive Strategies for Late Entry Into Market With a Dominant Brand" *Management Science*.

Carratu, V (1987) "Commercial Counterfeiting" in *Branding: A Key Marketing Tool* (ed Murphy, J) McGraw-Hill, London.

Carroll, J M (1985) *What's in a Name?* Freeman, New York.

Cauzard, D, Perret, J and Ronin, Y (1989) *Image de marque et marque d'image* Ramsay, Paris.

Channon, C (1987) *Advertising Works 4*, Cassell, London.

Chanterac, V (1989) "La marque à travers le droit" in *La Marque* (eds Kapferer, J N and Thoenig, J C) McGraw-Hill, Paris.

Chateau, J (1972) *Les sources de l'imaginaire* Editions Universitaires, Paris.

Clarke, D G (1976) "Econometric Measurement of the Duration of Advertising Effect on Sales" *Journal of Marketing Research* Vol. XIII, November, pp345–50.

Conseil National de la Comptabilité (1989) "La formation du capital commercial dans l'entreprise" 27. A.89.16, September.

Cooper, M (1989) "The Basis of Brand Evaluation" *Accountancy* March, p32.

Cooper, M (1989) "Brand Valuation in the Balance" *Accountancy* July, p28.

Crimmins, J (1992) "Better Measurement and Management of Brand Value", *Journal of Advertising Research*, July/August, 32(4), pp11–19.

Crozier, M (1989) *L'Entreprise à l'Ecoute: Apprendre le Management Post-Industriel*, InterEditions, Paris.

Davidson, J H (1987) *Offensive Marketing*, Gower Press, London.

Defever, P (1989) "L'utilisation de la communication électronique sur les lieux de vente" *Revue française du marketing* vol 123 (3), pp5–15.

Dhalla, N K (1978) "Assessing the Long Term Value of Advertising" *Business Review*, Vol 56, Jan–Feb, 1978, pp87–95.

Diefenbach, J (1987) "The Corporate Identity as the Brand" in *Branding: a Key Marketing Tool* (ed Murphy, J), McGraw-Hill, London.

Durand, G (1964) *L'imagination symbolique* PUF, Paris.

Durand, G (1969) *Les Structures Anthropologiques de l'Imaginaire* Bordas, Paris.

Duvillier, J P (1987) "L'absence d'enregistrement à l'actif du fonds de commerce" *Revue française de comptabilité* October, 183, p36.

Eliade, M (1952) *Images et Symboles*, Gallimard, Paris.

Farquhar, P H (1989) "Managing Brand Equity" *Marketing Research* September, Vol 1 (3), pp24–33.

Feral, F (1989) "Les signes de qualité en France à la veille du grand marché communautaire et à la lumière d'autres systèmes" *CER-VAC*, Université d'Aix Marseille 3, October.

Fourcade, A and Cabat, O (1981) *Anthropologie de la publicité* Fondation Jours de France pour la recherche en publicité.

Frey, J B (1989) "Measuring Corporate Reputation and its Value", Marketing Science Conference, Duke University, 17 March.

Fry, J N (1967) "Family Branding and Consumer Brand Choice" *Journal of Marketing Research* IV, August, pp237–47.

Fry, J N, Shaw, D, Haehling, C and Dipchand, C (1973) "Customer Loyalty to Banks: A Longitudinal Study" *The Journal of Business* 46, pp517–25.

Gamble, T (1967) "Brand Extension", in *Plotting Marketing Strategy* (ed. Adler, L), Interpublic Press Book, New York.

Garbett, T (1981) *Corporate Advertising*, McGraw-Hill, New York.

Geary, M (1990) "Fusions et acquisitions: le problème de Goodwill", in *Séminaire: Le traitement du Goodwill* 1 February, PF Publications Conférences, Paris.

Gelle, T (1990) "La comptabilisation des marques" HEC research paper, under the direction of Collins, L, May, Jouy-en-Josas.

Greener, M (1989) "The Bomb in the Balance Sheet" *Accountancy*, August, p30.

Guest, L (1964) "Brand Loyalty Revisited: A Twenty Years Report" *Journal of Applied Psychology*, Vol 48 (2), pp93–7.

Hamel, G and Prahalad, C (1985) "Do You Really Have a Global Strategy?" *Harvard Business Review*, Jul–Aug.

Heather, E (1958) "What's in a Brand Name" *Management Review*, June, pp33–5.

Heller, R (1986) "On the Awareness Effects of Mere Distribution" *Marketing Science*, vol 5, summer, p273.

Hite, R and Fraser, C (1988) "International Advertising Strategies of Multinational Corporations" *Journal of Advertising Research*, August/September, vol 28 (4), pp9–17.

Hout, T, Porter, M and Rudder, E (1982) "How Global Companies Win Out" *Harvard Business Review*, Sept–Oct.

Jacobson, R and Aaker, D (1985) "Is Market Share All that It's Cracked Up to Be?" *Journal of Marketing*, vol 45, 4, Fall, pp11–22.

Jacoby, J and Chestnut, R (1978) *Brand Loyalty and Measurement* John Wiley, New York.

Jaubert, M J (1985) *Slogan, mon Amour* Bernard Barrault Editeur, Paris.

Jones, J P (1986) *What's in a Name: Advertising and the Concept of Brands* Lexington Books, Lexington.

Kapferer, J N (1983) "Le Nom de L'Entreprise, Premier Véhicule de son Influence" 3ᵉ journée d'Etudes du CRCS, November, Paris, pp105–18.

Kapferer, J N (1984) *Les chemins de la persuasion* Dunod Entreprise, Paris.

Kapferer, J N (1985) "Réfléchissez au Nom de votre Société" *Harvard—l'Expansion*, Autumn, pp104–18.

Kapferer, J N (1986) "Beyond Positioning, Retailer's Identity" *Esomar Seminar Proceedings*, Brussels, 4–6 June, pp167–76.

Kapferer, J N (1988) "Maîtriser l'Image de l'Entreprise: le Prisme d'Identité" *Revue Française de Gestion*, Nov–Dec, pp76–82.

Kapferer, J N (1989) "Consommateurs: l'Etonnant Silence" *Le Nouvel Economiste*, 22 December.

Kapferer, J N (1990) "La Marque est-elle encore à la portée des PME?" in *Le Défi de la Moyenne et Petite Entreprise*, Paris, pp193–6.

Kapferer, J N (1990) "Marque de Fabrication ou Marque de Distributeur?" *Le Monde*, 8 March.

Kapferer, J N (1990) "Une opposition Idéologique: le Produit ou la Marque" *Revue Vinicole Internationale*, March, pp84–5.

Kapferer, J N (1990) "La Marque Malade de la Publicité" *Fortune*, April, 25, p23.

Kapferer, J N (1990) "Le Grand Commerce est-il Consumériste" *Revue Française de Gestion*, May.

Kapferer, J N (1990) "Vraies Marques ou Fausses Marques" *Humanisme et Entreprise*, 181, June, pp17–26.

Kapferer, J N (1990) "Marque, Consommation, Consumérisme" *Revue de l'E.N.A.*, Sept–Oct.

Kapferer, J N and Laurent, G (1983) *Comment Mesurer le Degré d'Implication des Consommateurs* Institut de Recherches et d'Etudes Publicitaires, Paris.

Kapferer, J N and Laurent, G (1983) *La Sensibilité aux Marques* Fondation Jours de France pour la Recherche en Publicité, Paris.

Kapferer, J N and Laurent, G (1988) "Consumers" Brand Sensitivity: A New Concept for Brand Management" in *Defining, Measuring and Managing Brand Equity*, Marketing Science Institute: A Conference Summary, Report pp88–104, MSI, Cambridge, MA.

Kapferer, J N and Thoenig, J C (1989) *La Marque* McGraw-Hill, Paris.

Kapferer, J N and Thoenig, J C *et al.* (1991) "Une analyse empirique des effets de l'imitation des marques par les contremarques: mesure des taux de confusion au tachystoscope" *Revue Francaise du Marketing*, January, 136, pp53–68.

Kapferer, J N and Variot, J F (1984) "Le prisme d'identité: nouvel outil de diagnostic et de maîtrise de l'image", Fourth CRCS study paper, November, pp17–36.

Kapferer, J N and Variot, J F (1985) "Les six facettes de l'image du distributeur" *Points de vente*, 15 October, 288, pp44–7.

Keller, K L and Aaker, D (1992) "The Effects of Sequential Introduction of Brand Extensions", *Journal of Marketing Research*, 29(1), February, pp35–50.

King, S (1973) *Developing New Brands* John Wiley and Sons, New York.

Kotler, P and Dubois, B (1991) *Marketing management* Publi-Union, Paris.

Krief, Y (1986) "L'Entreprise, l'institution, la marque" *Revue française du marketing*, 109, pp77–96.

Krief, Y and Barjansky, M (1981) "La marque: nature et fonction" *Stratégies*, 261 and 262, pp37–41, 32–6.

Kripke, S (1980) *Naming and Necessity*, Harvard University Press, Cambridge, MA.

Laurent, G and Kapferer, J N (1985) "Measuring Consumer Involvement Profiles" *Journal of Marketing Research*, Vol XXII, pp41–53.

Laurent, G, Kapferer, J N and Roussel, F (1987) "Thresholds in Brand Awareness" 40th ESOMAR Marketing Research Congress Proceedings, Montreux, September 13–17, pp677–99.

Leclerc, F, Schmitt, B H and Dube-Rioux, L (1989) "Brand name à la française? Oui, but for the right product!" *Advances in Consumer Research*, vol 16, pp253–7.

Levitt, T (1967) "Market Stretching" in *Plotting Marketing Strategy*, (ed. Adler, L) Interpublic Press Book, New York.

Levitt, T (1969) "The Augmented Product Concept", in *The Marketing Mode: Pathways to Corporate Growth*, McGraw-Hill, New York.

Levitt, T (1981) "Marketing Intangible Products and Product Intangibles" *Harvard Business Review* vol 59 (3) May/June, pp94–102.

Levitt, T (1983) "The Globalization of Markets" *Harvard Business Review* May/June.

Lindsay, M (1990) "Establish Brand Equity Through Advertising" *Marketing News* January 22, pp16–17.

Loden, D J (1992) *Mega Brands*, Irwin, Illinois, USA.

Mac Innis, D J and Nakamoto P K (1990) "Examining Factors that Influence the Perceived Goodness of Brand Extensions" Working Paper No 54, University of Arizona.

Macrae, C (1991) *World Class Brands*, Addison-Wesley, England.

McWilliam G (1989) "Managing the Brand Manager" in *Brand Valuation* (ed Murphy, J), Hutchinson Business Books, London, pp154–65.

Magrath, A J (1990) "Brands Can Either Grow Old Gracefully or Become Dinosaurs" *Marketing News*, January 22, pp16–17.

Margolis, S E (1989) "Monopolistic Competition and Multiproduct Brand Names" *Journal of Business* vol 62 (2), pp199–210.

Marketing Mix (1987) "Monter une gamme: un problème majeur", 17, November, pp40–6.

Marion, G (1989) *Les images de l'entreprise* Les Editions d'Organisation.

Martin, D N (1989) *Romancing the Brand* American Management Association, New York.

Mauguère, H (1990) *L'évaluation des entreprises non cotées* Dunod Entreprise, Paris.

Maurice, A (1989) "Enquête sur les contremarques: Les apprentis sorciers" *Références*, May, pp16–20.

Mazanec, J A and Schweiger, G C (1981) "Improved Marketing Efficiency Through Multi-product Brand Names?" *European Research* January, pp32–44.

Meffert, H and Bruhn, M (1984) *Marken Strategien in Wettbewerb* Gabler, Wiesbaden.

Melin, B (1990) "Comment Evaluer les Marques" Research paper, under the direction of Kapferer, J N, HEC, June, Jouy-en-Josas.

Meyers-Levy, J (1989) "Investigating Dimensions of Brand Names that Influence the Perceived Familiarity of Brands" *Advances in Consumer Research*, vol 16, Association for Consumer Research, pp258–63.

Mongibeaux, J F (1990) "Contrefaçons et contremarques" *Revue de l'E.N.A.*, Sept–Oct.

Moorhouse, M (1989) "Brand Accounting" in *Brand Valuation*, (ed. Murphy, J) Hutchinson Business Books, London, pp143–53.

Muller, M and Mainz, A (1989) "Brands, Bids and Balance Sheets: Putting a Price on Protected Products" *Acquisitions Monthly* April, 24, pp26–7.

Murphy, J (1989) *Brand Valuation* Hutchinson Business Books, London.

Murphy, J (1990) *Brand Strategy*, Director Books, London.

Nedungadi, P and Hutchinson, J W (1985) "The Prototypicality of Brands" in *Advances in Consumer Research*, Vol 12 (eds Hirschman, E and Holbrook, M), Association for Consumer Research, pp498–503.

Neuhaus, C F and Taylor, J R (1972) "Variables Affecting Sales of Family-Branded Products" *Journal of Marketing Research* 14 (November), pp419–22.

Nussenbaum, M (1990) "Comment évaluer les marques" *Option Finance* 7 May, 113, pp20–2.

Olins, W (1978) *The Corporate Personality* Mayflower Books, New York.

Olins, W (1989) *Corporate Identity* Thames and Hudson, London.

Oliver, T (1987) "The Wide World of Branding" in *Branding: a Key Marketing Tool* (ed. Murphy, J) McGraw-Hill, London.

Pariente, S (1989) *La concurrence dans les relations industrie-commerce* Institut du commerce et de la consommation, Paris.

Park, C W, Javorskey, B J and Mac Innis, D J (1986) "Strategic Brand Concept-Image Management" *Journal of Marketing*, 50 (October) pp135–45.

Park, C W, Milberg, S and Lawson, R (1991) "Evaluation of Brand Extensions", *Journal of Consumer Research*, 18, September, pp185–193.

Peckham, J O (1981) *The Wheel of Marketing*, The Nielsen Company, Chicago.

Penrose, N (1989) "Valuation of Brand Names and Trade Marks" in *Brand Valuation* (ed Murphy, J) Hutchinson Business Books, London, pp32–45.

Perrier, R (1989) "Valuation and Licensing" in *Brand Valuation* (ed Murphy, J) Hutchinson Business Books, London, pp104–12.

Porter, M (1980) *Choix stratégiques et concurrence* Economica, Paris.

Pourquery, D (1987) "Mais où est donc passé Béatrice Foods?" *Le monde affaires*, 7 November, pp10–12.

Publicis (1988) "Advertising in Europe" September, 1.

Quelch, J and Hoff, E (1986) "Customizing Global Marketing" *Harvard Business Review* May/June.

Rangaswamy, A, Burke, R and Oliva, T A (1990) "Brand Equity and the Extendability of Brand Names", Working Paper No 90–019, Marketing Department, The Wharton School, University of Pennsylvania.

Rao, V R, Mahajan, V and Varaiya, N (1990) "A Balance Model for Evaluating Firms for Acquisition", Working Paper, Graduate School of Management, Cornell University, January.

Rastoin, N (1981) "Sortez vos griffes" *Coopération—distribution—consommation* 5, pp26–35.

Rege, P (1989) *A vos marques*, Favre, Lausanne.

Regouby, C (1988) *La Communication globale*, Les Editions d'Organisation, Paris.

Revue Française de Comptabilité (1989) "Le Débat sur les Marques en Grande-Bretagne" October, 205, p19.

Revue Française de Comptabilité (1990) "Incorporels identifiables: le projet australien" January, 208, p11.

Ries, A and Trout, J (1987) *Le Positionnement* McGraw-Hill, Paris.

Rutteman, P (1989) "Mergers, Acquisitions, Brand and Goodwill" *Accountancy* September, p27.

Rutteman, P (1990) "Boosting the Profits of the Brands Industry" *Accountancy* January, pp26–7.

Saporito, B (1986) "Has Been Brands Go Back to Work" *Fortune*, 28 April, pp123–4.

Schlossberg, H (1990) "Brand Value can be Worth more than Physical Assets" *Marketing News* 5 March, p6.

Schwebig, P (1988) *Les communications de l'entreprise* McGraw-Hill, Paris.

Seguela, J (1982) *Hollywood Lave Plus Blanc* Flammarion, Paris.

Selame, E and Selame, J (1988) *The Company Image* John Wiley and Sons, New York.

Simon, C J and Sullivan, M W (1989) "The Measurement and Determinants of Brand Equity: A Financial Approach" Working Paper, October, University of Chicago.

Smith, D and Park, C W (1992) "The Effects of Brand Extensions on Market Share and Advertising Efficiency", *Journal of Marketing Research*, 29, August, pp296–313.

Stobart, P (1989) "Brand Valuation: A True and Fair View" *Accountancy* October, p27.

Sudovar, B (1987) "Branding in the Pharmaceutical Industry", in *Branding: a Key Marketing Tool* (ed Murphy, J) McGraw-Hill, London.

Sullivan, M (1988) "Measuring Image Spillovers in Umbrella Branded Products", Working Paper, The Graduate School of Business, University of Chicago.

Swiners, J L (1979) "Bilan critique du rôle de la copy-stratégie dans la pratique publicitaire actuelle" *IREP*, June, 19.

Tauber, E (1988) "Brand Leverage: Strategy for Growth in a Cost-Control World", *Journal of Advertising Research* Aug–Sept, vol 28 (4), pp26–30.

Taylor, R (1987) "The Branding of Services" in *Branding: a Key Marketing Tool* (ed. Murphy, J) McGraw-Hill, London.

Thil, E and Baroux, C (1983) *Un Pavé dans la Marque* Flammarion, Paris.

Thiolon, B (1990) "La Marque et la Banque" *Humanisme et Entreprise*, 181, June, pp29–32.

Thoenig, J C (1990) *Les performances économiques de l'industrie de produits de marque et de la distribution*, ILEC, Paris.

Touche Ross Europe (1989) *Accounting for Europe Success by A.D. 2000*. Internal Report, London.

Tuvee, L (1987) L'Histoire du Marketing Global: Bibliographie Commentée *Revue Française du Marketing*, vol 114 (4), pp19–48.

Sapolsky, H M (1986) *Consuming Fears: The Politics of Product Risks*, Basic Books, New York.

Sappington, D and Wernerfelt, B (1985) "To Brand or Not to Brand?" *Journal of Business*, 58 (July), pp279–93.

University of Minnesota Consumer Behavior Seminar (1987) "Affect Generalization to Similar and Dissimilar Brand Extensions" *Psychology and Marketing*, 4 (Fall), pp225–37.

Ville, G (1986) "Maîtriser et optimiser l'avenir d'une marque" Esomar Congress Proceedings, pp527–41.

Ward, K (1989) "Can the Cash Flows of Brands Really be Capitalized?" in *Brand Valuation*, (ed Murphy, J) Hutchinson Business Books, London pp70–80.

Watkins T (1986) *The Economics of the Brands: A Marketing Analysis* McGraw-Hill, Maidenhead.

Wentz, L (1989) "How Experts Value Brands" *Advertising Age* 16 January, p24.

Wernerfelt, B (1988) "Umbrella Branding as a Signal of New Product Quality" *Rand Journal of Economics*, 19, (Autumn), pp458–66.

Wernerfelt B (1990) "Advertising Content When Brand Choice is a Signal" *Journal of Business*, vol 63 (1), pp91–8.

Winram, S (1987) "The Opportunity for World Brands" in *Branding: a Key Marketing Tool* (ed Murphy, J) McGraw-Hill, London.

Yoshimori, M (1989) "Concepts et stratégies de marque au Japon" in *La marque* (eds Kapferer, J N and Thoenig, J C) McGraw-Hill, Paris.

Young, R (1967) "Multibrand Entries" in *Plotting Marketing Strategy* (ed Adler, L) Interpublic Press Book, New York.

Yovovich, B G (1988) "What is Your Brand Really Worth?" *Adweek's Marketing Week* August 8, pp18–24.

Zareer, P (1987) "De la valeur des marques de commerce" *C A Magazine* February, p72.

Index

About the Author

Jean-Noël Kapferer is an internationally recognized authority on brands and brand marketing. A professor of marketing strategy at the HEC Graduate School of Management in France, Kapferer holds a Ph.D. from Northwestern University and is also an active consultant to various U.S. corporations. He is the author of six books and several articles on branding, advertising, and communication.